CONVEYANCING SOLUTIONS
3: REMEDIES UNDER THE CONTRACT

AUSTRALIA AND NEW ZEALAND
The Law Book Company Ltd.
Sydney : Melbourne : Perth

CANADA AND U.S.A.
The Carswell Company Ltd.
Agincourt, Ontario

INDIA
N.M. Tripathi Private Ltd.
Bombay
and
Eastern Law House Private Ltd.
Calcutta and Delhi
M.P.P. House
Bangalore

ISRAEL
Steimatzky's Agency Ltd.
Jerusalem : Tel Aviv : Haifa

MALAYSIA : SINGAPORE : BRUNEI
Malayan Law Journal (Pte.) Ltd.
Singapore and Kuala Lumpur

CONVEYANCING SOLUTIONS 3: REMEDIES UNDER THE CONTRACT

RUTH ANNAND, B.A.

Solicitor,
Lecturer in Law, University of Bristol

BRIAN CAIN, LL.B.

Solicitor

LONDON   SWEET & MAXWELL   1988

Published in 1988 by
Sweet & Maxwell Limited
11 New Fetter Lane, London
Computerset by Promenade Graphics Limited, Cheltenham
Printed in Great Britain by
Butler and Tanner Limited
Frome, Somerset

British Library Cataloguing in Publication Data
Annand, Ruth
    Remedies under the contract.—
    (Conveyancing solutions; v. 3).
    1. England. Real property. Conveyancing. Law
    I. Title II. Cain, Brian III. Series
    344.2064'38

    ISBN 0-421-38110-8

CONTENTS

TABLE OF CASES

TABLE OF STATUTES

TABLE OF STANDARD CONDITIONS OF SALE

The standard conditions are set out in full at Appendices B and C.

1 INTRODUCTION

This is the third in a series of conveyancing manuals for practitioners. The idea for the series was formulated at a time of growing public dissatisfaction with the system of residential conveyancing. The Administration of Justice Act 1985 contains provisions which extend the procedures for dealing with complaints against solicitors[1] and allow licensed non-solicitors to undertake conveyancing for reward.[2] The manuals concentrate in the main on residential conveyancing, although much of what is said applies equally to commercial and agricultural conveyancing.

There follows in chart form, a basic description of the conveyancing process. The areas affected by this manual—remedies under the contract—are identified in bold type.

Conveyancing procedure

Preliminary agreement to buy

Vendor and Purchaser instruct conveyancers

Vendor's conveyancer	*Purchaser's conveyancer*
Send **draft contract** with copy Register entries and filed plan and, or other copy documents to ⟶	
	Peruses draft contract and other documents
	Private surveyor instructed
	Application for mortgage made
PRELIMINARY	Searches Public Index Map (unregistered land)
	Makes local land charges search and enquiries of the local authority
	⟵ Raises enquiries before contract
Answers enquiries before contract ⟶ **(refers to client where necessary)**	
	Search of Commons Register and, or register of rents?
	Other enquiries?
	Considers replies to searches and enquiries with client together with mortgage offer and surveyor's report
Agrees contract	Agrees contract
Obtains vendor's signature to contract	Obtains purchaser's signature to contract and **deposit**

---

[1] s.5.
[2] s.7.

EXCHANGE OF CONTRACTS

Insurance is necessary as from
date of contract as risk passes
to purchaser
Protection of contract by
registration?

Supplies abstract of title or
authority to inspect Register ⟶

Investigates title
Prepares draft conveyance
or transfer and **requisitions on
title**. Reserves right to raise
further requisitions on behalf
of mortgagee

⟵ Notifies mortgagee of
redemption and obtains
redemption figure and "daily
rate"
Replies to requisitions and
approves conveyance or
transfer ⟶

If not acting for mortgagee—
sends all documents to
mortgagee's conveyancer;
receives mortgagee's
requisitions and
draft mortgage from
mortgagee's conveyancer,
replies to mortgagee's
requisitions by raising **further
requisitions with vendor's
conveyancer** if necessary;
mortgagee agrees loan
If acting for purchaser and
mortgagee—reports on
vendor's title to mortgagee;
drafts mortgage

**Replies to any additional
requisitions** ⟶

Makes land charges search or
official search of register (and
"bankruptcy only" land
charges search if necessary)
Search of companies register?

Prepares completion statement ⟶

Mortgage executed
Dispatches engrossed
⟵ conveyance or transfer
(sometimes bearing purchaser's
signature)

**Makes final arrangements for
completion**

**Confirms arrangements for
completion
Obtains completion moneys**
from mortgagee and purchaser

**CONTRACT
TO
COMPLETION**

COMPLETION

**AFTER
COMPLETION**

Redeems mortgage
Accounts to client

If not acting for mortgagee
sends all documents to
mortgagee's conveyancer
Otherwise attends to stamping
and registration where
appropriate

Forwards receipted mortgage
or Form 53 ⟶

Reform The only specific proposal for reform in this area towards the simplification of conveyancing is the abolition of the rule in *Bain* v. *Fothergill*.[3] The rule in that case limits the damages recoverable by a purchaser of land when the vendor cannot fulfil his contractual obligation to show a good title.

---

[3] (1874) L.R. 7 H.L. 158. See Law Commission Report No. 166 (1987), reproduced in Appendix E.

2 FAILURE TO PAY THE DEPOSIT

Function of a deposit

Why take a deposit?

The functions of a deposit under a contract of sale of land are, first, to provide a security for performance by the purchaser, and a security moreover that can be enforced without the delay and cost of proceedings and secondly, to act (if the contract proceeds to completion) as part payment of the purchase price. This dual function was made clear by Cotton L.J. in *Howe* v. *Smith*[1]:

> "What is the deposit? The deposit, as I understand it . . . is a guarantee that the contract shall be performed. If the sale goes on . . . it goes in part payment of the purchase price for which it is deposited; but if on the default of the purchaser the contract goes off, that is to say, if he repudiates the contract, then . . . he can have no right to recover the deposit."

It is however the security aspect of a deposit that is more often stressed in the cases on the subject. "Everybody knows what a deposit is," pronounced Lord Mcnaghten in *Soper* v. *Arnold*,[2] "its primary purpose is this, it is a guarantee that the purchaser means business." If the purchaser terminates the contract because of the vendor's default, he may recover his deposit with interest.[3]

Requirement for a deposit

Deposit needs express provision

Under an open contract no deposit is payable.[4] The statutory conditions of sale of land implied into contracts by correspondence by section 46 of the Law of Property Act 1925 leave open the question of a deposit. But standard form contracts invariably require the payment of a deposit upon entering into the contract.[5] In *Morris* v. *Duke Cohan & Co.*[6] solicitors were held negligent in failing to warn a vendor of the dangers of not taking a deposit from a prospective purchaser.

Status of a deposit

Until recently there was some dispute as to the effect of the purchaser's failure to pay the deposit where the parties had stipulated for payment of a deposit.

---

[1] (1884) 27 Ch.D. 89 at 95. See also, "Deposits on exchange of contracts in residential conveyancing—time for a change", Conveyancing Standing Committee (1988).

[2] (1889) 14 App.Cas. 429 at 435.

[3] *Soper* v. *Arnold* (1887) 37 Ch.D. 96 at 100 (affmd. (1889) 14 App.Cas. 429).

[4] *Perry* v. *Suffields Ltd.* [1916] 2 Ch. 187 at 189.

[5] See p. 11 below.

[6] (1975) 119 S.J. 826.

Myton Ltd. v. Schwab-Morris

In *Myton Ltd.* v. *Schwab-Morris*,[7] there was a written agreement for the grant of an underlease of a maisonette. The agreement required the payment of a deposit on the signing of the agreement. The purchaser gave a cheque for the deposit but it was dishonoured. The vendor informed the purchaser that the contract was rescinded because of failure to pay the deposit. Subsequently the purchaser registered a caution against the land to protect its alleged interest under the agreement. The vendor applied for removal of the caution. The vendor's first argument was that due payment of the deposit was a condition precedent to the operation of the agreement as a contract. Goulding J. agreed and said that a vendor who stipulates for a deposit takes it as evidence of the purchaser's intention and ability to complete in due course. The vendor never intends to be bound by the contract in the first place, unless he gets a deposit.

Condition precedent or fundamental term?

Goulding J. also accepted the vendor's second argument whilst preferring the first. The second argument was that the provision for payment of the deposit was a fundamental term of the contract, the breach of which entitled the vendor to renounce the contract.

Practical importance

Unfortunately these two views of the status of a deposit are poles apart in their practical consequences. If failure to pay the deposit is failure of a condition precedent then the deposit cannot be claimed because there is no contract in existence. If, however, it is a fundamental breach then there is a contract, and the money can be claimed as a forfeited deposit.

Myton's case was not cited in *Pollway Ltd.* v. *Abdullah*[8] but the Court of Appeal did shed some light on the condition precedent/fundamental term controversy. The purchaser bought property at an auction and gave a cheque for the deposit made out to the auctioneers. He subsequently stopped payment of the cheque. He was given time to comply with the obligation but refused. It was held by the Court of Appeal that the auctioneers were entitled to sue on the cheque. Roskill L.J. whose judgment was concurred in by the other members of the court said[9]:

> "The case appears to have been argued before the learned judge on the footing that the consideration for the cheque was the vendors' obligation to complete the sale. I will assume for the moment that this is correct. On this assumption the contract of sale . . . still subsisted when the cheque was stopped. But they did not immediately exercise that right. So long as they refrained from so doing their obligation to perform the sale contract remained."

Conflicting dicta

Obviously this statement is inconsistent with the view that, the deposit not having been paid, no contract existed, although the point was apparently not argued. Contrast *Edgewater Developments Co.* v. *Bailey*[10] where the fact that no deposit had been paid was taken to indicate that no complete contract had been made.

---

[7] [1974] 1 W.L.R. 331; (1974) 124 New L.J. 811, H.W. Wilkinson.
[8] [1974] 1 W.L.R. 493.
[9] *Ibid.* at 496.
[10] (1974) 118 S.J. 312.

Millichamp v. Jones

In *Millichamp* v. *Jones*,[11] the plaintiffs had the benefit of an option to purchase agricultural land from the defendant, on the giving of prescribed notice; the agreement also provided that a 10 per cent. deposit should be paid. Notice was duly given but no deposit was paid. Warner J. held that payment of the deposit was not a condition precedent to the creation of a contract. Having reviewed the authorities, he said[12]:

" . . . it seems to me that unless a distinction is to be made between sales by auction and sales by private treaty, the weight of authority is in favour of the view that a requirement in a contract for the sale of land that a deposit should be paid by the purchaser does not constitute a condition precedent, failure to fulfil which prevents the contract from coming into existence, but is in general to be taken as a fundamental term of the contract, breach of which entitles the vendor, if he so elects, to treat the contract as at an end and to sue for damages including the amount of the unpaid deposit. Nor do I see that anything, either in the authorities or in principle, calls for a distinction to be made in that respect between sales by auction and sales by private treaty."

Reference should also be made to *Portaria Shipping Co.* v. *Gulf Pacific Navigation Co. Ltd., The Selene G.*[13] Clause 2 of the written agreement in that case provided:

Portaria Shipping v Gulf Pacific

"As security for the correct fulfillment of this contract the Buyers shall pay a deposit of 10% . . . of the Purchase Money within 48 hours . . . after signing this Memorandum of Agreement . . . ."

The buyers failed to pay the deposit and the sellers rescinded. Robert Goff J. held that the provision for payment of the deposit was an essential term of the agreement. It was not argued that the payment of the deposit was a condition precedent to the formation of the contract.

Of the cases mentioned, the condition precedent question was only directly in issue in *Myton Ltd.* v. *Schwab-Morris* and *Millichamp* v. *Jones*. Each judge at first instance in each case arrived at a diametrically opposed conclusion. For this reason, an appellate decision on the point was welcome. True, *Damon Cia. Naviera S.A.* v. *Hapag-Lloyd International S.A.*[14] concerned a contract for the sale of three ships, but the courts have in the past assimilated the contractual position of parties in land and ship transactions. In *Damon*, the Court of Appeal applied the decision of Warner J. in *Millichamp* v. *Jones* and held that the provision for payment of the deposit was not a condition precedent to the formation of the contract; it was a fundamental term of a concluded contract.

An appellate decision

Australia

It is noteworthy that seven years earlier in *Brien* v. *Dwyer*[15] the High Court of Australia decided that the deposit condition in

---

[11] [1982] 1 W.L.R. 1422.
[12] *Ibid.* at 1430.
[13] [1981] 2 Lloyd's Rep. 180.
[14] [1985] 1 W.L.R. 435.
[15] (1978) 141 C.L.R. 378.

a standard contract of sale of land was a fundamental term of the contract. *Brien* v. *Dwyer* was not cited in any of the above cases.

Prior notice

Breach of the fundamental term must be sufficiently fundamental

Once it is accepted that failure to pay the deposit as required by the contract is a breach of a fundamental term, it should follow that the vendor be entitled to terminate the contract forthwith. Not so. The deposit in *Millichamp* v. *Jones*[16] should have been paid in April 1980 when notice exercising the option was given. The non-payment was not discovered until June 1980 when the parties agreed to extend the original completion date to allow the defendant to harvest his crops. The plaintiffs proffered a cheque for the deposit, but it was refused. Warner J. held that while non-payment of the deposit will *often* entitle the vendor to rescind the contract, this was not so in the instant case. The plaintiffs had never refused to pay or even been out of funds; the non-payment was a mere oversight in which the defendant had shared. It was therefore:

" . . . incumbent on the defendant, before he could treat the plaintiffs' failure to pay the deposit as a repudiation of the contract, to tell them that he was minded so to do and to give them an opportunity of complying with their obligation. Only if they then showed in some way that they were unwilling or unable to comply with it would he become entitled to consider their conduct a sufficiently clear breach of the contract to entitle him to treat it as discharged."[17]

John Wilmott Homes v. Read

This passage from Warner J.'s judgment in *Millichamp* v. *Jones* was cited with approval and applied by Whitford J. in *John Wilmott Homes Ltd.* v. *Read*.[18] The last day for payment of the deposit under the option agreement there, was October 4, 1984. Although the option was exercised on September 27, 1984, the deposit was not paid until October 5. The vendor purported to rescind the agreement. Whitford J. held that the parties had never considered time to be of the essence of payment, that the delay of 24 hours could not be said to have deprived the vendor of any part of the benefit which it was intended he should obtain under the contract, and that *Millichamp* v. *Jones* showed that the vendor would have been entitled to rescind only if he had first given notice that he must have payment by a specified date, and he had not done this.

Practical difficulties

The difficulty these cases present is twofold. First, *Millichamp* v. *Jones* suggests that there will be circumstances when the purchaser's failure to pay the deposit will be sufficiently repudiatory to entitle the vendor to terminate the contract without giving notice. What are they? Secondly, assuming time is, prima facie, not of the essence for payment of the deposit (*John Wilmott Homes Ltd.* v. *Read*) and by analogy with the procedure for serving common law completion notices,[19] must

[16] [1982] 1 W.L.R. 1422.
[17] *Ibid.* at 1431–1432.
[18] (1986) 51 P. & C.R. 90.
[19] See pp. 33–36 below.

the vendor wait for a reasonable time to elapse from the contractual date for payment of the deposit before serving his notice, and must the notice give the purchaser a reasonable time for payment? In the context of the transaction in *Damon Cia. Naviera S.A.* v. *Hapag-Lloyd International S.A.*[20] a three day notice by telex apparently sufficed.

Contrast the Australian position

By way of contrast, the Australian position[21] is that whatever be the date for payment of the deposit, payment must be made on the due date, the purpose of the deposit as a security for the purchaser's performance of the contract negates any implication of a term allowing payment within a reasonable time after that prescribed by the contract. And, if payment is not made on the due date then the vendor may terminate the contract without the need for any prior notice; the failure to pay being breach of a fundamental term of the contract.

Suing for the unpaid deposit

A vendor who chooses to terminate the contract for failure to pay the deposit, can clearly forfeit any part of the deposit he is *actually holding*. But he cannot "forfeit" a deposit which has not been paid. Can he sue for and recover an unpaid deposit?

Damon Cia. v. Hapag-Lloyd

In *Damon Cia. Naviera S.A.* v. *Hapag-Lloyd International S.A.*[22] the sellers had agreed to sell three ships to undisclosed buyers for $US 2,365,000. The contract was negotiated by two brothers who had power to nominate the buyers. A Panamanian company, Damon, was nominated and it was agreed that a new memorandum of agreement should be signed, upon which task being performed, a 10 per cent. deposit was payable. Damon failed to sign the memorandum of agreement or pay the deposit, and in consequence the sellers sold all three ships elsewhere for $US 2,295,000. The sellers sued for $US 236,500, which represented the agreed deposit; Damon argued that they were only liable for the sellers' loss on re-sale, which an arbitrator had set at $US 60,000. The Court of Appeal, Robert Goff L.J. dissenting, held affirming the decision of Legatt J., that the sellers could recover the whole 10 per cent. deposit.

Past decisions conflicted as to recovery of unpaid deposit

The question had in the past produced a divergence of judicial opinion. In *Dewar* v. *Mintoft*[23] Horridge J. held that a vendor, who had rescinded a contract for the sale of a farm upon the purchaser's breach, was entitled to recover the amount of the unpaid deposit. The reason given was that the purchaser "could not put himself in a better position by refusing to pay the deposit than if the deposit had in fact been paid, in which case it could be retained by the seller . . . ." Nevertheless, *Dewar* v. *Mintoft* was not followed by Pennycuick J. in *Lowe* v. *Hope*,[24] on the ground that a vendor who has elected to put an end to a contract by

[20] [1985] 1 W.L.R. 435.
[21] *Brien* v. *Dwyer* (1978) 141 C.L.R. 378. See Butt, *The Standard Contract for Sale in New South Wales* (1985).
[22] [1985] 1 W.L.R. 435; considered in [1985] Conv. 286.
[23] [1912] 2 K.B. 373.
[24] [1970] Ch. 94.

rescission is not entitled thereafter to insist on performance of the contract in relation to the deposit. Pennycuick J. said[25]:

" . . . it seems to me that the vendor, having elected to bring the contract to an end by rescission, is not entitled to insist on the performance of the contract in relation to the deposit. This is admittedly so, insofar as the deposit bears the character of part of the unpaid purchase price. It seems to me that it must equally be so, insofar as the deposit bears the character of a pledge; for once the vendor has rescinded the contract there are no outstanding obligations on the purchaser in respect of which the vendor can be entitled to be protected by a pledge."

Fallacy behind Lowe v. Hope exposed

It is now clear that *Lowe* v. *Hope*, in holding that an unpaid deposit is irrecoverable, proceeded upon a misunderstanding of the effect of "rescission" (or "termination") of a contract for breach, as opposed to "rescission" of a contract for some vitiating factor such as mistake. The difference was explained by Dixon J. in *McDonald* v. *Dennys Lascelles Ltd.*[26]:

"When a party to a simple contract, upon a breach by the other contracting party of a condition of the contract, elects to treat the contract as no longer binding upon him, the contract is not rescinded as from the beginning. Both parties are discharged from further performance of the contract, but rights are not divested or discharged which have already been unconditionally acquired. Rights and obligations which arise from the partial execution of the contract and causes of action which have accrued from its breach alike continue unaffected. When a contract is rescinded because of matters which affect its formation, as in the case of fraud, the parties are to be rehabilitated and restored, so far as may be, to the position they occupied before the contract was made. But when a contract, which is not void or voidable at law, or liable to be set aside in equity, is dissolved at the election of one party because the other has not observed an essential condition or has committed a breach going to its root, the contract is determined so far as it is executory only and the party in default is liable for damages for its breach."

This was approved by the House of Lords in *Johnson* v. *Agnew.*[27]

The deposit in *Damon Cia.* v. *Hapag-Lloyd* was obviously a contentious issue; the amount of the deposit exceeded the sellers' actual loss by \$US170,000. All three members of the Court of Appeal held, as a matter of construction, that the obligation to pay the deposit was conditional upon the memorandum being signed (both were terms of a concluded contract between Damon and the sellers); they differed however as to the effect of that finding.

The decision in Damon Cia. v. Hapag-Lloyd

Fox and Stephenson L.JJ. held that Damon had breached its obligation to sign a memorandum containing a term requiring payment of a 10 per cent. deposit, and the sellers were entitled to be put in the same position as if the memorandum had been

---

[25] *Ibid.* at 98.
[26] (1933) 48 C.L.R. 457 at 476–477.
[27] [1980] A.C. 367 at 396. See also *Millichamp* v. *Jones* [1982] 1 W.L.R. 1422.

executed. Had the memorandum been executed and the deposit not paid, the sellers could have sued in debt for the deposit. Therefore even though the memorandum had not been executed, the sellers were entitled to damages in the amount of the deposit, and not merely in the amount of their actual loss.

Robert Goff L.J. dissented from this. He was of the opinion that executing the memorandum was a condition precedent to the obligation to pay the deposit. As this had not been satisfied, that obligation did not arise. Damages were accordingly to be assessed on the basis of ordinary principles, which would enable the sellers to recover their loss on resale, that is $US60,000. Were it not for the condition precedent factor, his Lordship would have awarded the sellers the full amount of the deposit.

Although the facts of *Damon Cia.* v. *Hapag-Lloyd* were out of the ordinary, the case is authority that under a contract of sale of land that requires payment of a deposit upon entry into the contract, a vendor who subsequently terminates can sue for and recover the amount of the agreed deposit.[28] The Court of Appeal preferred *Dewar* v. *Mintoft* to *Lowe* v. *Hope* and applied the passage from Dixon J.'s judgment in *McDonald* v. *Dennys Lascelles Ltd.* as to the effect of termination on rights already acquired under the contract.

The right to sue for and recover an unpaid deposit will be particularly valuable to a vendor whose loss is less than the stipulated deposit.

Failure to pay the deposit under the standard conditions

National condition 2

"2. Deposit
(1) Unless the Special Conditions otherwise provide, the purchaser shall on the date of the contract pay a deposit of 10 per cent. of the purchase price, on a sale by auction, to the auctioneer, or on a sale by private treaty, to the vendor's solicitor and, in either case, as stakeholder
(2) In case a cheque taken for the deposit (having been presented, and whether or not it has been re-presented) has not been honoured, then and on that account the vendor may elect
either (i) to treat the contract as discharged by breach thereof on the purchaser's part
or (ii) to enforce payment of the deposit as a deposit, by suing on the cheque or otherwise."

Law Society general condition 9

"9. DEPOSIT
(1) The purchaser shall on or before the date of the contract pay by way of deposit to the vendor's solicitors as stakeholders the normal deposit, or such lesser sum as the vendor shall have agreed in writing. On a sale by private treaty, payment shall be made by

---

[28] No argument appears to have been presented that the deposit was a penalty; see p. 48 below.

banker's draft or by cheque drawn on a solicitor's bank account.

(2) Upon service by the vendor of a completion notice, the purchaser shall pay to the vendor any difference between the normal deposit and any amount actually paid (if less).

(3) If any draft, cheque or other instrument tendered in or towards payment of any sum payable under this condition is dishonoured when first presented the vendor shall have the right by notice to the purchaser within seven working days thereafter to treat the contract as repudiated."

A 10 per cent. deposit

Both conditions reflect the normal practice of requiring a 10 per cent. deposit to be paid to the vendor's solicitor as stakeholder. In the case of an auction sale governed by the National conditions, it is the auctioneer who holds the money as stakeholder. The 10 per cent. is calculated exclusive of any amount payable for chattels, fixtures and fittings[29] and any preliminary deposit paid to an estate agent.[30] The Law Society

Reduced deposits

condition additionally allows (sales by private treaty only) for payment of a lesser sum than the "normal deposit" (defined by general condition 1(f)) of 10 per cent. A balancing payment to make up the full 10 per cent. becomes due (under 9(2)), if the vendor serves a completion notice under general condition 23.[30a] The vendor has in any event, the right to sue for and recover the unpaid balance of an agreed deposit at common law.[31] The efficacy of sub-condition 9(2) (and the common law right) is questionable in the face of a purchasers actual or potential impecuniosity. Just as, in *Morris* v. *Duke-Cohan & Co.*[32] solicitors were negligent in not advising a vendor of the dangers of not taking any deposit at all, so it may also be wise to alert a vendor to the risk of accepting a reduced deposit.

Time for payment of the deposit

The money becomes due under the National condition "on the date of the contract"; under the Law Society condition, "on or before the date of the contract." The "date of the contract" is prescribed by National condition 1(7) and Law Society general condition 10 respectively. In summary this will be, either[33]:

(1) the date agreed between the parties and inserted in the contract; or

(2) the date when counterpart contracts are formally exchanged; or

(3) where contracts are exchanged by post, the date when the last part is posted; or

(4) where the Law Society Contract is exchanged through a document exchange, the date when the last part is

---

[29] This is by implication under the National conditions, because of the separation of chattels from purchase price on the front page of the contract form.

[30] Again, by implication under the National conditions; see condition 5(3)(i).

[30a] However a provision for payment of a deposit, or the balance of it, when a contract is rescinded is probably unenforceable as a penalty.

[31] *Millichamp* v. *Jones* [1982] 1 W.L.R. 1422. *Damon Cia.* v. *Hapag-Lloyd* [1985] 1 W.L.R. 435.

[32] (1975) 119 S.J. 826.

[33] For a more detailed discussion see Annand & Whish, *Conveyancing Solutions 2: The Contract* (1987).

delivered to the exchange. The National conditions make no mention of document exchanges. Apparently the date of a National Contract exchanged by this method will be when, according to the rules of the exchange, the last part is delivered to the other side[34]; or

(5) for telephonic or telex exchanges, the date when both parties agree that the Contract is immediately binding, usually the date of the telephone conversation or telex message.

Non-payment or late payment of the deposit—standard conditions inapplicable

What if the purchaser fails to pay the deposit on time? Interpreted in the light of the security function of a deposit, the words "on the date of the contract" and "on or before the date of the contract," whilst permitting payment at any time up to and including the date of the contract, surely preclude payment thereafter. The security purpose of a deposit can only be fulfilled if the deposit is held by or on behalf of the vendor at the time the contract is entered into; this purpose is frustrated if the deposit is not paid until sometime (be it only a "reasonable" time) after entry into the contract. The conditions themselves do not specify the position where the contract has been formed, but no deposit has been paid. This is presumably based on the assumption that the vendor will not proceed to exchange until a deposit cheque is forthcoming; unfortunately not always the case in practice. The common law rule is that whereas payment of the deposit is a fundamental term of the contract, payment of the money by the due date is not. The vendor must serve prior notice requiring payment by a specified date, before proceeding to terminate the contract for late payment or for non-payment of the deposit.[35]

Suggested addition to standard conditions

To avoid any ambiguity as to when a breach of the condition as to payment of the deposit has occurred it would be advisable to extend the deposit conditions as follows: "if part or all of the deposit is not paid within seven working days of the date hereof the vendor shall have the right by notice to the purchaser to treat the contract as repudiated."

Bouncing deposits

The deposit conditions do deal with bouncing deposit cheques; the Law Society condition also covers bouncing bankers' drafts and other instruments. National condition 2(2), drafted in the wake of the condition precedent/fundamental term controversy,[36] makes it clear that payment of the deposit is a fundamental term of the contract; in the event of the deposit cheque being dishonoured, the vendor has the choice of either terminating the contract, or of keeping the contract alive and suing on the cheque. No time limit is placed on the time in which the vendor must make the election (he may represent the cheque), but presumably he must make his choice within a reasonable time and his conduct may be relevant. He may waive his right to terminate for the purchaser's default in payment of the deposit, if he proceeds with the sale in the normal way.[37]

Under National condition 2(2)

The wording of National condition 2(2) suggests that it only applies where one cheque is given for the total amount of the

---

[34] *John Wilmott Homes Ltd.* v. *Read* (1986) 51 P. & C.R. 90.
[35] *Ibid.* following *Millichamp* v. *Jones* [1982] 1 W.L.R. 1422.
[36] See pp. 4–7 above.
[37] *Johnson* v. *Agnew* [1980] A.C. 367.

Trustbridge Ltd. v. Bhattessa

deposit and that cheque is dishonoured. This point arose for decision by the Court of Appeal in *Trustbridge Ltd.* v. *Bhattessa*.[38] A contract for the sale of a motel, incorporating the National Conditions of Sale (20th edition) provided for the payment of a deposit of £40,000. The purchaser paid the deposit by two cheques of £20,000 each. Following dishonour of one of these cheques the vendor by letter required the purchaser to provide (i) a banker's draft for the amount in question within two days and (ii) evidence that the balance of the purchase price would be available before completion. After the vendor company had received the banker's draft it informed the purchaser of its election to treat the contract as discharged under National condition 2(2). The Court of Appeal held that the vendor company had the right under the clause to treat the contract as discharged. The dishonoured cheque was "a cheque taken for the deposit" within the terms of the clause. The argument that condition 2(2) applied only where one cheque was given for the whole of the deposit could not be accepted. Furthermore, the vendor company had not by its conduct affirmed the contract. It had reserved its position under National condition 2(2) until its two requirements had been fulfilled; satisfactory evidence of the purchaser's means had not been produced.

National condition 2(2) obviates the necessity at common law for giving prior notice before terminating the contract.[39]

Under Law Society condition 9(3)

Law Society general condition 9 underwent extensive revision in 1984. Sub-condition 9(3) now omits any reference to fundamental breach in deference to Warner J.'s decision in *Millichamp* v. *Jones*.[40] It is expressed to apply where any draft, cheque or other instrument tendered *in or towards payment* of the deposit is dishonoured. In this event the vendor is given the right to treat the contract as repudiated. To exercise this right he must serve notice on the purchaser within seven days of the dishonour. He is not given the opportunity to represent the draft, cheque or other instrument.

Avoid the problem

In fact, the problem of bouncing deposits is to a large extent avoided by the Law Society condition. Sub-condition 9(1) provides that on a sale by private treaty the deposit shall be paid by banker's draft or solicitor's cheque. The likelihood of such instruments not being met is small. Only on a sale by auction is the purchaser's own cheque acceptable. A provision in these terms could usefully be incorporated into the National Contract. At present the National conditions prescribe no method for payment of the deposit.

---

[38] (1985) 82 L.S.Gaz. 2580.
[39] See p. 7 above.
[40] [1982] 1 W.L.R. 1422.

3 FAILURE TO ANSWER REQUISITIONS

Requisitions: nature and type

Nature of requisitions

After delivery of the abstract of title the purchaser gets a second chance to make enquiries of the vendor, this time by means of "requisitions on title."[1] In theory requisitions should be confined to specific matters of title.[2] But in practice requisitions normally consist of a combination of requests for information genuinely needed, statements of the obvious, and general enquiries.[3]

Time limits

Under an open contract requisitions must be raised within a reasonable time of delivery of the abstract.[4] "Reasonableness" governs the time for answering requisitions[5] and for making observations on the replies. Not surprisingly, the standard conditions of sale set precise time limits.[6] They also specify the subject matter of requisitions[7] (although probably not exclusively[8]) and provide for consequences to follow a failure to answer requisitions even going so far as to permit rescission.[9] Generally speaking these conditions apply only to requisitions on title.

Categories of requisitions

The scenario for this chapter is the purchaser raising a requisition which the vendor feels is beyond him to answer, or the vendor giving a reply which the purchaser feels it is not possible for him to accept. In order to appreciate how the rules dictate the balance between the parties, it will be helpful to consider briefly what types of requisitions the purchaser should raise and which the vendor is obliged to answer:

(1) Requisitions on title "As the name itself indicates, requisitions on title are questions concerning the *title* to the land."[10] These the vendor must reply to. Matters "going to title" include, for example, the existence of easements or covenants

---

[1] The first chance is in preliminary enquiries. See Annand & Cain, *Conveyancing Solutions 1: Enquiries before Contract* (1986).

[2] *Re Ford and Hill* (1879) 10 Ch.D. 365.

[3] Witness Oyez's Con 28B "Requisitions on Title." *Williams on Vendor and Purchaser* (4th ed.), Vol. 1, states at p. 212: "Besides the requisitions properly so called, asking for the production of some particular piece of evidence to complete the title, it is generally desirable for the purchaser's advisers to make certain enquiries of the vendor respecting the property sold." An example given is that if the property is sold subject to easements, tenancies etc., the vendor should be asked if any such exist.

[4] *Spurrier* v. *Hancock* (1799) 4 Ves. 667.

[5] *Re Stone and Saville's Contract* [1962] 1 W.L.R. 460.

[6] National condition 9(1) and (3), Law Society general condition 15(2)(3).

[7] National conditions 9(2) and 15(2), Law Society general condition 15(2).

[8] The conditions do not say that requisitions can only be made on the subjects mentioned.

[9] National condition 10, Law Society general condition 16.

[10] *Emmet on Title* (19th ed.), para. 5/101, citing Oliver J. in *Ridley* v. *Oster* [1939] 1 All E.R. 618 at 623.

affecting the property,[11] or the existence of a perpetual rent charge on the land.[12] The purchaser may not raise a requisition which constitutes an insinuation that the vendor has improperly failed to abstract a material matter known to him, such as: "Is there to the knowledge of the vendors or their conveyancers any settlement, deed, fact, omission, or any encumbrance affecting the property not disclosed by the abstract?"[13] This is not a specific question on title and need not be answered; "The introduction of new-fangled requisitions of this kind is dangerous and ought to be discouraged," said James L.J. in *Re Ford and Hill*.[14]

Planning   It is generally accepted that the way in which the property is affected by town and country planning restrictions does not "go to title." Note however that National condition 15(2) permits requisitions about authorised use of the property for the purposes of the Planning Acts.

(2) General enquiries about the state of the property which the vendor is not obliged to answer,[15] but which it may be incumbent on the purchaser to ask   The need for this type of requisition arises from *Goody* v. *Baring*.[16] There Danckwerts J. said: "It is still the duty, however, of a purchaser's solicitor to make the appropriate requisitions and enquiries after the formal contract is signed, even if preliminary enquiries have been so complete that it is only necessary to ask whether the answers thus received are still complete and accurate."[17] Question 1 of Oyez's

Oyez Con 28B   standard form of "Requisitions on title"[18] incorporates preliminary enquiries by reference and asks the vendor to detail any changes in the replies. A longer version of the form is available for use where enquiries have not been made before contract.

(3) Requisitions on conveyance   "[These] assume that the vendor has shown that he can, either alone or jointly with other persons whose concurrence he can require, make title to the property, and the only question is as to the persons to make the conveyance and the form which it is to take."[19] Examples of "conveyance" requisitions would include, for example: a query as to the absence of, or need for, parties to join in or consent to the conveyance[20]; a query as to the appointment of an additional trustee; a query whether a mortgage or charge over the property

---

[11] *Re Brewer and Hankin's Contract* (1899) 80 L.T. 127 (sewerage easement); *Re Belcham and Gawley's Contract* [1930] 1 Ch. 56 (sewerage easement); *Re Courcier and Harrold's Contract* [1923] 1 Ch. 565 at 572–573 (restrictive covenant).
[12] *Re Great Northern Rly. Co.* v. *Sanderson* (1884) 25 Ch.D. 788.
[13] *Re Ford and Hill* (1874) 10 Ch.D. 365.
[14] *Ibid.* at 370.
[15] *Luff* v. *Raymond* (1982) 79 L.S. Gaz. 1330.
[16] [1956] 1 W.L.R. 448.
[17] *Ibid.* at 456.
[18] The current form 28B is reproduced in Appendix D.
[19] *Halsbury's Laws of England* (3rd ed.), Vol. 34, p. 271.
[20] E.G. *Kitchen* v. *Palmer* (1877) 46 L.J. Ch. 611—vendor being equitable owner under a trust, a requisition that the trustees of the legal estate concur in the conveyance.

has been/will be discharged.[21] These requisitions do no more than point out to the vendor what the law requires of him in any event.

(4) **Reminders to the vendor to fulfil his obligations under the contract**   For example, as to vacant possession, the documents to be handed over on completion and suggested ways in which completion of the contract may be facilitated such as method of payment of the purchase price. These are again strictly not necessary but do ensure that chains of interdependent transactions are speedily and efficiently concluded.

(5) **Requisitions about the rights of those in actual occupation**   Depending on the nature of the rights, these may be general requisitions on title (*Re Ford and Hill*), requisitions on title proper, or a repetition of preliminary enquiries and the vendor's duty to answer will vary accordingly. Note that National condition 9(2) provides that the vendor "may be required . . . to deal with requisitions and observations concerning persons who are or may be in occupation or actual occupation of the property . . . ."

Objections and requisitions distinguished

For the purposes of the standard conditions it is further necessary to distinguish between an "objection" and a "requisition."

"**Requisition**"   A "requisition," in the strict sense, is a request by the purchaser for some information to be given or some action to be

"**Objection**"   taken by the vendor. An "objection," is an assertion by the purchaser that the vendor is, for reasons given in the objection, unable to complete the contract in accordance with its terms.

Conveyancers tend to treat the terms "requisition" and "objection" as interchangeable. But a distinction exists and can be important. For example in *Waddell* v. *Wolfe*,[22] it was held that a condition in a contract precluding any "requisition or inquiry" concerning the title did not preclude an objection to title.

Vendor and purchaser summons

Law of Property   A vendor and purchaser summons under section 49 of the Law of
Act 1925, s.49   Property Act 1925 is a summary remedy which may be used to settle disputes arising out of the making and answering of requisitions. Section 49 provides:

> "**49**—(1) A vendor or purchaser of any interest in land, or their representatives respectively, may apply in a summary way to the court, in respect of any requisitions or objections, or any claim for compensation, or any other question arising out of or connected with the contract (not being a question affecting the existence or validity of the contract) and the

[21] *Re Daniel, Daniel* v. *Vassall* [1917] 2 Ch. 405; *Leominster Properties Ltd.* v. *Broadway Finance Ltd.* (1981) 42 P. & C.R. 372.
[22] (1874) L.R. 9 Q.B. 515.

court may make such order upon the application as to the court may appear just, and may order how and by whom all or any of the costs of and incident to the application are to be borne and paid

(2) . . .

(3) This section applies to a contract for the sale or exchange of an interest in land."

By originating application to Chancery Division or county court

The remedy is sought by originating application to the Chancery Division or county court. The summons must be entitled "In the matter of the Agreement and in the matter of the Law of Property Act 1925" and in the body of the summons the section (that is, section 49) under which the application is made must be specified.[23] On a proceeding under the section the parties are in the same position as they would have been under a reference as to title in a suit for specific performance; evidence may be given by affidavit and deponents may be cross-examined.[24] But the court has never awarded a decree of specific performance under section 49.

When can section 49 be used?

Suitable for resolving individual problems arising out of the abstract

The section is intended for the decision of isolated points arising out of or connected with the contract. It can be used to determine, *inter alia*: the validity of a vendor's notice to rescind for unwillingness to comply with the purchaser's requisitions[25]; matters arising on the form of the conveyance, such as whether or not a particular covenant should be included in the conveyance[26]; or the question of whether a mistake on the part of the vendor enables him to rescind his contract of sale.[27] It should not normally be used to seek a declaration in general terms as to the validity of the vendor's title,[28] although actions framed in such general terms have been allowed under the section.[29]

Questions of construction involving "real difficulty" should be settled by "construction" summons

Where the vendor's title depends upon a question of construction involving real difficulty the proper mode of settling the question is by "construction" summons, not by a vendor and purchaser summons. An order made on a vendor and purchaser summons would be binding only between a vendor and purchaser, and—"it is not right for the Court to force a title upon a purchaser which merely may mean that he is buying a lawsuit."[30] In *Re Nichols' and Von Joel's Contract*,[31] the vendors title depended on the construction of an obscure will. The purchaser objected to the title and the vendors took out a vendor and purchaser summons for the purpose of getting the question of construction determined. The court offered to adjourn the summons to enable the vendors to clear their title by means of a

---

[23] See *Emmet on Title* (19th ed.), para. 8/151.

[24] *Re Burroughs, Lynn, and Sexton* (1877) 5 Ch.D. 601.

[25] *Re Jackson and Woodburn's Contract* (1887) 37 Ch.D. 44.

[26] *Re Wallis and Barnard's Contract* [1899] 2 Ch. 515.

[27] *Ibid.*

[28] *Ibid.*

[29] *Re Hargreaves and Thompson's Contract* (1886) 32 Ch.D. 454; *Re Burroughs, Lynn and Sexton* (1877) 5 Ch. D.601.

[30] *Re Nichols' and Von Joel's Contract* [1910] 2 Ch. 43 at 46, *per* Cozens-Hardy M.R.

[31] *Ibid.*

"construction" summons. This having been done, the court declared that the vendors had shown a good title, but ordered them to pay costs. A similar offer was made to the vendor in *Wilson* v. *Thomas*.[32] He however insisted on proceeding by vendor and purchaser summons and his title was declared too doubtful to force upon the purchaser.

Section 49 cannot be used to test the validity of the contract

The court will not allow an action under section 49 where the only area of dispute is the enforceability of the contract itself.[33] In *Re Hughes and Ashley's Contract*[34] the question to be decided on summons was whether the purchaser was entitled to have included in the conveyance to him a particular right of way. At the hearing it became apparent that the purchaser might have a claim against the vendor for misrepresentation and for rescission of the contract. But the Court of Appeal still felt able to settle the form of the conveyance in accordance with the terms of the contract as it stood.

What can the court do?

Types of orders which may be made by the court

The court may make whatever order it thinks fit in order to settle the dispute, including an order for costs (section 49). The court has power not only to answer the question submitted to it, but also to direct such things to be done as are the natural consequence of the decision, for example to make an order rescinding the contract, and to order the vendor to return the deposit with interest, and to pay the purchaser's costs of investigating the title and the costs of the summons.[35] However Stirling J., in *Re Davis and Cavey*,[36] made it clear that there is no hard and fast rule that, in all cases where the vendor fails to show good title, an order must be made for return of the deposit. In that case the court refused to order the vendor to return the deposit, but without prejudice to the purchasers right to bring an action to recover the same.

Expeditious and cheap?

M.E.P.C. Ltd. v. **Christian-Edwards**

The vendor and purchaser summons procedure is supposed to be expeditious and cheap: in practice, it may turn out to be neither.[37] The purchasers in *M.E.P.C. Ltd.* v. *Christian-Edwards*,[38] contracted to buy freehold premises for £710,000 in 1973. On examining the title it was discovered that a contract was entered into for the sale of the property to P in 1912. No copy or note of the contract had survived, the last reference to it was in 1930, and P had died in 1942. The purchasers objected to the title on the grounds that there was no evidence that the 1912 contract had ever been abandoned, and no guarantee that if a representative of P turned up with the 1912 contract having

---

[32] [1958] 1 W.L.R. 422.
[33] *Re Sandbach and Edmondson's Contract* [1891] 1 Ch. 99 at 102.
[34] [1900] 2 Ch. 595.
[35] *Re Hargreaves and Thompson's Contract* (1886) 32 Ch.D. 454; *Re Marshall and Salt's Contract* [1900] 2 Ch. 202; *Re Walker and Oakshott's Contract* [1901] 2 Ch. 383.
[36] (1888) 40 Ch.D. 601.
[37] (1961) 25 Conv. (N.S.) 90.
[38] [1981] A.C. 205.

obtained a grant to his estate, specific performance would not be ordered: and this was especially so since there was evidence in the 1930 document that the contract had been suspended on unknown terms. The vendors took out a vendor and purchaser summons asking for it to be declared that they had made out a title to the property under the contract for its sale to the purchaser sufficient to entitle them to enforce the contract against the purchaser. In 1977,[39] Goulding J. decided that they had not. In 1978[40] the Court of Appeal decided the contrary. And finally in 1981, the House of Lords confirmed the Court of Appeal's decision.

The vendor's right to rescind

Introduction

No right to rescind under the general law
Under an open contract the vendor has no right to withdraw after exchange unless the purchaser repudiates the contract. However conditions of sale permitting the vendor to rescind following the purchaser's insistence upon unwelcome objections or requisitions, have been common in contracts for the sale of land for over a century.[41]

Conditions, like National condition 10 and Law Society general condition 16, permitting the vendor to rescind, originated out of the same circumstances as the rule in *Bain* v. *Fothergill*,[42] namely the complexities of land law and the difficulty of an owner knowing the true state of his title. The rule in *Bain* v. *Fothergill* limits the damages recoverable by a purchaser, where, through no fault of his part, the vendor is unable to show good title to the **History behind conditions of sale permitting rescission** land sold. Similarly conditions, such as National condition 10 and Law Society condition 16, were devised to allow vendors to withdraw from the contract (thereby escaping liability for failure to make good title) where purchasers insisted upon objections and requisitions, which because of the complexity of the title, the vendor was unable or unwilling to answer. But as with the rule in *Bain* v. *Fothergill* the origin of these conditions led to their restrictive interpretation; the courts strove to limit their operation for the purpose for which they were intended and prevented their use for other, sometimes improper, purposes.

General principles

The circumstances in which the vendor is entitled to rescind, and the purchaser's rights in the event of such rescission, depend upon the exact wording of the condition.

In *Re Starr-Bowkett Building Society and Sibun's Contract*[43] land was contracted to be sold under a condition which enabled

---

[39] [1977] 1 W.L.R. 1328.
[40] [1978] Ch. 281.
[41] See *e.g. Tanner* v. *Smith* (1840) 10 Sim. 410.
[42] (1874) L.R. 7 H.L. 158.
[43] (1889) 42 Ch.D. 375.

"Should the purchaser make any requisition" etc.

the vendors to rescind if the purchaser *made* any unwelcome objection or requisition. Nineteen requisitions were raised; some the vendors could not answer, others they could answer only at great expense and trouble. Without attempting to answer any of the requisitions, the vendors gave notice to rescind the contract. The Court of Appeal in construing the condition, held that the right to rescind arose immediately the requisitions were made and that the vendors were not bound to give any reasons for rescinding; the contract had been duly annulled. As Fry L.J. commented, this type of condition is a stringent one: the purchaser is not given the opportunity to withdraw the offending objection or requisition and if the vendor enters into negotiations to resolve the dispute he probably waives his right to rescind.

"Should the purchaser insist upon any objection or requisition"

By way of contrast, the relevant condition in *Duddell* v. *Simpson*[44] allowed the vendor to rescind if the purchaser *insisted* upon any unwelcome objection or requisition. Here it was held that the right to rescind did not arise until the purchaser *had* insisted upon an objection or requisition. This involved four matters being present:

> "First, there must be an objection to the title; secondly, there must be an inability, or unwillingness on the part of the vendor to remove that objection; thirdly, there must be a communication to the purchaser of the existence of this inability or unwillingness; and fourthly, there must be an insisting by the purchaser on his objection, notwithstanding this communication."[45]

This type of rescission clause is of obvious benefit to both parties: negotiations can take place to settle any dispute; the purchaser can withdraw his objection or requisition, but if he does the vendor cannot rescind.

The vendor must not use his contractual power of rescission unreasonably[46]: "he must exercise the power bona fide for the purpose for which it was made part of the contract."[47]

Principles governing rescission— *Selkirk* v. *Romar Investments Ltd.*

The effect of the numerous authorities was summarised by Viscount Radcliffe, in *Selkirk* v. *Romar Investments Ltd.*,[48] as follows:

> "It does not appear to their Lordships . . . that there is any room for uncertainty as to the nature of the equitable principle that is invoked in these cases. It has frequently been analysed, and frequently applied, by Chancery judges, and, although the epithets that describe the vendor's offending action have shown some variety of expression, they are all related to the same underlying idea, and their variety is only due to the fact that, as each case is decided according to the whole context of its circumstances and the course of conduct of the vendor, one may illustrate more

---

[44] (1886) 2 Ch.App. 102. See also *Re Dames and Wood* (1885) 29 Ch.D. 626; *Procter* v. *Pugh* [1921] 2 Ch. 256.
[45] *Duddell* v. *Simpson* (1886) 2 Ch.App. 102, *per* Cairns L.J. at 109.
[46] *Quinion* v. *Horne* [1906] 1 Ch. 596; *Re Dames* v. *Wood* (1885) 29 Ch.D. 626.
[47] *Emmet on Title* (19th ed.), para. 8/33, citing *Bowman* v. *Hyland* (1878) 8 Ch.D. 588.
[48] [1963] 1 W.L.R. 1415 at 1422.

vividly than another some particular aspect of that idea. Thus it has been said that a vendor, in seeking to rescind, must not act arbitrarily, or capriciously or unreasonably. Much less can he act in bad faith. He may not use the power of rescission to get out of a sale 'brevi manu' since by doing so he makes a nullity of the whole elaborate and protracted transaction. Above all, perhaps, he must not be guilty of 'recklessness' in entering into his contract, a term frequently resorted to in discussions of the legal principle and which their Lordships understand to connote an unacceptable indifference to the situation of a purchaser who is allowed to enter into a contract with the expectation of obtaining a title which the vendor has no reasonable anticipation of being able to deliver. A vendor who has so acted is not allowed to call off the whole transaction by resorting to the contractual right of rescission."

Two points in time for judging vendor's conduct

It is apparent from this passage that there are two points in time at which the vendor's conduct should be judged: first, at entry into the contract; and secondly, at exercise of the power of rescission. The vendor cannot rescind if he has entered into the contract "recklessly," and even if he has not entered into the contract, he must not be "arbitrary," "capricious," or "unreasonable" in seeking recision.

"Recklessness" in entering into the contract

In *Selkirk* v. *Romar Investments Ltd.*,[49] the purchaser's requisition called for evidence to establish the date of death of the Crown grantee of the property and to prove the death of the grantee. The vendor company was unable to satisfy the purchaser's requisition, although it made serious attempts to do so, and in due course, it rescinded under the vendor's rescission clause in the contract. It appeared that the vendor knew at the time it entered into the contract that it was doubtful whether it would be able to obtain this evidence, but it had no knowledge of any outstanding claim to the property; it knew that there had been earlier sales of the property (including the sale to it) without any stronger evidence being available on these points, and there was in existence a conveyance nearly 20 years old which contained a recital concerning the matters of which the purchaser sought proof and which would, on the expiration of 20 years to presumptive evidence in favour of a vendor in any subsequent resale. The Privy Council held that the vendor had not been reckless in entering into the contract:

Vendor not "reckless" in Selkirk v. Romar Investments Ltd.

"It is true that [it] might properly have brought the title situation directly to the purchaser's mind by putting forward a special condition to cover the missing points of evidence: but it does not follow that just because [it] did not take this step the vendor's action in entering into the sale contract is to be characterised as reckless in its indifference to the rights or interests of the purchaser. In their Lordships' opinion it is impossible to characterise its conduct as marked by any such culpable indifference . . ."[50]

---

[49] [1963] 1 W.L.R. 1415.
[50] *Ibid.* at 1424.

Vendor reckless in
Baines v. Tweddle

There was a "reckless" vendor in *Baines* v. *Tweddle*.[51] He contracted to sell land under the 1953 edition of the Law Society's general conditions. The land, with other land, was subject to two mortgages and the vendor was in arrears with his mortgage repayments. He failed to check with the mortgagees before contract, that on completion they would release the land to be sold and in fact the mortgagees refused to concur in the sale. He served notice under the rescission condition, condition 10, purporting to rescind the contract as he was unable to comply with the purchaser's objection to taking the land subject to the mortgages. The Court of Appeal held that he could not rescind under condition 10; he had been reckless in signing the contract without being certain that his mortgagees would concur in the sale.

Is a vendor
affected by his
conveyancer's
recklessness?

A question that was raised but not answered by the Court of Appeal in *Baines* v. *Tweddle* was: can a vendor rely on a rescission condition if he enters into a contract upon reckless advice as to his capacity to sell? Does the seeking of legal advice absolve him of any finding of recklessness, or is he affected with the recklessness of his conveyancer. In *Re Milner and Organ's Contract*[52] the vendors were held not to have acted recklessly in entering into a contract on the basis of mistaken advice. But in that case there was no suggestion that the advice had been given recklessly and the position if it had was not discussed. In *Selkirk* v. *Romar Investments Ltd.*[53] where the vendor was a limited company, only the actions of its solicitor were considered. Nevertheless it is suggested that in such a situation the vendor should not usually be affected by the recklessness of his conveyancer. As Lord Evershed said in *Baines* v. *Tweddle*[54] a vendor has "sufficiently cleared his conscience" by going to a competent conveyancer and acting upon that conveyancer's advice that it is proper for him to enter into the contract.

The above cases were all concerned with the vendor's recklessness in entering into the contract. However the Privy Council, in *Selkirk* v. *Romar Investments Ltd*,[55] said:

Unreasonableness
in rescinding

> "No doubt recklessness in entering into the contract may not be the only thing to be regarded when a vendor's right to exercise a contractual power of rescission is brought into question. It is the use of that right that is not to be arbitrary or without reason, and courts have expressed themselves from time to time as being unwilling to allow a vendor to call the whole contract off in the face of some requisition to which he takes what is merely a capricious or fanciful objection."

Thus, in *Quinion* v. *Horne*[56] a vendor, being a trustee under a will, was held to be acting unreasonably in purporting to rescind in the face of a requisition for information concerning the birth of children of the testator, upon which information the

---

[51] [1959] 1 Ch. 679.
[52] (1920) 89 L.J. Ch. 315.
[53] [1963] 1 W.L.R. 1415.
[54] [1959] 1 Ch. 679 at 690.
[55] [1963] 1 W.L.R. 1422 at 1424.
[56] [1906] 1 Ch. 596.

vendor's power to sell depended: the information could have been obtained by the vendor without expense or trouble.

What if the vendor has no title at all? It seems that the vendor cannot rely on a rescission clause where he has no title at all[57]: his withdrawal from the contract is a breach and full damages are payable to the purchaser. It further seems that a rescission clause will be inapplicable where the vendor fails to disclose defects known to him at the date of the contract. In *Re Jackson and Haden's Contract*[58] the vendors contracted to sell land by a description which would include mines and minerals under it. There was no dishonesty on their part in entering into the contract on these terms: they had assumed that the purchaser was aware of this lack of title since it was well known that in the district mines and minerals were customarily reserved. However the purchaser did not know of the lack of title. It was held that the vendors could not use their contractual right to rescind upon receipt of an objection concerning the lack of title to the minerals: they had recklessly and erroneously described the property, assuming that the purchaser would not be misled and they could not make use of their own error to avoid the contract. A similar decision was arrived at in *Re Des Reaux and Setchfield's Contract*.[59] The vendor purported to sell a fee simple knowing he only had a life estate. But he did believe that he would be able to obtain the concurrence of the person with power to pass the balance of the fee simple. However, he had not consulted that person, nor had he sought legal advice as to the state of the title, before making the contract. The purchaser objected to his lack of title to the fee simple. It was held that the vendor could not exercise his contractual right to rescind: he had entered into the contract knowing he himself had no title.

It is suggested that the above cases do not create a separate rule but are part of the wider rule that a vendor must not act "recklessly" in entering into the contract.

Misdescription v. rescission If a contract contains a condition that misdescription shall not annul the sale but shall be the subject of compensation, and also a condition for rescission, the vendor can defeat the purchaser's claim for compensation by exercising his right to rescind the contract.[60]

Specific performance If the vendor commences an action for specific performance, then so long as that plea is on the record he cannot exercise his contractual right of rescission.

Statutory limitations There are, in addition, statutory limitations on the application of rescission conditions. Sections 42, 45 and 125 of the Law of Property Act 1925 give the purchaser a non-excludable right to raise objections and requisitions in relation to certain matters (the sections are reproduced in Appendix A). The vendor cannot exercise his contractual right to rescind to avoid satisfying such requisitions and objections.

---

[57] *Bowman* v. *Hyland* (1878) 8 Ch.D. 588.
[58] [1906] 1 Ch. 412.
[59] [1926] Ch. 178.
[60] *Ashburner* v. *Sewell* [1891] 3 Ch. 405; *Re Terry and White's Contract* (1886) 32 Ch.D. 14.

Rescission under the standard conditions

**National condition
10(1)**

"10 Vendor's right to rescind.
(1) If the purchaser shall persist in any objection to the
title which the vendor shall be unable or unwilling, on
reasonable grounds, to remove, and shall not withdraw
the same within 10 working days of being required so
to do, the vendor may, subject to the purchaser's
rights under Law of Property Act 1925, ss.42 and 125,
by notice in writing to the purchaser or his solicitor,
and notwithstanding any intermediate negotiation or
litigation, rescind the contract."

**Law Society
general condition
16(1)**

"16 RESCISSION
(1) If the vendor is unable, or on some reasonable ground
unwilling, to satisfy any requisition or objection made
by the purchaser, the vendor may give the purchaser
notice (specifying the reason for his inability or the
ground of his unwillingness) to withdraw the same. If
the purchaser does not withdraw the same within
seven working days of service, either party may
thereafter, notwithstanding any intermediate
negotiation or litigation, rescind the contract by notice
to the other."

**Scope of National
condition 10(1)
Leominster v.
Broadway Finance
Ltd.**

National condition 10(1) permits rescission for the
purchaser's insistence upon any "objection to the title." It was
held in *Leominster Properties Ltd.* v. *Broadway Finance Ltd.*[61] that
the same condition in the 19th edition of the National conditions
did not permit rescission for objections to *conveyance*. The
vendor in that case contracted under the National Conditions,
19th edition, to sell land as a mortgagee. The land was subject to
a prior mortgage in favour of M. The purchaser insisted that
either this be discharged or M should execute the conveyance of
the property. As M was unwilling to join in the conveyance the
vendor gave notice to rescind under condition 10(1). Slade L.J.
held that the phrase "if the purchaser shall persist in any
objection to the title" at the beginning of condition 10(1) must be
read as meaning "if the purchaser shall refuse to accept the title
on any particular ground"; that here the purchaser had not
refused to accept the vendor's title but had objected to matters of
conveyance; and that accordingly the vendor was not entitled to
rescind the contract.

It is submitted that the wording of National condition 10(1)
also precludes rescission for "*requisitions* on title" properly so
called. Questions raised under National condition 9(2) in relation
to occupational interests may only be the subject of rescission if
they amount to objections to the title.

In *Leominster* assistance was sought from a comparison with
general condition 18 of the Law Society's 1973 Revision which
permitted rescission for requisitions or objections "as to title,
conveyance or otherwise." Its present equivalent, general

**Scope of Law
Society general
condition 16(1)**

condition 16(1), merely refers to "any requisition or objection"
which suggests that this condition is not confined to requisitions
or objections to title. If, however, the reasoning of Slade L.J. in

[61] (1981) 42 P. & C.R. 372.

Leominster is to be followed, general condition 16(1) must be construed with the immediately preceding general condition 15, which refers restrictively to "any requisitions or objections relating to the title, evidence of title or the abstract."

Statutory rights of the purchaser

The purchaser's right to raise objections relating to the matters contained in sections 42 and 125 of the Law of Property Act 1925 is expressly reserved by National condition 10(1). The same effect is achieved under Law Society general condition 16(1) by leaving the general law to operate.

"persist"/"make"

The National condition contains the words "if the purchaser shall *persist* . . . ", whereas the Law Society condition uses the words "any requisition or objection *made* by the purchaser . . . " But the distinction mentioned earlier[62] is inapplicable here because both conditions give the purchaser time to withdraw his requisition or objection once notice has been served.[63] It does however seem that under the former condition the purchaser needs to repeat his objection but not under the latter.

Reasonableness

The vendor must act reasonably in seeking to rescind.[64] Although the wording of the conditions suggests that "reasonableness" only qualifies unwillingness to comply with requisitions and objections, case-law goes against a vendor being able to rescind for unreasonable inability to comply.[65]

Mechanics of the conditions

Both conditions state that if the vendor gives notice to the purchaser to withdraw his objection or requisition and the purchaser fails to do so within the time specified (time not being of the essence[66]) rescission may follow. Under National condition 10(1) the purchaser has 10 working days to withdraw his objection after being required to do so. The vendor's request need not be written, nor must reasons be given. If the purchaser refuses to withdraw, the vendor may rescind "by notice in writing." He should exercise this right within a reasonable time after expiry of the 10 working days. Law Society general condition 16(1) provides that the vendor may give the purchaser notice to withdraw and that the purchaser has seven working days from service of the notice in which to do so. The vendor's notice must be in writing, service being governed by Law Society general condition 2. The notice must also specify the reason for the vendor's unwillingness or inability to comply. If the purchaser does not withdraw his requisition, *either party*[67] may rescind the contract by notice to the other. The same criteria of reasonableness probably applies to a purchaser who rescinds under this condition.

"negotiation or litigation"

The right to rescission under either condition is "notwithstanding any intermediate negotiation or litigation." These words are designed to preclude the operation of the rule that if a vendor (or purchaser) being entitled to rescind because of an objection or requisition, negotiates upon it, he loses his right

---

[62] See pp. 19–20.

[63] This was pointed out by H.W. Wilkinson in *Standard Conditions of Sale of Land* (3rd ed.), p. 97.

[64] See p. 22 above.

[65] See *e.g. Baines* v. *Tweddle* [1959] Ch. 679 and *Re Jackson and Haden's Contract* [1906] 1 Ch. 412.

[66] s.41 of the Law of Property Act 1925.

[67] Giving the purchaser the right to rescind was new to the 1980 Edition of the Law Society conditions.

to rescind.[68] But they do not prevent the rule operating if the vendor expressly or impliedly chooses not to rescind.[69]

Disputes   A dispute concerning the use of the right to rescind may be settled by the court under section 49 of the Law of Property Act 1925.[70]

Parties' rights in the event of rescission under the standard conditions

National condition 10(2)   "10(2) Upon such rescission the vendor shall return the deposit but without interest, costs or investigating title or other compensation or payment, and the purchaser shall return the abstract and other papers furnished to him."

Law Society general condition 16(2)   "16(2) Upon rescission under any power given by these conditions or any special condition—
(a) the vendor shall repay to the purchaser any sums paid by way of deposit or otherwise under the contract, with interest on such sums at the contract rate from four working days after recission until payment
(b) the purchaser shall forthwith return all documents delivered to him by the vendor and at his own expense procure the cancellation of any entry relating to the contract in any register."

"Rescission ab initio"   A valid rescission under National condition 10(1) or Law Society general condition 16(1) invokes the provisions of conditions 10(2) or 16(2). The rescission is in general terms a rescission *ab initio*: the deposit and other sums paid by the purchaser must be refunded and neither party is liable to the other for damages, costs and expenses.

Interest   Law Society general condition 16(2) newly[71] provides for the vendor to pay interest[72] at the contract rate on the deposit, from four working days after rescission until payment to the purchaser. This is apparently so whether it is the vendor or the purchaser who rescinds. No interest is payable under National condition 10(2).

Equitable lien for the deposit   Until the deposit is paid to the purchaser, he has an equitable lien over the vendor's property, which may be enforced by an order of sale. In *Whitbread & Co. Ltd.* v. *Watt*[73] the plaintiffs contracted to buy a public house and paid a deposit. Subsequently the property was sold to another purchaser, Watt, who took with notice of the plaintiff's contract. The plaintiffs validly rescinded the contract under a clause empowering them to do so, and claimed repayment of the deposit from Watt. It was held that the purchaser had a lien on the property for the deposit he had paid, which could be enforced by foreclosure or sale. Such a lien must now be protected by registration of a Class C (iii) land charge in the case of unregistered land, or notice or caution in registered land.

[68] *Gardom* v. *Lee* (1865) 3 H. & C. 651.
[69] *Tanner* v. *Smith* (1840) 10 Sim. 410.
[70] See pp. 17–19 above.
[71] First introduced in the 1980 Edition.
[72] Defined by general condition 1(*b*).
[73] [1902] 1 Ch. 835.

Purchaser must return abstracted etc.

The purchaser for his part must return all the vendor's documents. Law Society general condition 16(2)(*b*) expressly obliges him to cancel any land charge, or notice or caution which he has registered to protect the contract or his lien for the deposit. In any event the vendor may procure its cancellation by an application to the court under section 49 of the Law of Property Act 1925.[74] The court may also order cancellation under section 1(6) of the land Charges Act 1972 (unregistered land) and section 82(1) of the Land Registration Act 1925 (registered land). It will not order the vacation of any entry in any register where the very existence of the contract is disputed.[75]

Cancellation of entries in registers

Estate agent's commission

Although a vendor who validly rescinds under National condition 10(1) or Law Society general condition 16(1) will free himself of further liability to the purchaser he may be left with a liability to pay estate agent's commission on the aborted sale. Liability will ultimately turn upon the construction of the agency agreement.

Position of estate agent

If it is agreed that the agent shall be paid commission for introducing a purchaser who will enter into a binding contract, and a binding contract is made, if the vendor subsequently rescinds the contract he must pay commission.[76] But if commission is payable "on the total purchase price obtained" and no completion takes place, no purchase price is obtained and no commission is payable.[77]

Even where commission is payable only on completion, a vendor whose wrongful rescission causes the purchaser to terminate the contract, will be liable in damages to the agent for the commission he has thereby lost.[78]

---

[74] See pp. 17–19 above.
[75] *Re Engall's Agreement* [1953] 1 W.L.R. 977 and *Re 462 Green Lane, Ilford, Gooding* v. *Borland* [1971] 2 W.L.R. 138; contrast *Heywood* v. *B.D.C. Properties Ltd.* [1963] 1 W.L.R. 975 and *Hooker* v. *Wyle* [1974] 1 W.L.R. 235.
[76] *McCallum* v. *Hicks* [1950] 2 K.B. 271.
[77] *Boots* v. *E. Christopher Ltd.* [1952] 1 K.B. 89.
[78] *Alpha Trading Ltd.* v. *Dunnshaw-Patten Ltd.* [1981] Q.B. 290.

4 FAILURE TO COMPLETE

The date for completion: Is it of the essence?

Historical introduction: the common law

At common law the stipulated date for completion[1] was always considered to be "of the essence" of a contract for the sale and purchase of land. By this it was meant that completion by the due date was a condition of the contract. Thus where a vendor was unable to complete on the contractual completion date, he was precluded from thereafter enforcing the contract against the purchaser[2] and was liable in damages to the purchaser[3] (subject to the rule in *Bain* v. *Fothergill*,[4] which absolved the vendor from liability for the purchaser's loss of bargain, where through no fault of his own, the vendor was unable to show good title); the purchaser, for his part, could terminate the contract and recover his deposit.[5] On the other side of the coin, if the purchaser failed to complete on time, he could not thereafter enforce the contract against the vendor and was liable in damages to the vendor, and the vendor could terminate the contract and forfeit the deposit.

In equity

Equity's treatment of the contractual completion date was different. "The legal *construction*[6] of the contract . . . must be, in equity the same as in a court of law"[7]—in equity, failure to complete on the due date was a breach of contract, the same as at law. But, in equity, the *effect* of the breach was different. Subject to the qualifications mentioned below, equity would grant specific performance of the contract at the suit of the delayor and as an incident of doing so, restrain proceedings at law based on the delay.[8] It was in this sense that it was said that in equity the time fixed for completion is not of essence of the contract.[9] However equitable intervention in this area was subject to the normal discretions and would be accompanied in an appropriate case by an award of damages to the purchaser to compensate him for his loss caused by the delay.[10]

Assimilation of the rules of law and equity was completed by section 25(7) of the Supreme Court of Judicature Act 1873, subsequently re-enacted (with slight amendments) in section 41 of the Law of Property Act 1925:

Law of Property Act 1925, s.41

"Stipulations in a contract, as to time or otherwise, which

---

[1] For conditions, express or implied, as to when completion is to take place, see Annand & Whish, *Conveyancing Solutions 2: The Contract* (1987).
[2] *Maryon* v. *Carter* (1830) 4 Car. & P. 295; 172 E.R. 711.
[3] *Raineri* v. *Miles* [1981] A.C. 1050.
[4] (1874) L.R. 7 H.L. 158.
[5] *Wilde* v. *Fort* (1812) 4 Taunt, 334; 128 E.R. 359.
[6] Own emphasis.
[7] *Tilley* v. *Thomas* (1867) L.R. 3 Ch.App. 61, *per* Lord Cairns at 67. Cited with approval in *Raineri* v. *Miles* [1981] A.C. 1050 at 1082, 1090.
[8] *Tilley* v. *Thomas* (1867) L.R. 3 Ch.App. 61 at 67; *Stickney* v. *Keeble* [1915] A.C. 386 at 415, 416.
[9] *Tilley* v. *Thomas* (1867) L.R. 3 Ch.App. 61; *Stickney* v. *Keeble* [1915] A.C. 386.
[10] *Phelps* v. *Prothero* (1855) 7 De. G.M. & G. 722 at 734; 44 E.R. 280 at 285; *Raineri* v. *Miles* [1981] A.C. 1050 at 1081.

according to rules of equity are not deemed to be or have become of the essence of the contract, are also construed and have effect at law in accordance with the same rules."

There is some uncertainty as to the precise operation of section 41. Lord Parker of Waddington said, in *Stickney* v. *Keeble*[11]:

Stickney v. Keeble

"The section[12] cannot in my opinion mean that the rules as to time laid down by Courts of Equity in certain cases, for certain purposes, and under certain circumstances only, shall be applied generally and without inquiry whether the particular case, purpose, or circumstances are such that equity would have applied the rules. If since the Judicature Acts the Court is asked to disregard a stipulation as to time in an action for common law relief, and it be established that equity would not under the then existing circumstances have prior to the Act granted specific performance or restrained the action, the section can, in my opinion, have no application, otherwise the stipulation in question would not, as provided in the section, receive the same effect as it would prior to the act have received in equity."

According to this view, the section can have no application (and time remains of the essence) where equity would not have intervened to restrain an action at law based on breach of the time stipulation—as where the party seeking relief from the consequences of breach of the time stipulation had lost his right to specific performance of the contract, by, for example, in the case of a vendor, selling the property elsewhere (as occurred in *Stickney* v. *Keeble*).

United Scientific Holdings Ltd. v. Burnley Borough Council

By way of contrast, the House of Lords, in *United Scientific Holdings Ltd.* v. *Burnley Borough Council*[13] acted on the view that since the enactment of section 41 stipulations in contracts as to time take effect in accordance with the rules of equity and this is *not* limited to those situations where relief was available before 1875. The *United Scientific* case concerned the construction of time stipulations in rent review clauses in leases but their Lordships' interpretation of section 41 would seem to apply equally to contracts for the sale of land. Lord Diplock[14] could see:

" . . . no relevant difference between the obligation undertaken by a tenant under a rent review clause in a lease and any other obligation in a synallagmatic contract[15] that is expressed to arise upon the occurrence of a described event, where a postponement of that event beyond the time stipulated in the contract is not so prolonged as to deprive the obligator of substantially the whole benefit that it was intended he should obtain by accepting the obligation."

Again, Lord Simon said:

---

[11] [1915] A.C. 386 at 417.
[12] His Lordship was of course referring to s.25(7), the predecessor of s.41.
[13] [1978] A.C. 904.
[14] *Ibid.* at 930.
[15] By "synallagmatic contract" Lord Diplock meant a contract imposing obligations on two or more parties; as opposed to a unilateral contract.

"I agree [with the arguments of Lord Diplock] culminating in the propositions that, in general, in modern English law time is prima facie not of the essence of a contract . . . ."[16]

and:

"I cannot read section 41 of the Law of Property Act as meaning other than that, whenever contractual stipulations as to time fall for consideration in any court, they shall not be construed as essential, except where equity would before 1875 have so construed them—*i.e.*, only when the strict observance of the stipulated time for performance was a matter of express agreement or of necessary implication."[17]

Three of their Lordships[18] considered that the law was correctly summarised in this passage from *Halsbury's Laws of England* (4th ed.), Vol. 9, para. 481, p. 338:

"Time will not be considered to be of the essence unless (1) the parties expressly stipulate that conditions as to time must be strictly complied with: or (2) the nature of the subject matter of the contract or the surrounding circumstances show that time should be considered to be of the essence . . . ."

Time of the essence at law and in equity

Notwithstanding this apparent divergence of opinion as to the exact operation of section 41, it is clear that, both at law and in equity, time *will be* or *will have become* of the essence for completion of a contract for the sale of land:

1. where the parties expressly provide for the completion date to be of the essence;
2. where the surrounding circumstances, including the nature of the property, indicate that the completion date is of the essence;
3. where either party has been guilty of unreasonable delay in completing the contract; or
4. where the correct notice procedure is followed.

Each of these circumstances will be considered in turn.

(1) Express provision

Time of the essence by express provision

The parties may agree that time shall be of the essence for completion of the contract. The normal way of doing this is to state that as regards completion "time shall be of the essence of the contract." If this formula is used any delay in completion will entitle the innocent party to terminate the contract. It is however not necessary for the formula "time shall be of the essence" to be used. Any expression that makes it clear that a timely completion is an essential term of the contract will suffice. In *Harold Wood Brick Co. Ltd.* v. *Ferris*[19] the contract stated that completion should be on August 13, 1933 and "if for any reason the actual completion of the purchase is delayed beyond August 31, 1933, then nevertheless on that date the purchase money . . . shall be

[16] [1978] A.C. 904 at 940.
[17] *Ibid.* at 943.
[18] Viscount Dilhorne, Lord Simon of Glaisdale and Lord Fraser of Tullybelton.
[19] [1935] 1 K.B. 198.

placed on deposit . . . but the purchase shall in any event actually be completed not later than September 15, 1933 . . . ." The Court of Appeal held the date, September 15, fixed for completion was of the essence and since the purchaser had failed to complete on that date, the vendor was entitled to treat himself as discharged from the contract and claim damages for the breach.

"On or before"   The view has been expressed that a provision for completion "on or before" a certain date, without more, makes times of the essence.[20] In *Lock* v. *Bell*[21] completion was scheduled to take place "on or about" November 10. Maugham J. equated the words "on or about" with the words "on or before" and came to the conclusion that time was of the essence of the contract. The purchaser had failed to complete "on or about" November 10 and therefore the vendor could forfeit his deposit. However in *James Macara Ltd.* v. *Barclay*[22] the Court of Appeal thought (*obiter*) that the words "on or before" did not make time of the essence. And in *Raineri* v. *Miles*[23] the point was not argued, for even though the contract provided for completion "on or before July 12, 1977," it was "common ground that time was not of the essence of the original contract between the appellants and the respondents."[24] *Lock* v. *Bell* concerned the sale of a public house as a going concern; *James Macara Ltd.* v. *Barclay* and *Raineri* v. *Miles* the sales of private dwelling-houses with vacant possession. This has led another writer[25] to suggest that the words "on or before" only make time of the essence for completion if coupled with other relevant circumstances, such as the nature of the property (see below). Indeed in *Pips (Leisure Productions) Ltd.* v. *Walton*,[26] where the agreement was that both parties "would use their best endeavour to complete the purchase by Monday December 3, 1979," Megarry V.-C. held that time was impliedly of the essence because the subject of the sale was a wasting asset (a short lease), not expressly because of the quoted words which were merely treated as not negativing the intention.

Waiver   A party may, by his conduct, be estopped from relying on the expressed essentiality of a completion date.

In *Offredy Developments Ltd.* v. *Steinbock*[27] it was agreed that completion should take place nine months after exchange of contracts, as the vendor was having another house built. The date was stated to be of the essence. On several occasions the vendor asked for an extension of the completion date but the purchaser refused. The vendor led the purchaser to believe that possession could not be given on the completion date, so the purchaser did not submit a draft transfer for approval by that date. The day after the date set for completion the vendor purported to rescind

---

[20] (1956) 20 Conv. (N.S.) 347; J.T. Farrand, *Contract and Conveyance* (4th ed.), p. 182, and see *Raineri* v. *Miles* [1981] A.C. 1050 at 1089, *per* Lord Fraser of Tullybelton, discussed at [1980] Conv. 238.
[21] [1931] 1 Ch. 35.
[22] [1945] K.B. 148.
[23] [1981] A.C. 1050.
[24] *Ibid.* at 1088.
[25] (1977) 127 New L.J. 471, H.W. Wilkinson.
[26] (1982) 43 P. & C.R. 415.
[27] (1971) 221 E.G. 963, C.A.

the contract for the purchaser's delay in completion. The vendor was estopped from exercising his right to terminate the contract.

(2) From the surrounding circumstances

Even though the parties may not have expressed the completion date to be of the essence, the surrounding circumstances, including the nature of the property may make it so. This is especially true where the subject matter of the sale is property "which by delay will not be of the same value as at the time of sale."[28] So, for instance, the completion date has been held to be

Time of the essence for sale of a business as a going concern

essential in a contract for the sale of a public house as a going concern[29] (because the business depends largely upon the powers of management of the licensee and the stock fluctuates daily) and similarly in a contract for the sale of a cafe[30]; in a contract for the sale of a leasehold mine which was being worked[31]; in a contract for the sale of a determinable interest, such as a life estate[32] and (in some circumstances) for the sale of a leasehold interest[33] and (probably) in a contract for the sale of a farm.[34]

However time will not be of the essence in such circumstances if the contract states that it shall not be of the

Special conditions may prevent time being of the essence

essence or if there are provisions in the contract from which it can be implied that time is not of the essence. *Shires* v. *Brock*[35] concerned the sale of a leasehold interest and hairdresser's business conducted thereon. A special condition in the contract provided that the vendor should retain possession until actual completion and that should completion not take place until after the date nominated in the contract, the vendor should carry on the business for the benefit of the purchaser. Time was held not to be of the essence. Similarly time was held not to be of the essence for the sale of an ironmongery and hardware business in *Ellis* v. *Lawrence*[36]: special conditions in the contract provided for the payment of interest if completion was delayed and for the giving of a notice to complete.

Negotiations prior to entry into the contract

Negotiations between the parties prior to entry into the contract may have the effect of making the completion date impliedly of the essence. Thus in *Tilley* v. *Thomas*,[37] time was found to be essential where the purchaser had already sold his house at the date of the contract and to the knowledge of the vendor needed another quickly. But the modern view appears to be that the completion date is not essential for the sale of

---

[28] *Withy* v. *Cottle* (1823) Tum & R. 78 at 80, *per* Lord Eldon L.C.
[29] *Coslake* v. *Till* (1826) 1 Russ. 376; *Lock* v. *Bell* [1931] 1 Ch. 35; *Cowles* v. *Gale* (1871) 7 Ch.App. 12; *Powell* v. *Marshall, Parkes & Co.* [1899] 1 Q.B. 710.
[30] *Vasilou* v. *Metz* (1960) 176 E.G. 260.
[31] *Macbryde* v. *Weekes* (1856) 22 Beav. 533; and see *Harold Wood Brick Co. Ltd.* v. *Ferris* [1935] 2 K.B. 198—sale of brickfield with modern machinery and arrangements for making wire-cut bricks.
[32] *Parkin* v. *Thorold* (1852) 16 Beav. 59 at 65.
[33] Probably only short leaseholds. In *Pips (Leisure Productions) Ltd.* v. *Walton* (1982) 43 P. & C.R. 415, Sir Robert Megarry held time to be of the essence for the sale of a lease for 21 years with less than $15\frac{1}{2}$ years to run.
[34] *Stickney* v. *Keeble* [1915] A.C. 386.
[35] (1977) 247 E.G. 127, C.A.
[36] (1969) 210 E.G. 215.
[37] (1867) L.R. 3 Ch.App. 61.

residential property[38] (unless expressed to be so) even where the subject contract is one in an interdependent chain of transactions,[38] for: "it would need very special circumstances to make time of the essence of the contract on a sale of an ordinary private dwelling house with vacant possession."[39]

(3) By unreasonable delay

A completion date may have become of the essence, when either party has been guilty of unreasonable delay.[40] If the delay *is* unreasonable, the innocent party is entitled to consider himself discharged from the contract without further ado. What amounts to unreasonable delay in a particular case must depend on its peculiar circumstances. In *Accuba Ltd.* v. *Allied Shoe Repairs Ltd.*[41] landlords were 18 months late in serving a notice to increase the rent for the second seven years of a 14 year underlease. Goff J. thought that this was a borderline case but ultimately decided that the delay was not unreasonable in the context of the length of the term. On the other hand, in *Inns* v. *D. Miles Griffiths, Piercy & Co.*,[42] the purchaser was guilty of unreasonable delay in completing a contract for the sale of a smallholding. The contract had not set a date for completion, so that the "crucial question" was, whether a reasonable time had passed in which the purchaser could have completed bearing in mind the conveyancing business to be done. An informal agreement between the respective solicitors had been ineffective to fix a completion date and the service of a notice to complete was thought by the judge to be irrelevant, but that agreement plus the fact that the solicitors were ready to complete led him to conclude that a reasonable time had elapsed.

Unreasonable delay—a question of fact

(4) By notice

Where the completion date is not of the essence under the contract, it may be made so by the serving of a notice to complete. Also where the right to rely on the essentiality of a completion date has been lost by conduct,[43] it may be reinstated by the serving of a notice to complete.

Completion notice

At common law three requirements are essential for the service of a valid notice to complete[44]:

Three essential requirements at common law

    (a) the recipient must be in default under the contract, such as to justify the serving of a notice; and

---

[38] This was assumed in *Raineri* v. *Miles* [1981] A.C. 1050 although Lord Edmund-Davies (at 1082) suggested that if the purchaser had argued that time was of the essence because his purchase was part of a chain transaction, he might have been successful.

[39] *Smith* v. *Hamilton* [1951] Ch. 174 at 179.

[40] *Farrant* v. *Oliver* [1922] W.N. 47, cited with approval in *Accuba Ltd.* v. *Allied Shoe Repairs* [1975] 1 W.L.R. 1559 at 1565; *Emmet on Title* (19th ed.), para. 7/92; and see [1980] Conv. 19, A. Sydenham.

[41] [1975] 1 W.L.R. 1565.

[42] (1980) 255 E.G. 623. See also *Cole* v. *Rose* [1978] 3 All E.R. 1121, D.C.

[43] See p. 31 above.

[44] *Re Barr's Contract* [1956] Ch. 551 at 556.

(b) the server of the notice must be able, ready and willing to proceed to completion; and

(c) the notice must specify a reasonable time for completion.

(a) **The recipient must be in default**   Where the parties have fixed a date for completion, a completion notice may be served on the party who has failed to complete as soon as that date has passed. At one time it was thought that a notice could not be served until completion had been unreasonably delayed: that is, until *both* the contractual completion date had passed *and* a reasonable time thereafter had expired.[45] This was because the contractual completion date was regarded as a target date only, requiring completion on that date or within a reasonable time thereafter, so that a party could not be in default in completing the contract until a reasonable time had expired.[46] However it is now known that the "target date" theory was based on a misconception as to the effect of the rule that time is not of the essence in equity.[47] The true position is that failure to complete on the contractual completion date (time not being of the essence) is a breach of contract, which, although not entitling the innocent party immediately to terminate the contract, does immediately sound in damages and does, *a fortiori*, justify the immediate serving of a notice to complete on the defaulter.[48]

Where the contract does not specify a date for completion, the law implies a term that completion shall take place within a reasonable time. This is a question of fact to be determined in the light of the conveyancing business yet to be attended to.[49] It would seem, by analogy with the position where the contract does fix a date for completion, that a defaulter can be served with notice to complete if he fails to complete within a "reasonable time" after exchange of contracts.

(b) **Readiness of server of notice**   The second requirement for the service of a valid notice to complete is that the server of the notice must be "able, ready and willing to proceed to completion . . . ."[50] Thus it has been held that a vendor cannot issue a notice to complete where he has refused to satisfy a requisition about a third party's claim to possession of the property[51]; or where he has failed to comply with his obligation to disclose existing tenancies.[52] In *Cole* v. *Rose*[53] the purchaser did not complete on the agreed completion date because he was

Margin notes:

When may a completion notice be served

Not only the scouts must "be prepared"

Cole v. *Rose*

---

[45] *Green* v. *Sevin* (1879) 13 Ch.D. 589.

[46] *Smith* v. *Hamilton* [1951] Ch. 174. See also *Babacomp Ltd.* v. *Rightside Properties Ltd.* [1973] 3 All E.R. 873 and *Woods* v. *Mackenzie Hill Ltd.* [1975] 1 W.L.R. 613 and [1978] Conv. 144–160, C.T. Emery.

[47] *Raineri* v. *Miles* [1981] A.C. 1050.

[48] *Inns* v. *D. Miles Griffiths, Piercy & Co.* (1980) 255 E.G. 623.

[49] *Johnson* v. *Humphrey* [1946] 1 All E.R. 460.

[50] *Re Barr's Contract* [1956] Ch. 551 at 556; and see (1973) 123 New L.J. 229, H.W. Wilkinson.

[51] *Horton* v. *Kurzke* [1971] 1 W.L.R. 769 (third party claiming grazing tenancy over part of property).

[52] *Pagebar Properties Ltd.* v. *Derby Investment Holdings Ltd.* [1972] 1 W.L.R. 1500. See also *Jneid* v. *Mirza* (1981) 131 New L.J. 472 (licence to assign not yet obtained by vendor).

[53] [1978] 3 All E.R. 1121; and see [1979] Conv. 161.

unable to raise the money. The vendors served a notice to complete and on failure by the purchaser to comply, resold the property and forfeited the purchaser's deposit. In an action brought by the purchaser to recover his deposit, it was held that the notice to complete was invalid because the vendors had not, at the date of its issue, obtained for themselves, and provided the purchaser with, details of charges affecting the property: they could not be ready to complete until they had those details. In that case Mervyn Davies Q.C. (sitting as deputy High Court judge) drew a distinction between a failure to be ready to complete because of outstanding "matters of substance" (into which category the charges in this case fell) and a failure to be ready to complete because of "administrative matters" (examples given were "a completion statement may have to be prepared and agreed or arrangements made for the discharge of mortgages (in the ordinary case),[54] or the time and place of completion agreed"[55]): only failure to attend to outstanding "matters of substance" prevents the service of a valid notice to complete.

**Misdescription—
Johns v. Deacon**

In *Johns* v. *Deacon*[56] a contract for the sale of a farm wrongly described the property as including a dismountable stable block: the vendor had, prior to exchange of contracts dismantled the stable block and sold it elsewhere. It was accepted that this was a misdescription of the kind which did not cause the sale to be annulled but gave rise to a right of compensation, by way of reduction to the purchase price. The Court of Appeal held that unless and until the reduction in the purchase price had been agreed, the vendor could not be ready to complete.

**Must the server
remain ready
whilst the notice is
running?**

There are dicta in *Quadrangle Development & Construction Co. Ltd.* v. *Jenner*[57] which suggest that a party who serves notice must be ready to complete *both* at the date of service *and* at all times during the currency of the notice. In *Oakdown Ltd.* v. *Bernstein & Co.*,[58] following a vendor's notice to complete, the purchaser nominated for completion the day before expiry of the 28 day period. The vendor refused to complete on that day for religious reasons. Scott J. felt unable to accept the purchaser's argument, based on the dicta in *Quadrangle*, that this entitled them to terminate the contract: the only obligation under the notice of which time was of the essence was to complete before the expiry of the notice.[59] As his Lordship pointed out, *Quadrangle* was in fact on the separate point (discussed below) of whether one party can make use of the other's notice.

**Reasonableness—
a question of fact**

(c) **The notice must allow a reasonable time for completion**   The third requirement for a valid notice to complete is that the time specified in the notice for completion

---

[54] Writer's addition.
[55] *Cole* v. *Rose* [1978] 3 All E.R. 1121 at 1128. Other examples may include, where it is the purchaser serving the notice, obtaining mortgage moneys or making a land charges or land registry search.
[56] [1985] C.A.T. 13, C.A.
[57] [1974] 1 W.L.R. 68, *per* Buckley L.J. at 73.
[58] (1984) 49 P. & C.R. 282.
[59] The purchaser was however entitled to treat the contract as at an end because the vendor failed to complete within the 28 day period at all.

must be reasonable. What is reasonable is a question of fact: regard must be had to all the circumstances of the case.[60]

Relevant circumstances

The purchaser's difficulty in obtaining finance may affect the length of the notice. In *Re Barr's Contract*[61] the purchasers were unable to complete on the agreed date because their proposed sub-sale of the property fell through. The vendors served them with a 28 day notice to complete. It was held that the notice was

Difficulty in raising purchase price

bad: it gave the purchasers insufficient time to raise the £50,000 required to complete. A similar case is *Smith* v. *Hamilton*,[62] where a 14 day notice was held to be unreasonable. Indeed Harman J. said in that case,[63] that he knew of "no instance where a delay as short as a fortnight has been held to entitle either a vendor or a purchaser to rescind." Nevertheless a vendor's six day notice to complete was upheld by the Privy Council in *Ajit* v. *Sammy*[64]: the purchaser had no money and no prospect of ever acquiring any.

However, it would seem that the purchaser's difficulty in raising the money will only be relevant, if it has been brought to the vendor's notice.[65]

Conveyancing difficulties

Conveyancing difficulties may also be one of the circumstances.[66] Thus in *Re Engall's Agreement*,[67] Vaisey J. doubted whether a 21 day notice given by the vendors 21 days after the contractual completion date was sufficient, in view of the fact that the draft conveyance had not been submitted for approval.

The reasonableness of the time for completion specified in the notice is computed having regard to the date of service of the notice, not the date of its issue. This is probably so even where the notice calls for completion "within X days of the date hereof."[68]

It remains to make brief mention of some miscellaneous points concerning notices to complete.

Form of notice

First, no particular form of notice is required at common law. Any writing will suffice provided it gives notice in clear, unequivocal and unambiguous terms.[69] There seems to be no reason why an oral notice to complete should not be effective, although there may be problems with section 40(1) of the Law of Property Act 1925.[70]

Secondly, a notice to complete which demands rights in excess of those possessed by the server will not necessarily be invalid. In *Inns* v. *D. Miles Griffiths, Piercy & Co.*,[71] a notice to complete served at common law claimed interest on the balance of the purchase price at the rate of 18 per cent. per annum from

---

[60] *Re Barr's Contract* [1956] Ch. 551, *per* Danckwerts J. at 558.
[61] [1956] Ch. 551.
[62] [1951] Ch. 174.
[63] *Ibid.* at 182.
[64] [1967] A.C. 255.
[65] *Re Roger Malcolm Development Ltd.'s Contract* (1960) 176 E.G. 1237.
[66] *Re Barr's Contract* [1956] Ch. 551 at 558.
[67] [1953] 1 W.L.R. 977 at 979.
[68] *Re Barr's Contract* [1956] Ch. 551 at 551 and *Dimsdale Developments (South East) Ltd.* v. *De Haan* (1984) 47 P. & C.R. 1; but see *Rightside Properties Ltd.* v. *Gray* [1975] Ch. 72.
[69] *Inns* v. *D. Miles Griffiths, Piercy & Co.* (1980) 255 E.G. 623.
[70] *Clearbrook Property Holdings Ltd.* v. *Verrier* [1974] 1 W.L.R. 243.
[71] (1980) 255 E.G. 624.

the contractual completion date. No rate of interest had been agreed under the contract. It was held that the notice was valid; the purchaser's remedy was to ignore the unjustified demand for interest, not to refuse to complete. As a practical matter, the purchaser should attend on completion as required by the notice, and tender the amount he (the purchaser) considers reasonable.[72]

Unjustified demands may be ignored

Relationship with specific performance

Thirdly, a notice to complete is not a necessary prelude to an action for specific performance.[73] Such an action may be brought if the contractual completion date has not been met, or even before it has arrived if one party has reasonable cause to suspect that the other will not complete on time.[74] However a notice to complete cannot be served after an order for specific performance has been obtained, because the carrying out of the contract has become essentially a matter for the court and not the parties. In *Singh (Sudagar)* v. *Nazeer*,[75] following the vendor's failure to complete on the contractual completion date, the purchaser applied for and obtained an order for specific performance of the contract. When the vendor was eventually ready to complete, the purchaser delayed, so the vendor served a 28 days' notice to complete under the contract. It was held that the notice was bad: the appropriate action for the vendor to have taken was to have applied for a court order fixing a date for completion.

Fourthly, where an effective notice to complete is served, time is of the essence under the contract for *both* parties. If the server does not complete on time, the party served can take advantage of his notice. In *Finkielkrant* v. *Monohan*[76] the vendor served a notice to complete on the purchaser. Errors in the engrossed conveyance were not noticed until the notice had started to run and were not corrected by the time it expired. For this reason the vendor could not complete and the purchaser (who was by this time "ready") gave the vendor three days' notice to complete. Still the vendor could not complete and it was held that the purchaser was entitled to terminate the contract.

Unreasonable delay

Fifthly, once a party's delay in completing has become unreasonable, the other may terminate the contract without first serving notice to complete.[77]

Damages

Sixthly, the issuing of a notice to complete following failure to complete on the (non-essential) completion date does not affect the innocent party's right to claim damages for delay.[78] Damages might include, the cost of bridging finance for the vendor, and the cost of alternative accommodation and of removal and storage of furniture.[79] It is doubtful whether the damages for such delay would be increased to cover any distress, anguish and frustration

[72] *Towli* v. *Fourth River Property Co. Ltd.*, *The Times*, November 24, 1976; *Schindler* v. *Pigault* (1975) 30 P. & C.R. 328.
[73] *Marks* v. *Lilley* [1959] 1 W.L.R. 749 at 753.
[74] *Hasham* v. *Zenab* [1960] A.C. 316; see also *Oakacre Ltd.* v. *Claire Cleaners (Holdings) Ltd.* [1982] Ch. 197, where it was held that the issue of a writ of specific performance before the contractual completion date was not premature and did not preclude a claim for damages for delay in completion.
[75] [1979] 1 Ch. 474.
[76] [1949] 2 All E.R. 234.
[77] See p. 33 above.
[78] *Raineri* v. *Miles* [1981] A.C. 1050.
[79] *Ibid.*

suffered.[80] In *Cochrane (Decorators) Ltd.* v. *Sarabandi*,[81] property was sold as suitable for conversion. Completion was delayed for 10 months, during which time, building costs increased, and the one-time buoyant property market declined. The purchasers had planned to make a profit of £100,000 on the conversion of the property into flats but, in the event, suffered a loss of £25,000. They were awarded damages of £112,000 for the delay: it was within the contemplation of the parties that the conversion was to be carried out for profit.

Duty to mitigate?　However, note should be taken of Templeman L.J.'s observation in the Court of Appeal in *Raineri* v. *Miles*[82] that: "In a good many cases a short delay will not cause damage and if sufficient warning is given a purchaser will be able to mitigate any damage and is under a duty to do so. But where . . . damage cannot be avoided, a vendor who chooses not to complete must take the consequences."

Extensions of time　Seventhly, at common law a notice can be extended to fixed dates, without affecting its validity. In *Buckland* v. *Farmar and Moody*[83] purchasers were served with notice to complete the purchase by December 1. They could not raise the money and proposed to assign the benefit of the contract to a third party, M. The vendor gave M two extensions of time, to enable him to make the necessary arrangements. M failed to complete and on February 7 the vendor gave the purchasers notice of it's intention to terminate the contract. It was held that neither the extensions of time granted to M, nor the lack of communication between the vendor and the purchasers from December 1 to February 7, precluded the vendor from relying on its rights under the notice. Furthermore even if the purchasers could take advantage of M's extensions of time, these were to fixed dates and time remained essential.

Or new bargain?　A contrasting case is *Luck* v. *White*.[84] There the parties negotiated a *new* completion date at the expiration of the vendor's notice to complete. Completion did not take place on the new date, because the purchaser disputed the amount of interest payable. The vendor purported to terminate the contract. Goulding L.J. said[85]:

> "If the party who is in the right allows the defaulting party to try to remedy his default after an essential date has passed, he cannot then call the bargain off without first warning the defaulting party by fixing a fresh limit reasonable in the circumstances."

The vendor had not done this and could not rely on the fact that at one time he had, by notice, made time of the essence. The purchaser was entitled to specific performance. *Luck* v. *White* was

---

[80] *Bliss* v. *South East Thames Regional Health Authority* (1985) I.R.L.R. 308, affirming *Addis* v. *Gramophone Co. Ltd.* [1909] A.C. 488. *Jarvis* v. *Swans Tours Co.* [1973] 1 Q.B. 233 not followed.
[81] (1983) 133 New L.J. 558.
[82] [1981] A.C. 1050 at 1064.
[83] [1979] 1 W.L.R. 221.
[84] (1973) 26 P. & C.R. 89.
[85] *Ibid.* at 96.

distinguished in *Prosper Homes* v. *Hambros Bank Executor & Trustee Co. Ltd.*[86]

It is doubtful whether an oral extension of time complies with the provisions of section 40(1) of the Law of Property Act 1925.[87]

Consequences of non-compliance

Finally, what are the consequences of failure to comply with a notice to complete? The delayee has two available options—to seek specific performance or to end the contract. In either case damages may be recoverable. If the contract is terminated the deposit may be forfeited or recovered as appropriate. If the delayor is the purchaser, the vendor may, "as owner," resell the property and claim as damages the difference between the contract price and the resale price (plus his expenses),[88] provided of course that the loss is attributable to the purchaser's breach. Credit must be given for the deposit.[89] If the vendor does not resell, the measure of damages is the difference between the contract price and the value of the property (generally) at the time the contract is lost.[90]

A reselling vendor is probably under a duty to obtain a proper market price for the property.[91]

Failure to complete under the standard conditions

National condition 5(2)

"(2) Unless the Special Conditions otherwise provide, in respect of the completion date time shall not be of the essence of the contract, but this provision shall operate subject and without prejudice to—
  (i) the provisions of condition 22 and
  (ii) the rights of either party to recover from the other damages for delay in fulfilling his obligations under the contract."

National condition 22

"22. Special notice to complete
(1) At any time on or after the completion date, either party, being ready and willing to fulfil his own outstanding obligations under the contract, may (without prejudice to any other right or remedy available to him) give to the other party or his solicitor notice in writing requiring completion of the contract in conformity with this condition
(2) Upon service of such notice as aforesaid it shall become and be a term of the contract, in respect of which time shall be of the essence thereof, that the party to whom the notice is given shall complete the contract within 16 working days after service of the notice (exclusive of the day of service): but this condition shall operate without prejudice

---

[86] (1979) 39 P. & C.R. 395.
[87] *Clearbrook Property Holdings Ltd.* v. *Verrier* [1974] 1 W.L.R. 243.
[88] *Harold Wood Brick Co. Ltd.* v. *Ferris* [1935] 1 K.B. 198.
[89] *Ockenden* v. *Henly* (1858) El. B. & El. 485.
[90] *Johnson* v. *Agnew* [1980] A.C. 367; *Domb* v. *Isoz* [1980] Ch. 548.
[91] By analogy with the position of a mortgagee exercising his statutory power of sale, *Cuckmere Brick Co. Ltd. and Another* v. *Mutual Finance Ltd.* [1971] Ch. 949. *Tse Wong Lam* v. *Wong Chit Sen* [1983] 1 W.L.R. 1394.

to any right of either party to rescind the contract in the meantime

(3) In case the purchaser refuses or fails to complete in conformity with this condition, then (without prejudice to any other right or remedy available to the vendor) the purchaser's deposit may be forfeited (unless the court otherwise directs) and, if the vendor resells the property within twelve months of the expiration of the said period of 16 working days, he shall be entitled (upon crediting the deposit) to recover from the purchaser hereunder the amount of any loss occasioned to the vendor by expenses of or incidental to such resale, or by diminution in the price."

Law Society general condition 23

"23. COMPLETION NOTICE

(1) This condition applies unless a special condition provides that time is of the essence in respect of contractual completion date.

(2) If the sale shall not be completed on contractual completion date, either party, being then himself ready able and willing to complete, may after the date serve on the other party notice to complete the transaction in accordance with this condition. A party shall be deemed to be ready, able and willing to complete—

(a) if he could be so but for some default or omission of the other party

(b) notwithstanding that any mortgage on the property is unredeemed when the completion notice is served if the aggregate of all sums necessary to redeem all such mortgages (to the extent that they relate to the property) does not exceed the sum payable on completion.

(3) Upon service of a completion notice it shall become a term of the contract that the transaction shall be completed within fifteen working days of service and in respect of such period time shall be of the essence.

(4) If the purchaser does not comply with a completion notice—

(a) the purchaser shall forthwith return all documents delivered to him by the vendor and at his own expense procure the cancellation of any entry relating to the contract in any register

(b) without prejudice to any other rights or remedies available to him, the vendor may—

   (i) forfeit and retain any deposit paid and/or
   (ii) re-sell the property by auction, tender or private treaty.

(5) If on any such re-sale contracted within one year after contractual completion date the vendor incurs a loss and so elects by notice to the purchaser within one month after the contract for such re-sale, the purchaser shall pay to the vendor liquidated damages. The amount payable shall be the aggregate of such loss, all costs and expenses reasonably incurred in any such re-sale and any attempted re-sale and interest at the contract rate on such part of the purchase money as is from time to time outstanding (giving credit for all sums received under any re-sale contract on account of the re-sale price) after contractual completion date.

(6) If the vendor does not comply with a completion notice, the purchaser, without prejudice to any other rights or remedies available to him, may give notice to the vendor forthwith to pay to the purchaser any sums paid by way of deposit or otherwise under the contract and interest on such sums at the contract rate from four working days after service of the notice until payment. On compliance with such notice the purchaser shall not be entitled to specific performance of the contract, but shall forthwith return all documents delivered to him by the vendor and at the expense of the vendor procure the cancellation of any entry relating to the contract in any register.

(7) Where after service of a completion notice the time for completion shall have been extended by agreement or implication, either party may again invoke the provisions of this condition which shall then take effect with the substitution of 'seven working days' for 'fifteen working days' in sub-condition (3)."

Is time of the essence?

National condition 5(2) negatives the common law rule that time is automatically of the essence in a contract for the sale of land where the circumstances of the transaction, including the nature of the property, make it so[92]—if a timely completion is essential to the parties, this must be provided for by special condition. The Law Society general conditions contain no equivalent provision. In any event, both contracts contain provisions (payment of interest/compensation for a delayed completion, service of completion notices) from which it can be implied that time is not of the essence.[93]

Damages for late completion

National condition 5(2)(ii) specifically preserves a party's right to sue the other at common law for damages for failure to complete on a non-essential completion date.[94] Law Society general condition 22 similarly obliges a party "in default" in completing to compensate the other for loss occasioned by "his delay," but delay by an innocent party before completion may lessen (or even cancel out) any damages the defaulting party has to pay.

National condition 22 and Law Society general condition 23 avoid many of the difficulties involved in serving common law completion notices. The better view is that the remedies provided by these conditions are only available if a valid notice to complete is served in accordance with the conditions.[95] Thus, National condition 22(1) speaks of a notice in writing being served and remedies following if the purchaser fails to complete "in conformity with this condition." Law Society general condition 23(4) and (5) sets out the vendor's remedies if the purchaser does not comply with "a completion notice" and 23(6) sets out the purchaser's remedies if the vendor is in default.

Remedies only available if valid notice served

Either party may serve a completion notice under the

[92] See p. 39 above.
[93] *Shires* v. *Brock* (1978) 247 E.G. 127 and *Ellis* v. *Lawrence* (1969) 210 E.G. 215 and see p. 32 above.
[94] *Raineri* v. *Miles* [1981] A.C. 1050.
[95] H.W. Wilkinson, *Standard Conditions of Sale of Land* (3rd ed.), p. 177.

When may notice be served? conditions once the contractual completion date has passed and has not been met. This settles any doubt that may still exist at common law as to whether the delayee must first wait until a reasonable time has elapsed.[96]

No question of reasonableness of time allowed by notice Once a valid notice to complete has been served, the delayor has 16 working days within which to complete the contract under the National conditions, and 15 working days under the Law Society's. No question arises as to the reasonableness of the period allowed by the notice, because the parties have agreed otherwise.[97] (National condition 22(2) and Law Society general condition 23(2)).

Other remedies still available Neither condition excludes a party's normal contractual remedies for delay. In *Woods* v. *Mackenzie Hill Ltd.*[98] a completion notice served under the Law Society's General Conditions of Sale (1973 revision) was invalid, because it was given by only two out of the three vendors. Without serving another notice, the vendors took proceedings for specific performance and were successful. Megarry J. said of the conditions:

> "In my judgment, such provisions add to the remedies available against a defaulting party without driving out the existing remedies, or altering the existing structure [of the contract] . . . I wholly reject any notion that the contractual completion date has lost its potency and that the service of a completion notice is now a prerequisite to the enforcement of any contract which contains provisions enabling such notice to be served."[99]

An effective notice to complete cannot be served under the conditions once a decree of specific performance has been made.[1]

Damages The service of a notice to complete under the conditions does not affect a delayee's right to claim damages for the delay.[1a]

Form of notice The notice must be in writing. Ideally it should refer expressly to condition 22 or condition 23, as the case may be, or set out the relevant condition in full, require completion within the appropriate period and state that in this regard time is to be of the essence.[2] In *Babacomp Ltd.* v. *Rightside Properties Ltd.*[3] a contract for the sale of land incorporated the National Conditions of Sale (18th ed.), condition 22 of which was in substantially the same terms as the present condition 22. The purchasers sent a letter giving "notice to complete" the contract "in accordance with its terms." It was held that this was a valid notice to complete within condition 22. *Babacomp* also establishes that it is **Reducing length of notice** possible, by special condition, to reduce the normal period of a notice served under the conditions. In that case 14 days was effectively substituted for the normal 28-day period.

A notice that fails to invoke the provisions of the desired

---

[96] See p. 34 above.
[97] *Cumberland Court (Brighton) Ltd.* v. *Taylor* [1964] Ch. 29; *Innisfail Laundry Ltd.* v. *Dawe* (1963) 107 S.J. 437; *Hooker* v. *Wyle* [1974] 1 W.L.R. 235.
[98] [1975] 1 W.L.R. 613.
[99] *Ibid.* at 615–616.
[1] *Singh (Sudagar)* v. *Nazeer* [1979] Ch. 474.
[1a] *Raineri* v. *Miles* [1981] A.C. 1050.
[2] *Babacomp* v. *Rightside Properties Ltd.* [1973] 3 All E.R. 873, *per* Goff J. at 876.
[3] [1974] 1 All E.R. 142, C.A.

Informal notices

condition may nonetheless be valid at common law. In *McKay* v. *Turner*[4] a contract was stated to be made "subject to the general conditions printed within." No conditions were printed within, but the vendors intended to have incorporated the Law Society's General Conditions of Sale (1973 revision). After delay, the purchaser purported to give notice to complete under condition 19, now 23. It was held that the Law Society's conditions had not been incorporated into the contract and that accordingly condition 19 would not apply. Since however, the notice specified a reasonable time for completion, it was valid at common law.

"Tricky" notices

It may be necessary to distinguish informal notices from "tricky" notices.[5] In *Rightside Properties Ltd.* v. *Gray*[6] the contract incorporated the Statutory Conditions of Sale and the vendor served a notice to complete under condition 9 thereof, which specifies "at least 21 days' notice in writing." Walton J. concluded that the notice was bad: it was too short for condition 9 since it required completion "*within* 21 days from the date *hereof*," the words "at least" in the condition indicated that the day of service and the date for completion were to be excluded from the computation of the period, and it could not be valid at common law because it specifically referred to condition 9.

The wording of condition 22(2) and 23(3) avoids the main difficulties of the *Gray* decision. But in any event *Gray* was not followed in *Dimsdale Developments (South East) Ltd.* v. *De Haan*.[7] The contract in that case was governed by the National Conditions of Sale (19th ed.) and the vendors served notice to complete under condition 22 calling for completion "within 28

Dimsdale v. De Haan

days from the date hereof. "Mr. Gerald Godfrey, Q.C., sitting as a deputy High Court judge held (i) that the date referred to could be taken as the date of service rather than the date stated on the notice, so that it was not a short notice for the purposes of condition 22 and (ii), even if he was wrong, the notice specified a reasonable time for completion and was valid and effective at common law.[8]

In computing the date fixed for completion by the notice it should be remembered that Saturday is not a normal working day for most conveyancers.[9]

Certainty of the conditions sullied

In *Pagebar Properties Ltd.* v. *Derby Investment Holdings Ltd.*[10] a notice requiring completion on August 11, was served upon the purchaser by the vendor under National condition 22. On August 11 the purchaser's solicitors' managing clerk attended the vendor's solicitors' office to effect completion, but discovered that part of the property to be purchased was subject to an undisclosed tenancy. He did not complete, deciding to take instructions over the weekend. The vendor then refused to complete and forfeited the purchaser's deposit. In fact the vendor's notice had been ineffectively served, so that the

---

[4] (1975) 120 S.J. 367.
[5] *Ibid.* at 368 *per* Fox J.
[6] [1975] 1 Ch. 72.
[7] (1984) 47 P. & C.R. 1.
[8] Following *Woods* v. *Mackenzie Hill Ltd.* [1975] 1 W.L.R. 613; (the conditions are not exclusive).
[9] *Per* Walton J. (*obiter*) in *Rightside Properties Ltd.* v. *Gray* [1975] Ch. 72 at 77–79.
[10] [1972] 1 W.L.R. 1500.

purchaser could get specific performance of the contract. But Goulding J. saw fit to add (*obiter*), that even if the notice had been valid and the purchaser without any fault on his part only discovered the existence of a defect in title on the last day for completion, he should have a reasonable time to consider the matter.

Readiness of server

National condition 22(1) requires a party, at the time of serving notice, to be "ready and willing to fulfil his own outstanding obligations under the contract." Despite the absence of reference to any "ability" to complete, it is not thought that his position is any different than at common law.[11] By Law Society general condition 23(2) a party is expressly deemed "ready, able and willing to complete" in two cases. The first is where he could complete but for some default or omission of the other party and the second where a mortgage is unredeemed when the notice is served but the sum required to redeem the mortgage does not exceed the sum payable on completion. This last provision takes account of the decision in *Cole* v. *Rose*.[12]

In *Naz* v. *Raja*[12a] it was held that failure to supply the purchaser with an authority to inspect the register did not prevent the vendor being "ready and willing" for the purpose of serving a notice to complete under National condition 22. The case was, however, somewhat unusual. The purchaser agreed to buy a property at an auction but then failed to communicate with the vendor or the vendor's solicitor until after the notice had expired. In *McGrath* v. *Shah*[12b] an alleged misrepresentation by the vendor was held not to invalidate his notice to complete served under National condition 22.

Re-invoking Law Society general condition 23

By Law Society general condition 23(7) where the period of a completion notice has been extended by agreement or by implication, either party may invoke the provisions of the condition again and serve a 7 working days' notice to complete (instead of 15 working days). The operation of this sub-condition was considered in *Chancery Lane Developments Ltd.* v. *Wades Stores Ltd.*[13] A contract for the sale of property in King's Lynn incorporated the Law Society's General Conditions of Sale (1984 rev). Completion was set for June 14. On June 14 the purchaser was unable to complete and the vendor served a notice to complete, which in accordance with general condition 23(2) expired on July 8. Still the purchaser could not complete and after lengthy negotiations the parties entered into a written agreement increasing the purchase price and fixing August 23 as the date for completion. The purchaser did not complete on August 23, and the vendor gave notice of its intention to terminate the contract and forfeit the deposit. It was held that the effect of the July agreement was to extend the original (non-essential) date for completion, and that sub-condition 23(7) "by necessary implication made it plain [that] time would *not* be of the essence for the purpose of an extended date for completion, and that it would only become of the essence if and when a new

---

[11] *Pagebar Properties Ltd.* v. *Derby Investment Holdings Ltd.* [1972] 1 W.L.R. 1500.

[12] [1978] 3 All E.R. 1121; see pp. 34–35 above.

[12a] *The Times*, April 11, 1987.

[12b] *The Times*, October 22, 1987.

[13] (1987) 53 P. & C.R. 306.

completion notice had been served and the abridged period of seven working days had expired thereafter."[14] In other words, under the Law Society's conditions, a notice can only be extended (as opposed to a fresh notice being served) without affecting its validity, if it is expressly stated that time is to remain of the essence. The National conditions contain no comparable provision therefore the general law applies.[15]

Non-compliance—Law Society general condition 23(4)–(6)

Law Society general condition 23(4)–(6) sets out a party's rights in the event of the other's non-compliance with a completion notice.

If the purchaser does not comply with a completion notice the vendor may forfeit the deposit[16] (23(4)) unless the court orders its return (see below). His right to sue for damages for breach of contract and loss of bargain is also preserved by this sub-condition.

If the vendor contracts to resell the property within one year of contractual completion date, *and so elects by notice in writing*, the purchaser is liable for *liquidated damages* for any loss, (23(5)). (The reason for a contractual condition for liquidated damages is to save the vendor the necessity of having to prove actual loss). The amount of damages is the aggregate of:

(1) the loss;
(2) all costs and expenses reasonably incurred in such resale and attempted resale; and
(3) interest at the contract rate on such part of the purchase money as is from time to time outstanding. Credit is given for any deposit paid and for all sums received on account of the purchase price, 23(4)(*b*)(i) and 23(5).

Interest—*Talley* v. *Wolsey-Neech*

This third head of liquidated damages was added in the 1980 edition of the conditions, to take account of the decision in *Talley* v. *Wolsey-Neech*.[17] In that case it was held that a vendor who chose to exercise his rights and remedies under general condition 19(4)(*c*) of the Law Society's General Conditions (1973 revision) (the predecessor of 23(5)) was only entitled to recover the liquidated damages defined by it, and was not, therefore, entitled to recover as further damages interest on the purchase price.

The new sub-condition puts a heavy burden on a defaulting purchaser and it is obviously in his interest to ensure that the vendor is making efforts to resell and is not simply letting the 12 months drift by whilst interest accumulates. Indeed a purchaser may seek to limit his liability, by special condition, to a fixed percentage of the purchase price.

Redressing the balance in the purchaser's favour

Law Society general condition 23(6) tilts the balance back in the purchaser's favour. Where it is the vendor who is in default, the purchaser may without prejudice to other remedies available to him, serve notice on the vendor requiring him to return the deposit and any other sums paid under the contract. The vendor then becomes liable to pay interest at the contract rate if he does not return the money within four working days of receiving the

---

[14] *Ibid.* at 316, *per* Slade L.J.
[15] See p. 38 below.
[16] Where a reduced deposit is paid, a balancing payment to make up the full 10 per cent. becomes due when the vendor serves a completion notice (condition 9(2)).
[17] (1978) 38 P. & C.R. 45.

purchaser's notice. Once the money is repaid, the purchaser loses his right to specific performance of the contract. He must return all documents to the vendor may cancel any entries in any register relating to the contract, but *at the vendor's expense.*

Non-compliance—National condition 22(3)

National condition 22(3) is different. It deals with a vendor's position, whereas a purchaser is left with his remedies at common law. It provides that where a purchaser does not comply with a completion notice, the vendor may forfeit the deposit (subject to the court ordering its return). On a resale within 12 months and 16 working days, the vendor may recover from the purchaser any difference between the contract price and the resale price, plus costs, but giving credit for the deposit. There is no requirement that resale costs and expenses should be paid as "liquidated damages," nor is any concession made for the payment of interest. Furthermore, the sub-condition begins: "without prejudice to any other right or remedy available to [the vendor]."

There are three recent cases on National condition 22(3), decided by three deputy High Court judges with different results.[18]

Bruce v. Waziri

First *Bruce* v. *Waziri*[19] where in addition to a loss incurred on re-sale the vendor also incurred substantial costs in borrowing to finance the purchase of new accommodation, this purchase being known to the purchaser. It was held that what is now National condition 22(3) was not a liquidated damages clause and so, following *Wadsworth* v. *Lydall*,[20] this head of damages was recoverable.[21] *Talley* v. *Wolsey-Neech* was distinguished: the difference in wording of Law Society general condition 19(4)(*c*), now 23(5), and National condition 22(3), meant that the two "could not be equated."[22]

Sakkas v. Donford Ltd.

These distinctions were noted, but rejected, in the second case, *Sakkas* v. *Donford Ltd.*,[23] where a vendor's claim for interest on the deposit and the balance of the purchase price was disallowed under National condition 22(3). Lord Grantchester Q.C., thought *Talley* v. *Wolsey-Neech*:

> "authority for the proposition that where a vendor elects to proceed under a condition similar to the condition in that case, what he then obtains thereunder is only the diffence between the initial sale price and the re-sale price and the costs of the re-sale."[24]

Wallace-Turner v. Cole

The facts of the third case, *Wallace-Turner* v. *Cole*,[25] were a little unusual, because the vendor, who had already obtained a judgment for damages at large (including the cost of bridging finance) at a time when he had not managed to resell, now claimed liquidated damages under condition 22(3) simply including the loss on a later resale. He was unsuccessful:

---

[18] See H.W. Wilkinson (1984) 134 New L.J. 252; [1984] Conv. 81; M.P. Thompson [1984] Conv. 311; J.E. Adams [1984] Conv. 376.

[19] (1983) 46 P. & C.R. 81.

[20] [1981] 1 W.L.R. 598.

[21] She also recovered the cost of staffing and maintaining insurance on the house, the subject matter of the sale.

[22] (1983) 46 P. & C.R. 81, *per* Mr. Julian Jeffs Q.C. at 86.

[23] (1983) 46 P. & C.R. 290.

[24] *Ibid.* at 309.

[25] (1983) 46 P. & C.R. 164.

"The basis of the decision in *Talley* v. *Wolsey-Neech*, as I understand it, is that a vendor is put to his election between his different remedies. It is common ground between counsel that he is put to an election between damages and specific performance. *Talley* v. *Wolsey-Neech* is, in my view, a decision that he is likewise put to his election between liquidated damages under this kind of condition and unliquidated damages at large for loss of bargain and breach of contract."[26]

Cost of bridging finance

Both *Bruce* v. *Waziri* and *Wallace-Turner* v. *Cole*, involved *inter alia* the cost of a bridging loan taken to enable the vendor to buy another property. It should be appreciated that this sort of expense (*i.e.* interest) is not covered by the new Law Society general condition 23(5).

On the wording of both conditions, there is no express requirement of good faith or reasonableness on the vendor's part when he resells. There was unfortunately no discussion on this point in the three cases above-mentioned. However the better view seems to be that such a requirement would be implied.[27]

Resale outside period

If the vendor resells outside the periods specified by the conditions, he can claim any loss on resale under the general law.[28]

Forfeiture of the deposit

General principles

Deposit is a guarantee for performance

As we have seen, both conditions contain express provision for the vendor to treat the deposit as forfeited to him. Indeed, the deposit is liable to be forfeited upon a termination by the vendor even without express provision: this follows from the nature of the deposit as a guarantee for the purchaser's performance of the contract.[29]

Distinction between "deposit" and payment on account of purchase price

Both under the standard conditions and at common law the vendor's power is to forfeit the "deposit." Accordingly a distinction must be drawn between a "deposit," properly so called, and a payment on account of the purchase price, even though a deposit does go in part payment of the purchase price if the sale is completed.[30] Thus, in *Mayson* v. *Clouet*,[31] a contract for the sale of land provided for a deposit to be paid on exchange and for the rest of the purchase price to be paid by three instalments. If the purchaser broke any of the conditions of the contract, the *deposit* was to be forfeited. The purchaser paid the deposit and two of the instalments but defaulted on the third, whereupon the vendor rescinded the contract. It was held that the rights of the parties depended on the contract, and that

---

[26] *Ibid.* at 168 *per* Mr. John Mowbray Q.C.
[27] *Cuckmere Brick Co. Ltd.* v. *Mutual Finance Ltd.* [1971] Ch. 949.
[28] *Michael Richards Properties Ltd.* v. *Corp. of Wardens of St. Saviour's Parish, Southwark* [1975] 3 All E.R. 416; and see Chapter 6 below.
[29] *Hall* v. *Burnell* [1911] 2 Ch. 551.
[30] *Soper* v. *Arnold* (1889) 14 App.Cas. 429 at 435.
[31] [1924] A.C. 980.

although the vendor was entitled to forfeit the deposit, the purchaser could recover the instalments.

Suing for unpaid deposit

For a vendor's right to sue for an unpaid deposit, see pages 8 to 10 above.

Apparently the court has equitable jurisdiction to grant relief against forfeiture of a deposit consequent upon termination of the contract for the purchaser's default, where the deposit is in the nature of a "penalty." In *Starside Properties Ltd.* v. *Mustapha*[32] the contract price of a house was £5,950. The purchaser was let into occupation as a licensee provided she paid an initial deposit of £350, a further £46 13s 4d monthly in interest on the balance of the purchase price and £15 13s 4d monthly towards a total deposit of £1,250. The purchaser was entitled to call for a conveyance once the total deposit had been paid but if prior to this there was any arrear of interest and/or deposit the vendors could rescind the contract and forfeit all sums paid. For a time the purchaser paid the instalments but then defaulted on two. The vendor started proceedings for possession and forfeiture of moneys. It was held that the provision for forfeiture was penal in character and the purchaser was given extra time to complete the purchase by way of re-sale at a higher figure.

Penalties

10 per cent. deposit unlikely to be a penalty

It is doubtful whether the court would treat a provision for the "normal" 10 per cent. deposit as a penalty clause, although in practice, in times of rising prices, this often exceeds a vendor's actual loss.[33] In *Windsor Securities Ltd.* v. *Loreldal and Lester Ltd.*,[34] the vendor managed to resell the property at £150,000 more than the original contract price. Still, Oliver J. refused to order the return of the purchaser's deposit of £235,000; he could see nothing in the circumstances to warrant the intervention of equity to relieve against forfeiture.

Statutory provision for recovery of deposit

Law of Property Act 1925, s.49(2)

Section 49(2) of the Law of Property Act 1925 provides:

> "Where the court refuses to grant specific performance of a contract, or in any action for the return of a deposit, the court may, if it thinks fit, order the repayment of any deposit."

How wide is the discretion conferred by the section?

The courts have in the past taken a narrow view of the scope of the discretion conferred by this section. For example, in *James Macara Ltd.* v. *Barclay*,[35] Vaisey J. expressed the view that:

> "the primary purpose of the provision was to remove the difficulty which had stood in the way of a purchaser who, though in a position successfully to resist specific

---

[32] [1974] 1 W.L.R. 816. See also *Stockloser* v. *Johnson* [1954] 1 Q.B. 476 at 491 where Lord Denning said that a provision for a 50 per cent. deposit might be regarded as a penalty.

[33] See J.E. Adams (1983) 80 L.S.Gaz. 2811 and "Deposits on exchange of contracts in residential conveyancing—time for a change," Conveyancing Standing Committee (1988).

[34] *The Times*, September 10, 1975.

[35] [1944] 2 All E.R. 31 at 32. On appeal it was not necessary to consider s.49(2); [1945] K.B. 148.

Narrow view

performance in equity, was at law precluded from recovering his deposit."

Again, in *Universal Corp.* v. *Five Ways Properties Ltd.*,[36] Walton J. said:

"It would indeed be surprising if Parliament had in this fashion conferred on the courts an absolutely unfettered jurisdiction to interfere in a bargain between vendor and purchaser in this way whenever it thought fit to do so, without the remotest hint of any guidelines as to how this quite extra-ordinary jurisdiction should be exercised."[37]

According to his Lordship, the proper approach to the exercise of the jurisdiction was to ask first: what, if anything, can be said against the vendor? And—

"Only when one had labelled the vendor as having been a party to some act or omission which, in the circumstances of the case, is not straightforward or is tricky or has some other mark of equitable disfavour attached to it, can one then turn to the purchaser and scrutinise the purchaser's conduct and see whether the case being made out, as it were, against the vendor is a reason why he should not be entitled to retain the deposit."[38]

Broad view

However a broader view of section 49(2) had earlier been taken by Megarry J., in *Schindler* v. *Pigault*.[39] He disagreed that the discretion was confined to cases where the other party's conduct had been unconscionable. The discretion was available

Schindler v. Pigault

"when justice required it" and was exercisable:

"on wider grounds . . . including a general consideration of the conduct of the parties (and especially the applicant), the gravity of the matters in question, and the amounts at stake. . . . The jurisdiction is, of course, statutory and is not the product of equity, but its discretionery character in relation to deposits on the sale of land makes it at least akin to equitable relief against forfeiture."[40]

Universal Corp. v. Five Ways Properties Ltd., C.A.

This approach of Megarry J. was preferred to that of Walton J. at first instance, by the Court of Appeal in *Universal Corp.* v. *Five Ways Properties Ltd.*[41] Buckley L.J. said that section 49(2) conferred a discretion "unqualified by any language of the subsection, to order or refuse repayment of the deposit, a discretion which must, of course, be exercised judicially and with regard to all relevant considerations, including the very important consideration of the terms of the contract into which the parties have chosen to enter."[42]

The discretion was one to be exercised where the justice of the case required, and his Lordship added:

[36] [1978] 3 All E.R. 1131.
[37] *Ibid.* at 1136.
[38] *Ibid.* at 1137.
[39] (1975) 30 P. & C.R. 328.
[40] *Ibid.* at 336.
[41] [1979] 1 All E.R. 552.
[42] *Ibid.* at 555.

"I take the word "justice" to be used in a wide sense, indicating that repayment must be ordered in any circumstances which make this the fairest course between the parties."[43]

Broad view applied—£125,000 deposit returned

Return of the purchaser's deposit (10 per cent. of £1,250,000) was considered to be "the fairest course between the parties," in *Maktoum* v. *South Lodge Flats Ltd.*[44] The fact that the value of the flats had risen since the termination of the contract by £250,000 and that the vendors expected to make a large profit on resale may well have been the persuasive reason.

Whole of deposit must be returned

There is one limitation on the courts powers under section 49(2): "while the court may order the return of the whole of the deposit, it is not, at any rate in terms, authorised to order the return of less than the whole."[45]

But—*Dimsdale Developments (South East) Ltd. v. De Haan*

However Mr. Gerald Godfrey Q.C., sitting as a deputy High Court judge, found a way round this limitation in *Dimsdale Developments (South East) Ltd.* v. *De Haan.*[46] The facts briefly here were that the purchasers had failed to comply with a completion notice and the vendors had forfeited their deposit of £12,250 and had resold elsewhere at a profit of £17,750. The judge ordered the vendors to return the whole of the purchaser's deposit but authorised them to deduct £6,500 from it to cover their expenses on resale.[47]

There is authority for the view that the operation of section 49(2) can be excluded by express agreement.[48]

Mareva injunction[49]

Outline of remedy

The Mareva injunction is an interim remedy which has been developed by the courts on a case by case basis over the past decade. It may be directed[50] to the defendant (whether vendor or purchaser) or his servants or agents (typically his bankers), to restrain the defendant from removing or hiding assets within the jurisdiction so as to frustrate the satisfaction of a judgment or execution of an order which the plaintiff will in all probability obtain. Originally the Mareva injunction was conceived in order to control foreign defendants but it can now be applied to any defendant. The plaintiff must show that he has a good arguable claim, that the defendant has assets in the jurisdiction, that there are reasonable grounds for believing that the defendant will remove those assets from the jurisdiction or will otherwise dissipate or dispose of them, and the court must conclude that refusal of a Mareva injunction involves a real risk that any

---

[43] *Universal Corp.* v. *Five Ways Properties Ltd.* [1979] 1 All E.R. 552.
[44] *The Times,* April 22, 1980.
[45] *James Macara Ltd.* v. *Barclay* [1944] 2 All E.R. 31 at 32.
[46] (1984) 47 P. & C.R. 1.
[47] Estate agent's and solicitor's fees and bank interest.
[48] *Michael Richards Properties Ltd.* v. *Corp. of Wardens of St. Saviour's Parish, Southwark* [1975] 3 All E.R. 416.
[49] See D.G. Powles, *Mareva Injunctions and Associated Orders* (1985); M.S.W. Hoyle, *The Mareva Injunction and Related Orders* (1985).
[50] A mareva injunction will be *ex parte* in the first instance but may be continued after an *inter partes* hearing.

judgment or order in favour of the defendant will be frustrated.[51] The assets frozen may be money in banks, land or shares.

The Mareva injunction has to date been used mainly in commercial causes but there is no reason why it would not be appropriate in litigation involving the sale of land.

---

[51] Supreme Court Act 1981, s.37.

5 MISREPRESENTATION, MISDESCRIPTION AND MISTAKE

Introduction

In Chapter 6 the position of the vendor and purchaser of land is examined where there has been a breach of the contract of sale. This chapter is concerned with the parties' position where there has been some misrepresentation or misdescription made in relation to the contract of sale. Additionally, the position of the parties where they have contracted on the basis of some mistake, which in the most extreme of cases may be sufficient to render the contract of sale void *ab initio*, is examined. The manner in which the common form standard conditions of sale seek to regulate the parties' rights in the event of representation or misdescription is also discussed.

In order to put the remedies of a vendor or purchaser of land into context it is first necessary briefly to look at the obligations which a vendor has imposed upon him to describe or disclose matters affecting his property or his title to it.

The vendor's duty of disclosure

The basic position in the law of contract is that there is no general rule requiring contracting parties to disclose to each other all matters which could possibly affect the course of negotiations between the parties. As Lord Atkin commented in *Bell* v. *Lever Brothers Ltd.*[1]: "The failure to disclose a material fact which might influence the mind of a prudent contractor does not give the right to avoid the contract." This tenet of the common law finds its most important manifestation in the rule of *caveat emptor*.

Caveat emptor   The rule of *caveat emptor* does not mean that the vendor of land has no duty of disclosure towards his purchaser. He must show good title which involves describing the physical extent of the property being sold and explaining to the purchaser the nature of his title and any defects in it.

The vendor's obligation to identify the property is twofold.

Vendor must identify the property   First he must correctly state the interest in the property he proposes to sell: "the legal description." Second, he must accurately describe by means of a sufficiently detailed plan or otherwise the physical extent of the property giving details, for example, of the property's boundaries: "the physical description."

The legal description   In the contractual particulars of sale the vendor must state the nature of the interest in the property to be sold; whether it is a freehold or leasehold interest or some more limited right such as a mere licence to occupy which may not confer upon the

---

[1] [1932] A.C. 161 at 227.

purchaser any proprietary right in the property at all. Additionally he must state certain other factors qualifying the interest he is selling so that the purchaser is not in any doubt as to the property he is acquiring. In *Re Brine and Davies' Contract*[2] the vendor agreed to sell a "registered freehold house." Unknown to the purchaser the title was possessory. Although what was said was true, the description was held to be misleading since the purchaser understood from it that the property was registered with absolute freehold title when this was not in fact the case. The purchaser was entitled to rescind the contract because of the vendor's lack of precision in describing the legal nature of his property.

Leaseholds   Particular care must be exercised by the vendor of leasehold property. The vendor of an underlease must ensure that he does not describe his property as simply being held under a "lease." To do so would expose him to a claim by his purchaser for misdescription.[3] It may not necessarily amount to an actionable misdescription to describe property held under a sub-underlease as held pursuant to an "underlease."[4] In practice, however, it is prudent to give full particulars of the document under which the vendor acquired his interest in the subject property; if held under a sub-underlease it should be so described in the contract. Problems may also arise in connection with sales of reversionary interests such as freeholds subject to tenancies. The extent and nature of such tenancies will need to be carefully described in the contract.[5]

A complete legal description sets out rights which the property enjoys and incumbrances which burden it. Failure to state easements and the like which benefit the property is not fatal. Incumbrances should be stated in the particulars but often appear elsewhere in the contract. Unlike benefits certain burdens *must* be detailed in the contract. A full account of this matter is given in the second volume in this series.

Physical description   It is essential that the vendor is able to convey all the property he contracts to sell, otherwise the purchaser, as we shall discuss later, may have a claim for rescission or compensation.[6] The vendor must be able to prove that the land he describes in the particulars of sale corresponds, is co-extensive with, or at least forms part of, the land described in the title deeds. A practice has developed, in unregistered conveyancing, of describing the property in the contract by reference to the description in the conveyance to the vendor. Provided that the vendor's conveyancer has confirmed beforehand that this description is accurate and the vendor is selling the whole of his property, there will be no difficulty. Careless copying of the description of the property from the vendor's title deeds can, however, lead to problems; for example, land could be included which the vendor has sold off previously. Alternatively the vendor might have acquired further property as occurred in *Wallington* v.

[2] [1935] Ch.388.
[3] *Re Russ and Brown's Contract* [1934] Ch.34; *Re Thompson and Cottrell's Contract* [1943] Ch.97.
[4] *Becker* v. *Partridge* [1966] 2 Q.B. 155.
[5] For an example of the type of problems which can arise in this area, see *Ridley* v. *Oster* [1939] 1 All E.R. 618.
[6] See below pp. 65–67; see also *Mustafa* v. *Baptist Union Corp. Ltd.* (1983) 266 E.G. 812.

Townsend.[7] Further suppose the description of the land in the conveyance to the vendor is inaccurate.[8] Later he agrees to sell the property, and the same description is incorporated into the contract (in the hope of ensuring that the vendor only contracts to sell the land which was conveyed to him). If the purchaser's solicitor on investigating the title discovers the inaccuracy the vendor may lose the sale or be forced to compensate the purchaser. In every case the most prudent course is for the vendor's solicitor completely to review the title deeds and examine all the facts to ensure that he is fully appraised of any matters affecting the contract description of the property.

Plans   If a written description is too uncertain or unreliable the property should be described by means of a plan. As Brightman J. pointed out in *Lloyd* v. *Stanbury,*[9] where the vendor is selling part only of his property the need for a plan is accentuated:

> "If there is a moral to this unfortunate story it is the danger of dispensing with a plan to a contract of sale particularly where natural boundaries are not obvious and the vendor is selling part only of his land."

Scarfe v. Adams   A plan used to control the description of the property being sold must be on a scale large enough for it to be of practical use. In *Scarfe* v. *Adams,*[10] purchasers at an auction each bought part of a property known as "The Coach House." The plan in the contract was an Ordinance Survey Map on a scale of 1:2,500. It showed a dotted line running through the grounds but not the house itself. If the line had been completed it would have divided the house not along an existing party wall, but along the middle of a tenanted flat in the house. A dispute arose as to the true extent of each of the purchaser's property. It was held that the division should follow the party wall. In delivering the judgment of the Court of Appeal, Brightman J. criticised the use of small scale plans in conveyancing transactions where the boundaries have to be defined with precision. A map on a scale of 1:1,250 should be adequate for most purposes.[11]

Registered land   Where the title to the vendor's property is registered, describing it in the contract for sale is made easier. As one writer has suggested,[12] "when on the register, do as the registrar does." Therefore, if the registered proprietor is selling the whole of his property, a reference in the contract to the title number is a sufficient description. However, the parties may want to use a plan to govern the description and again the Land Registry can be of assistance. They keep detailed maps of all registered estates and the "filed plan" may be incorporated into the contract. Once again the "filed plan" should be examined by the vendor's solicitor to ensure its accuracy.[13]

The case of *A. J. Dunning & Sons (Shopfitters) Ltd.* v. *Sykes*

---

[7] [1939] Ch. 588.
[8] *Spall* v. *Owen* (1982) 44 P. & C.R. 36; see the note at (1983) 127 S.J. (Aldridge).
[9] [1971] 1 W.L.R. 535 at 544.
[10] (1980) 125 S.J. 32.
[11] See also H. W. Wilkinson, (1981) 131 New L.J. 438.
[12] J. T. Farrand, *Contract and Conveyance* (4th ed.), p. 148.
[13] *Lee* v. *Barrey* [1957] Ch. 251.

A. J. Dunning v. Sykes *& Son (Poole) Ltd.*[14] is an interesting example of the type of problems which can occur when registered land is sold by reference to a plan. In this case, a vendor of registered land had prior to the sale in question sold off part of the land formerly within the same title to a third party. Unfortunately, when that sale had been completed the fences separating the vendor's retained land from the third party's land had been put in the wrong place and some of the land on the vendor's side of the fence in fact belonged to the third party. On a sale by the vendor of his retained land, the plan in the contract was drawn up by reference to the fence (and thus showed the vendor's land to be more extensive than it was). The purchaser brought an action against the vendor for damages for breach of the vendor's implied beneficial owner covenants for title. The Court of Appeal decided that despite the vendor's argument that he was protected by the provisions of rule 77[15] of the Land Registration Rules 1925 the purchaser was entitled to recover damages arising out of the vendor's misdescription of the property which he was selling.

Plans On a sale of part of a registered estate a plan *must* be used. As in unregistered conveyancing, the parties must be in no doubt as to the physical extent of their properties. Additionally, rule 79 of the Land Registration Rules 1925 requires an instrument dealing with part of a registered title to be accompanied by a plan; this matter should be dealt with at the contract stage.

Further evidence of identity Under an open contract where the contract description materially differs from that in the title deeds the purchaser has a right to call for further evidence of identity. Contractual conditions which try to exclude this right are strictly construed by the courts. Thus, in *Flower* v. *Hartopp*[16] where the description of the property in the title deeds differed from that in the contract the vendor could not enforce the contract, despite a condition that "no further evidence of identity was to be required than was afforded by the abstract and documents therein." In effect such a condition amounts to a term stating that the title deeds will show a sufficient identification of the property described in the contract.[17]

Effect of the standard conditions on the vendor's obligation to establish the identity of the property

National condition 13
"13. Identity: boundaries: condition of the property
(1) The purchaser shall admit the identity of the property with that comprised in the muniments offered by the vendor as the title thereto upon the evidence afforded by the descriptions contained in such muniments, and of a statutory declaration, to be made (if required) at the purchaser's expense, that the property has been enjoyed according to the title for at least twelve years
(2) The vendor shall not be bound to show any title to

[14] [1987] 1 All E.R. 700.
[15] "77(1) Any covenant implied by virtue of section 76 of the Law of Property Act 1925, in a disposition of registered land shall take effect as though the disposition was expressly made subject to—(a) all charges and other interests appearing or protected on the register at the time of the execution of the disposition and affecting the title of the covenantor . . ."
[16] (1843) 6 Beav. 476.
[17] *Curling* v. *Austin* (1862) 2 Drew. & S. 129.

boundaries, fences, ditches, hedges, or walls, or to distinguish parts of the property held under different titles further than he may be able to do from information in his possession."

Law Society general condition 13

"13 IDENTITY AND BOUNDARIES
(1) The vendor shall produce such evidence as may be reasonably necessary to establish the identity and extent of the property, but shall not be required to define exact boundaries, or the ownership of fences, ditches, hedges or walls, nor, beyond the evidence afforded by the information in his possession, separately to identify parts of the property held under different titles.
(2) If reasonably required by the purchaser because of the insufficiency of the evidence produced under sub-condition (1), the vendor shall at his own expense provide and hand over on completion a statutory declaration as to the relevant facts, in a form agreed by the purchaser, such agreement not to be unreasonably withheld."

National condition 13(1) was considered in *Re Bramwell's Contract*.[18] In this case the property described in the contract was probably identified by the vendor's title deeds. Despite National condition 13(1) the vendor was unable to force the property on the purchaser.

Law Society condition 13(1) provides that the vendor shall produce such evidence as may be reasonably necessary to establish the identity of the property. Again it would not enable the vendor to force the property on the purchaser if it was not adequately identified by reference to the former's title deeds.

If the title deeds prove inadequate, both conditions give the purchaser the right to call for further evidence of identity in the form of statutory declaration. Under National condition 13(1) the declaration shall state that the property has been enjoyed consistently with the title for at least 12 years. Law Society condition 13(2) is similar although no 12 year limit is imposed and unlike the National condition it is the vendor who must pay for the declaration. The purchaser may require a person other than the vendor to make the declaration under both conditions.[19]

Under an open contract the vendor may be obliged to distinguish parts of the property held under different titles. Both conditions relieve him of this duty (if it exists) when he cannot distinguish the different parts from the information in his possession.

Description of boundaries

No duty to define ownership of boundaries at common law

Under an open contract it is doubtful that the vendor is under a duty to define the ownership of the boundaries to the property.[20] National condition 13(2) resolves this doubt in favour of the vendor by providing that he is not required to define boundaries. Law Society condition 13(1) is less favourable to the vendor, providing that he is not "required to define exact

[18] [1969] 1 W.L.R. 1659.
[19] *Hobson* v. *Bell* (1839) 2 Beav. 17.
[20] *Dawson* v. *Brinckman* (1850) 3 M. & G. 53.

boundaries." He must produce some evidence of the identity of boundaries though this need not be conclusive. A purchaser should investigate the position and ownership of boundaries to the property prior to making the contract.

Boundary disputes are the source of much acrimonious litigation between neighbouring landowners. In the absence of conclusive evidence of the position and ownership of boundaries in the vendor's title deeds, the following rebuttable presumptions will apply:

Rebuttable presumptions

(i) **Dividing walls** These are often referred to as "party walls." They are divided down the middle vertically. The owner of the property on either side of the wall has rights of support and user over the rest of the wall.[21]

(ii) **Hedges, banks and ditches** The boundary is presumed to run along the edge of the ditch furthest from the hedge or bank. The presumption only arises where there is a single ditch which is man-made.[22] If an Ordinance Survey Map is used to describe the property, the boundary line is *prima facie* the centre of the hedge or ditch.[23]

(iii) **Rivers** Where the land is bordered by a non–tidal river the boundary is the middle of the river bed. If the river suddenly changes course drastically, the boundary remains where it was before the change.[24] Changes in the course of the river over a prolonged period will result in the alteration of boundaries.

(iv) **Highways** The owner of land adjacent to a road is presumed to own half of the subsoil of the road. On building estates developers will retain ownership of the subsoil of the estate roads in order to complete construction. Where the road is bordered by fences or hedges, the boundary is presumed to be the fence or hedge itself unless the circumstances indicate to the contrary.

(v) **Fences** If the fence is maintained by the vendor the presumption is that it belongs to him. There is no legal basis for the common presumption that a fence belongs to the owner of the land on which the supporting posts stand. It is possible that a fence may be declared a "party fence." The owner's rights are then the same as with "party walls."

Commonly, "T" marks are placed on plans to indicate ownership of fences. However, if the plan is not supported by a reference in the deed or transfer relating to their presence, such marks are not conclusive evidence of ownership.

(vi) **Registered land** Except where it is noted on the Property Register that the boundaries have been fixed, the filed plan will indicate general boundaries only. This means that a filed plan cannot be used to resolve boundary disputes. The exact line of the boundary is left undetermined even if the whole or a part of any ditch, wall, fence, road, stream or other boundary is expressly included or excluded from the title.

---

[21] Law of Property Act 1925, s. 38.
[22] *Marshall* v. *Taylor* [1985] 1 Ch. 641.
[23] *Davey* v. *Harrow Corp.* [1958] 1 Q.B. 60.
[24] *Ford* v. *Lacey* (1861) 7 H. & N. 151.

Boundaries may be fixed by the Land Registry. An official measures out the boundaries exactly from a fixed point, using measurements provided by the owner. Since this process necessarily "fixes" neighbouring owners' boundaries it has proved unpopular and is rare in practice.

Defects in title

The process by which the vendor of land deduces title and the matters which he is obliged to disclose to his purchaser will be dealt with elsewhere in the *Conveyancing Solutions* series.[25] It is not proposed in this book to give anything other than a very general outline of the vendor's obligations in this regard.

Starting point   The basic starting point is that a vendor of land selling under an open contract implicitly agrees to sell to the purchaser the freehold interest in the property free from all incumbrances,[26] unless his purchaser is made aware at the time of the contract that he intended to sell some lesser interest.[27]

Patent defects   The purchaser is taken to be aware of all patent defects in title affecting the property to be sold whether he actually knew of them or not. A defect is patent if it could be discovered by a purchaser on making a reasonably careful inspection of the property. The classic statement of the law on this point is that of Sargent J. in *Yandle & Sons* v. *Sutton*:

> "a patent defect, which can be thrust upon the purchaser, must be a defect which arises either to the eye, or by necessary implication from something which is visible to the eye."[28]

Latent defects in title   A vendor has a duty to disclose all latent defects in title. Failure to disclose latent defects results in the vendor being in breach of the term implied into the contract at common law, and gives the purchaser the right to rescind the contract and/or claim damages depending upon the seriousness of the vendor's non-disclosure.[29]

A defect is latent if it could not be discovered by a purchaser upon his making a reasonably careful inspection of the property. A restrictive covenant burdening the property to be sold is obviously a latent defect and must therefore be disclosed.[30]

Special conditions   In practice, where a vendor has a flaw in his title he will disclose it to the purchaser in the special conditions and then state that the purchaser is not allowed to raise objections or requisitions on it. By revealing the defect he ensures that the purchaser cannot later back out of the contract.[31]

The following is a list of some of the most important matters which would require disclosure by a vendor of land:

---

[25] See forthcoming title (Conveyancing Solutions 4).
[26] *Purvis* v. *Rayer* (1821) 9 Price 488; *Hughes* v. *Parker* (1841) 8 M. & W. 244.
[27] *Timmins* v. *Moreland Street Property Co. Ltd.* [1958] Ch. 110.
[28] [1922] 2 Ch. 199 at 210.
[29] *Re White and Smith's Contract* [1896] 1 Ch. 637.
[30] *Re Stone and Saville's Contract* [1963] 1 W.L.R. 163.
[31] *Re Marsh and Earl Granville* (1883) 24 Ch.D. 11; *Faruqi* v. *English Real Estates* [1979] 1 W.L.R. 963.

(a) Any latent easements, rights, privileges or other liabilities, to which the property is subject.[32]
(b) All tenancies affecting the property to be sold.[33]
(c) Any restrictive covenant, the burden of which will bind the purchaser. In *Re Higgins and Hitchman's Contract*[34] the subject-matter of the sale was a semi-detached house. The vendor failed to reveal the existence of a restrictive covenant, entered into by his predecessor in title, not to use the property as, or for the erection of, a public house. This was held to be a fatal defect entitling the purchaser to resist specific performance.
(d) Some local land charges[35] constitute latent defects in title. Where this is the case the vendor must disclose them. One type of local land charge requiring disclosure, frequently encountered in practice, is a financial charge registered by a local authority to recoup the expense of making up a road from the frontagers.

Having looked at some of the vendor's obligations in relation to information which he has to disclose to his purchaser, the remedies of the purchaser in the event of a misrepresentation or misdescription of the property may now be discussed.

Misrepresentation

A party to a contract may be able to claim relief if he was induced to enter into the contract by a statement which was misleading.

Pre-requisites to a claim

To have a claim for relief the purchaser to whom a (mis)representation is made must show that:

(a) the representation was of a kind which the law recognises as giving rise to liability;
(b) it was material; and
(c) he relied upon it when making the contract.

An actionable misrepresentation can only consist of a misleading statement of fact. Statements of opinion, intention or of law cannot themselves ground an action for misrepresentation.

Expression of opinion

If a vendor expresses an opinion concerning his property to the purchaser which later turns out to have been incorrect he does not necessarily expose himself to a claim for misrepresentation. For example, a wrong description of land as "uncommonly rich water meadow" did not ground an action.[36] However, a vendor should temper his praise for his property since the cases do show a reluctance to allow a vendor to escape liability for misrepresentations if such praise of the property turns out to be unfounded.[37] A vendor who makes a statement of opinion may, if he is in a position to know the full facts, be held

[32] *Ward* v. *Kirkland* [1967] Ch. 194; *E.R. Ives Investment Ltd.* v. *High* [1967] 2 Q.B. 379.
[33] *Farrell* v. *Green* (1974) 232 E.G. 587; see also National condition 18 (1) and Law Society condition 6 (2).
[34] (1882) 51 L.J. (N.S.) 772; see also National condition 12 (2).
[35] For a full discussion of local land charges see Annand and Cain, *Conveyancing Solutions 1: Enquiries before Contract* (1986).
[36] *Scott* v. *Hanson* (1829) 1 Russ. & M. 128.
[37] *Bisset* v. *Wilkinson* [1927] A.C. 177.

liable if he is not aware of facts which could justify his opinion. For example, where the vendor of a house described it as "let to a most desirable tenant" when in fact the tenant was in lengthy arrears with the rent, he was held to have made (impliedly) an actionable (mis)representation.[38]

Statements as to future action   A vendor's promise to do something in the future can never ground an action for misrepresentation whether the promise is by nature contractually binding or not. If the purchaser is to have a remedy for such a promise then he must insist on the vendor stating his intention in the contract.[39]

Representation of law   If during negotiations the vendor makes a representation of law, which induces the purchaser to enter into the contract, and it later transpires that the representation was wrong, the purchaser cannot claim relief for misrepresentation. In practice, statements of law are difficult to distinguish from statements of fact. For example, in *Laurence* v. *Lexcourt Holdings Ltd.*[40] the vendor stated that the property had the benefit of a planning permission which allowed it to be used as offices when it did not. This was held to be a representation of fact giving rise to an actional misrepresentation, and not as had been suggested a representation as to the law.[41]

Materiality   In the absence of any allegation of fraud the plaintiff in a misrepresentation action must establish that the misrepresentation was material. A misrepresentation is material if it would affect the judgment of a reasonable man in deciding whether or not to enter into the contract. Additionally, a statement will be regarded as material and so giving rise to a claim if the other party is induced to enter into the contract in terms other than those upon which he would otherwise have contracted had the statement not been made.

Reliance   In addition to proving that a misrepresentation is material a plaintiff must also establish that he was induced to enter into a contract as a result of the misrepresentation.[42] Where, for example, the purchaser of a property is in no way influenced by a vendor's erroneous statements, either because he was unaware of them or because he took no notice of them, he will have no claim against the vendor.[43] In deciding whether or not to enter into a contract a party will take into account numerous factors. The law does not require a plaintiff bringing a claim in misrepresentation to show that the *only* reason he contracted was as a result of the misrepresentation which has been made to him. He must, however, prove that the misrepresentation was one of the factors which operated on his mind in deciding to contract.[44]

Fraudulent, negligent and innocent misrepresentation

The law recognises three types of misrepresentation: fraudulent, negligent and innocent. The type of misrepresentation made will

---

[38] *Smith* v. *Land & House Property Corp.* (1884) 28 Ch. D. 7.
[39] *Maddison* v. *Alderson* (1883) 8 App. Cas. 467.
[40] [1977] 1 W.L.R. 1128.
[41] See also *Brikom Investments Ltd.* v. *Seaford* [1981] 1 W.L.R. 863 and *China Pacific S.A.* v. *Food Corp. of India* [1981] Q.B. 403.
[42] *Arkwright* v. *Newbold* (1880) 17 Ch.D.301.
[43] *Smith* v. *Chadwick* (1884) 9 App. Cas. 187; *Hartlelid* v. *Sawyer & McClockin Real Estate Ltd.* [1957] 5 W.W.R. 481.
[44] *Edgington* v. *Fitzmaurice* (1885) 29 Ch.D. 459.

have an important bearing upon the nature of the remedy available to a plaintiff.

Fraudulent misrepresentation

A fraudulent misrepresentation is one made knowingly, or without belief in its truth, or recklessly, careless whether it be true or false. An absence of honest belief on the part of the person making the representation is essential to establish the element of fraud. In *Derry* v *Peek*[45] a company issued a prospectus stating that it had the required governmental approvals to operate a steam tramway. In fact it did not, but the company did have grounds for believing that the necessary approvals would be forthcoming. An action was brought by the purchasers of shares which proved to be worthless, the company having been wound up after authorisation to operate the tramway was refused. The House of Lords refused to find the directors liable in damages for fraudulent misrepresentation because they had held an honest belief that the company would be entitled to operate the steam trams.

Derry v. *Peek*

At common law a purchaser has a right both to rescind the contract and to claim damages in the tort of deceit if he proves a vendor has made a fraudulent misrepresentation. Alternatively, damages for breach of contract may be claimed where the fraudulent misrepresentation has been incorporated as a contractual term.

Negligent misrepresentation at common law

At common law a negligent misrepresentation is one made in breach of a duty owed by the representor to the representee to take reasonable care that statements made are accurate.[46] If, when making a statement, a party or his agent purports to have some special knowledge and knows, or ought to know, that the other contracting party is going to rely on it, the duty of care arises. If the duty is breached the party who suffers loss as a result may sue for damages in the tort of negligence. In *Esso Petroleum Co. Ltd.* v. *Mardon*[47] the plaintiff company let a garage to M. One of the company's agents, an experienced salesman, told M. that the turnover would be approximately 200,000 gallons a year. In the event, it was found to be less than half of that. It was held that the plaintiffs owed a duty of care to M. since they knew he would rely on their estimates in deciding to take a lease of the garage. The advice was clearly inaccurate because the salesman had negligently failed to take into account all the relevant factors. The plaintiffs were liable to pay damages for M.'s loss.

Esso Petroleum v. *Mardon*

Misrepresentation Act 1967

The position of a contracting party who has suffered as a result of a negligent misrepresentation was ameliorated by the Misrepresentation Act 1967.

Section 2 (1)

Where a party or his agent makes a negligent misrepresentation, section 2(1) of the 1967 Act provides:

> "Where a person has entered into a contract after a misrepresentation has been made to him by another party thereto and as result thereof he has suffered loss, then, if the person making the misrepresentation would be liable to damages in respect thereof had the misrepresentation been made fraudulently, that person shall be so liable

---

[45] (1889) 14 App. Cas. 337.
[46] *Hedley Byrne & Co. Ltd.* v. *Heller & Partners Ltd.* [1964] A.C. 465.
[47] [1976] Q.B. 801.

notwithstanding that the misrepresentation was not made fraudulently, unless he proves that he had reasonable ground to believe and did believe up to the time the contract was made that the facts represented were true."

Advantages

Two advantages accure to a party suing under the Act rather than at common law. The first is the lack of need to prove that a duty of care is owed to him. The second is the reversal of the onus of proof; under the Act the representor or his agent must prove he had reasonable grounds to believe (and did believe) that the facts represented by him were true.

Section 2(2)

At one time the only remedy available for any non-fraudulent misrepresentation was rescission of the contract. The right to rescind for a non-fraudulent misrepresentation is preserved by section 2(2) of the Act of 1967 which provides that:

"Where a person has entered into a contract after a misrepresentation has been made to him otherwise than fraudulently, and he would be entitled by reason of the misrepresentation to rescind the contract, then if it is claimed in any of the proceedings arising out of the contract that the contract ought to be or has been rescinded, the court or arbitrator may declare the contract subsisting and award damages in lieu of rescission, if of the opinion that it would be equitable to do so, having regard to the nature of the misrepresentation and the loss that would be caused by it if the contract were upheld as well as the loss that rescission would cause to the other party."

If the court thinks it equitable to do so it may declare the contract subsisting and award damages instead of ordering rescission.

Although a purchaser suing under the Act may obtain damages under both section 2(1) and 2(2) the award is not cumulative. Section 2(3) requires that a court, in assessing damages under section 2(2), take into account damages awarded under section 2(1).

Misrepresentation repeated in contract

The remedies conferred under sections 2(1) and (2) of the 1967 Act are still available to the representee where the misrepresentation has been incorporated into the contract as a term. Section 1 of the 1967 Act preserves the representee's remedies in this respect. Further, the fact that the contract has been completed will not prevent a representee from pursuing his remedies under the statute.

However, if the misrepresentation is repeated in the contract the representor may be liable for breach of contract and the purchaser may prefer to sue for damages on the contract as an alternative to suing for misrepresentation under the Act although, of course, he would not be entitled to sue both under the Act and for breach of contract in order to make a double recovery of damages.

Innocent misrepresentation

An innocent misrepresentation is one made without any degree of fault on the part of the representor. Prior to the passage of the 1967 Act, rescission was the only remedy available to the representee for this type of misrepresentation. The right is now statutory and is set out in section 2(2) of the Act (above). Again the court's discretionary power to award damages in lieu of rescission may be exercised. It is not possible both to rescind *and* claim damages for innocent misrepresentation.

Where an innocent misrepresentation has been incorporated into the contract the representee may be able to recover damages for breach of contract. In this case the representee will not be dependant upon the court exercising its discretion in his favour to award damages in lieu of rescission.

Conduct　　A misrepresentation may be made by conduct.[48] Where the vendor of a house papered over cracks in a wall to conceal defective foundations, he was held to have made a fraudulent misrepresentation and his purchaser was accordingly entitled to relief.[49]

Watts v. Spence　　In *Watts* v. *Spence*[50] Graham J. held that one of two joint tenants, who alone contracted to sell a house, made a representation by his conduct (negotiating and subsequently making the contract), that he was the owner and so able to sell the property. He further held that this misrepresentation was made carelessly and so fell within the scope of section 2(1) of the Misrepresentation Act 1967.

The later case of *Malhotra* v. *Choudhury*,[51] distinguished *Watt's* case and suggested that the courts would in future be less ready to hold that entering into a contract, by itself, constituted an actionable misrepresentation of fact. This case concerned the enforceability of an option to purchase, granted by one partner to another, allowing the other to purchase the partnership practice and premises. The Court of Appeal endorsed Blackett-Ord V.-C.'s statement at first instance that:

> "this option itself cannot I think be treated as a representation, otherwise every contract would imply a representation and every vendor would be warranting his title."

Watt's case was further disapproved of in *Sharneyford Supplies Ltd.* v. *Edge*.[52]

Silence　　It has been said that remaining silent on a matter can constitute a misrepresentation, in that it distorts a positive statement already made about the property. In one recent case[53] a vendor of land, in his replies to preliminary enquiries, stated that the central heating system installed in his house was in a good condition. Prior to exchange the pipes in the house froze and the pipes in the system burst. The vendor was held liable for damages for misrepresentation despite the fact that at the time of making his replies to preliminary enquiries the central heating system was not damaged and his statement was true. The *ratio* for this decision appears to be that the representation made by the vendor was a continuing representation and that the vendor was, therefore, under a positive duty to inform his purchaser of the damage to the central heating system once it occurred.

A vendor of land who reveals only half the truth may be guilty of misrepresentation. In *Nottingham Patent Brick & Tile*

---

[48] *Bodger* v. *Nicholls* (1873) 28 L.T. 441.
[49] *Ridge* v. *Crawley* (1959) 173 E.G.959; *Gordon* v. *Selico* (1986) 278 E.G. 53.
[50] [1976] Ch. 165. See also *Errington* v. *Martell-Wilson* (1980) 130 New L.J. 545.
[51] [1980] Ch. 52.
[52] [1985] 1 All E.R. 976 and see below p. 92.
[53] *Corner* v. *Mundy*, discussed at (1988) 8 P.L.B. 50.

Half the truth

Co. v. *Butler*[54] a vendor's solicitor stated that he was not aware of any restrictive convenants burdening the land to be sold. He did not reveal that he had not looked at the title deeds. Restrictive covenants did burden the land and would have prevented the plaintiff company from practising its trade. The vendor's solicitor's statement though true was held to be sufficiently misleading to allow the purchaser to rescind.

Agents

In most conveyancing transactions both parties will employ agents to act on their behalf (*e.g.* solicitors and estate agents). What happens if an agent either makes a misrepresentation or is made aware of information to correct a mistatement previously made by the representor but does not pass on this information to his principal?

Resolute Martime inc v. Nippon Kaiji Kyokai

Resolute Maritime Inc. v. *Nippon Kaiji Kyokai*,[55] (*The Skopas*) shows that an agent (as opposed to his principal) will not be liable himself for a negligent misrepresentation under the Misrepresentation Act 1967, provided that when making the misrepresentation he is acting within his actual or ostensible authority. The purpose of the 1967 Act was to fill the gap in the remedies available to a contracting party before 1967; he could not claim damages from the other party for a non-fraudulent misrepresentation whether made by that other or his agent. Agents are, of course, liable for their own negligent statements under the principles laid down in *Hedley Byrne & Co. Ltd.* v. *Heller & Partners Ltd.*[56]

The importance of the *Skopas* case is that if a purchaser wishes to pursue his remedies under the Misrepresentation Act 1967 for a non–fraudulent innocent or negligent misrepresentation made by the representor's agent then he must proceed directly against the representor. The vendor who is thus subjected to liability will be able to gain compensation from the agent in the tort of negligence but only where the misrepresentation was made by his agent negligently. Where the misrepresentation was made by the agent innocently the vendor has no recourse at all.

Strover v. Harrington

In *Strover* v. *Harrington*[57] the vendor's particulars of sale incorrectly stated that their property had mains drainage. Prior to exchange of contracts the estate agents acting for the vendors wrote to the purchaser's solicitors pointing out the error. The purchaser's solicitors did not inform their clients of the error having been corrected. The purchasers brought an action against the vendors for misrepresentation. The court held that the purchasers were to be treated as having known of the estate agents' correction to the particulars despite the fact that the purchasers' solicitors had not passed on this information. In the course of his judgement Sir Nicholas Browne-Wilkinson V.C. stated[58]:

> "In this, as in all other normal conveyancing transactions, after there has been a subject to contract agreement the

---

[54] (1886) 16 Q.B.D. 778; see also *South Western General Property Co. Ltd.* v. *Marton* (1982) 263 E.G. 1090.
[55] [1983] 1 W.L.R. 857.
[56] [1964] A.C. 465.
[57] [1988] 2 W.L.R. 572.
[58] *Ibid.* at 586.

parties hand the matter over to their solicitors who become the normal channel for communication between vendor and purchaser in all matters relating to the transaction. In so doing, in my judgement the parties impliedly give actual authority to those solicitors to receive on their behalf all revelant information from the other party relating to the transaction. The solicitors are under an obligation to communicate that relevant information to their own clients. At the very least, the solicitors are held out as having ostensible authority to receive such information. Where there be express or ostensible authority, the purchaser is in my judgement estopped from denying that he received the information relating to the transaction which has been communicated to his solicitors acting in the same transaction. In my judgment, such knowledge would be imputed to the principal."

The principle underlying the decision is clearly correct given the normal conveyancing procedures involved. However, it is possible to conceive circumstances in which a purchaser may be without a remedy both as against his vendor and his solicitor. For example, the purchaser would still have knowledge of facts disclosed to his solicitor which the solicitor had recorded in a letter duly sent to his client but lost in the post.

Remedies

(1) Recission   If a misrepresentation has been made the **Election** purchaser may elect to treat the contract as subsisting or to rescind the contract. If the purchaser rescinds, the contract is terminated. The parties are restored to the position in which they stood before the contract was entered into.[59] In all cases the purchaser should communicate his intention to rescind to the vendor.[60]

Rescission is available at common law for fraudulent misrepresentation. In the case of negligent and innocent misrepresentation the Misrepresentation Act 1967 (discussed above) governs the position. In any action in which rescission is claimed the court is given a discretion by section 2(2) of the Act to award damages instead. This power to award damages in lieu of recission may put severe limitations on the availability of the remedy. The discretion may be exercised, for example, where the vendor has bought a new house with the proceeds of sale and to require repayment of the whole purchase price would in most cases cause him severe hardship.

The right to rescind for misrepresentation (fraudulent, negligent or innocent) is not lost because the contract for sale has **After completion** been performed and a conveyance or transfer executed.[61] This is of importance to a purchaser whose vendor has made a misrepresentation prior to the contract which is repeated in the contract. The purchaser has the choice of suing under the Misrepresentation Act 1967 or treating the inaccuracy as a misdescription and claiming a rescission or damages for breach of

---

[59] *Redgrave* v. *Hurd* (1881) 20 Ch. D.1.
[60] But this will not always be required or be possible; *Car & Universal Finance Co. Ltd.* v. *Caldwell* [1965] 1 Q.B. 525.
[61] s.1(*b*) of the Misrepresentation Act 1967.

contract. However, a remedy for misdescription is only available prior to completion. Even though the contract has been completed the purchaser can still claim rescission or damages under the Misrepresentation Act.

Limitations on availability of rescission

Although performance of the contract is no bar to rescission there are a number of limitations on the availability of the remedy.

Third parties

The right to rescind is lost if an innocent third party acquires a right in the land before the election to terminate the contract is made. A purchaser buying with the aid of a mortgage will, therefore, be unable to rescind the contract once his lender has acquired a charge over the property. In practice this happens almost immediately the transaction is completed since both conveyance and mortgage are executed simultaneously.

Return to status quo

An essential element of rescission is the restoration of the parties to the position they were in before the contract was made. If it is not possible substantially to return to the status quo ante, rescission will not be available. Thus, in *Clarke* v. *Dickson*[62] it was held that a purchaser of shares in a mining company could not rescind for misrepresentation because he had exhausted the mine.

Delay

The representee who delays in communicating his decision to rescind a contract may find that the remedy is no longer available to him. He may be taken to have affirmed the contract. Time does not begin to run until the purchaser discovers the truth.[63] However, where innocent misrepresentation is concerned it seems that time may begin to run even before the purchaser discovers the truth.[64]

2. Damages The availability and level of damages recoverable in an action for breach of a contract for the sale of property is discussed in Chapter 6. In this section we will discuss damages as a remedy in an action for misrepresentation.

Tortious basis of assessment

Generally, under the Misrepresentation Act the representee recovers damages calculated in accordance with tortious principles.

Example

The representee purchaser will be entitled to such damages as will put him in the position he would have been in had the misrepresentation not been made. This is not the same as the contractual method of assessing damages, where the aim is to put the purchaser in the position he would have been in if the statement in the contract had been true. An example will show the difference between the two rules. A buys a house from B for £10,000. B induces A to enter the contract by making a misrepresentation. If the misrepresentation had actually been true the house would have been worth £15,000. As it is the house is worth only £8,000. If A sues for misrepresentation under the Act he can only recover the tortious measure of damages, *i.e.* £2,000. On the other hand if the misrepresentation has become a term of the contract, A will be able to recover the contractual measure i.e. £5,000 for his "loss of bargain". Clearly a representee will want to bring a claim for breach of contract if the representation has become a term of the contract.

---

[62] (1858) El. B. & El.148.
[63] *Armstrong* v. *Jackson* [1917] 2 K.B. 822.
[64] *Leaf* v. *International Galleries* [1950] 2 K.B. 86.

The tortious method of assessing damages applies to claims for fraudulent and negligent misrepresentation, both at common law (on the *Hedley Byrne* principle) and under section 2(1) of the 1967 Act. Damages under section 2(2), awarded in lieu of rescission, are unlikely to exceed those which would be awarded using this method but the precise method of assessment is uncertain. The possibility of avoiding the rule in *Bain* v. *Fothergill*[65] by way of suing for misrepresentation is discussed in the next chapter.[66]

Clauses limiting or excluding liability

It has been said that a contracting party who attempted to limit his liability took "a very ordinary business precaution."[67–68] Those seeking to rely on exclusion clauses today may well view this statement with a certain amount of scepticism. The Misrepresentation Act 1967 and the Unfair Contract Terms Act 1977 severely limit the extent to which a party to a contract may exclude or restrict his liability both for breaches of contract (a representation may become a term of the contract) and misrepresentation. The ingenuity of lawyers has resulted in a number of mechanisms being adopted, some more successful than others, by contracting parties to exclude or limit liability in **Popular methods** this respect. The more popular methods involve clauses in contracts which:–

(a) limit the liability of the party in breach or making the representation to a specified monetary amount;

(b) exclude liability altogether;

(c) state that no representations have been made by a vendor of land (usually save for written replies to a purchaser's preliminary enquiries);

(d) operate as express statements by the purchaser that to the extent representations have been made by the vendor they have not been relied upon by the purchaser or induced him to enter into the contract;

(e) operate so as to result in the purchaser or some third party indemnifying the vendor against any liability he may incur as a result of any breach of contract or misrepresentation.

Both sets of standard conditions contain clauses which attempt to limit the vendor's liability for misrepresentation, non-disclosure or misdescription. National condition 17 and Law Society condition 7 are attempts to exclude a vendor's liability for misleading statements.

However first the statutory provisions which apply to limit the effect of clauses if the type described above need to be considered.

---

[65] (1874) L.R. 7 H.L.
[66] See below pp. 90–93.
[67–68] *Cellulose Acetate Silk Co.Ltd.* v. *Widnes Foundry (1925) Ltd.* [1933] A.C. 20, *per* Lord Atkin at 25.

Statutory provisions

Misrepresentation Act 1967

Section 3 (as substituted by section 8 of the Unfair Contract Terms Act 1977) provides:

> "If a contract contains a term which would exclude or restrict:
> (a) any liability to which a party to a contract may be subject by reason of any misrepresentation made by him before the contract was made; or
> (b) any remedy available to any party to the contract by reason of such misrepresentation that term shall be of no effect except insofar as it satisfies the requirement of reasonableness as stated in section 11(1) of the Unfair Contract Terms Act 1977 ..."

Section 11(1) of the 1977 Act provides that "reasonableness" means that "the term shall have been a fair and reasonable one to be included, having regard to the circumstances which were, or ought reasonably to have been, known to or in the contemplation of the parties when the contract was made."

The person seeking to rely on the clause must establish its reasonableness. Because the court in each case must have regard to the circumstances in which the contract was made, the same exclusion clause may be held reasonable in one case and unreasonable in another.

In *George Mitchell (Chesterhall) Ltd.* v. *Finney Lock Seeds Ltd.*[69] the House of Lords warned that appellate courts would only interfere with the original decision if it was based on some incorrect principle or "plainly and obviously" wrong.

Analysis and efficacy of clauses

Representation denied

One type of clause used by vendors to try to escape liability for misrepresentation purports to deny that any representation has been made. In *Cremdean Properties Ltd.* v. *Nash*[70] particulars of sale at an auction stated that they were for the convenience of purchasers but that "their accuracy is not guaranteed and any error, omission or misdescription shall not annul the sale . . . any intending purchaser . . . must satisfy himself as to the correctness of each of the statements contained in these particulars ." The vendor contended that the clause effectively denied any (mis)representation and that therefore the Misrepresentation Act 1967 could not apply. The court did not agree. They decided that such a clause could not protect the vendor. The clause was in effect saying that the vendor was making a representation which the purchaser was invited to verify.

Reliance excluded

Another type of exclusion clause is one in which the purchaser states he has not been induced to enter into the contract by any representation made by the vendor, whether the representation is made orally or in writing, and whether the representation is made by the vendor himself or on his behalf. This kind of clause is not guaranteed to afford a vendor complete

---

[69] [1983] 2 A.C. 803.
[70] (1977) 244 E.G. 547.

protection. A court will always enquire whether the purchaser did, or did not, in fact rely on the representation once it is established that one was in fact made.[71]

Reasonableness

Insofar as such a clause has the effect of excluding or limiting a vendor's liability it would also be subject to the test of reasonableness in section 11 of the Unfair Contract Terms Act 1977. Whether or not a clause such as this could be held "reasonable" would, obviously, depend upon the particular circumstances of each case. However, as we saw earlier once it is proved that a representation is *material*, reliance upon it is normally very easily established by the representee.[72] Given this it may in practice be very difficult to persuade a court that such a term is reasonable and so effective. When, for example a purchaser has specialist knowledge of the property in question or access to more information on it than his vendor such a clause may prove effective. In such cases a vendor could argue strongly that it is reasonable to require a purchaser to verify the accuracy of statement made by him.

Agents

There is one method available to a vendor of limiting or excluding his liability; this is by channelling all statements about the property through an agent. In *Overbrooke Estates Ltd.* v. *Glencombe Properties Ltd.*[73] Brightman J. held that a clause, providing that auctioneers had no authority to make or give any representations or warranty in relation to the property being sold, effectively protected the vendor from liability, when the auctioneers made statements about the property which misled the purchaser. The 1967 Act did not alter the vendor's ability publicly to limit the scope of his agent's authority. The purchaser was taken to have bought knowing that anything the auctioneer said could not bind the vendor. The decision has been criticised as allowing a vendor to "put into circulation facts about the property which can only be intended to affect the minds of potential purchasers." without the risk of incurring liability for misrepresentation.[74] The vendor must not, however, give his agent authority to put these statements into circulation. Once he does this the clause will not protect him; the agent's representations will be binding on him.

The standard conditions

National condition 17

"17. Errors, mis-statements or omissions
    (1) Without prejudice to any express right of either party, or to any right of the purchaser in reliance on Law of Property Act 1969, s.24, to rescind the contract before completion and subject to the provisions of paragraph (2) of this condition, no error, mis–statement or omission in any preliminary answer concerning the property, or in the sale plan or the Special Conditions, shall annul the sale, nor (save where the error, mis-statement or omission relates to a matter materially affecting the description or value of the

---

[71] See above pp. 59–60.
[72] *Lowe* v. *Lombank Ltd.* [1960] 1 W.L.R. 196.
[73] [1974] 1 W.L.R. 1335; *Collins* v. *Howell-Jones* (1980) 259 E.G. 331; see also J.E. Adams (1970) 67 L.S.Gaz. 257 and 318.
[74] H.W.Wilkinson [1984] Conv.12; J.E. Adams [1981] Conv.326.

property) shall any damages be payable, or compensation allowed by either party, in respect thereof

(2) Paragraph (1) of this condition shall not apply to any error, mis-statement or, omission which is recklessly or fraudulently made, or to any matter or thing by which the purchaser is prevented from getting substantially what he contracted to buy

(3) In this condition a "a preliminary answer" means and includes any statement made by or on behalf of the vendor to the purchaser or his agents or advisers, whether in answer to formal preliminary enquiries or otherwise, before the purchaser entered into the contract."

Law Society general condition 7

"7 ERRORS, OMISSIONS AND MISSTATEMENTS

(1) No error, omission or misstatement herein or in any plan unfurnished or any statement made in the course of the negotiations leading to the contract shall annul the sale or entitle the purchaser to be discharged from the purchase.

(2) Any such error, omission or misstatement shown to be material shall entitle the purchaser or the vendor, as the case may be, to proper compensation, provided that the purchaser shall not in any event be entitled to compensation for matters falling within conditions 5(2) or 6(3).

(3) No immaterial error, omission or misstatement (including a mistake in any plan furnished for identification only) shall entitle either party to compensation.

(4) Sub-condition (1) shall not apply where compensation for any error, omission or misstatement shown to be material cannot be assessed nor enable either party to compel the other to accept or convey property differing substantially (in quantity, quality tenure or otherwise) from the property agreed to be sold if the other property would be prejudiced by the difference.

(5) The purchaser acknowledges that in making the contract he has not relied on any statement made to him save one made or confirmed in writing ."

National condition 17 (1) entitles the purchaser to compensation for any misrepresentation, made by or on behalf of the vendor (17(3)), which materially affects the value of the property. Sub-condition (2) gives the purchaser a right to rescind in any case where the vendor or his agent misled him fraudulently or recklessly. A right of rescission is also reserved to the purchaser where the misrepresentation leads the purchaser to believe he is buying property fundamentally different from that which he in fact contracts to buy. The purchaser's right to rescind on discovery of an undisclosed land charge, given by section 24 of the Law of Property Act 1969, is unaffected.

The misrepresentation may be contained in the contract itself, in a plan sent with the contract or in answers written or oral given by the vendor or his agent to any enquiries before the purchaser entered into the contract.

The condition was drafted in its present form following the

Walker* v. *Boyle   decision in *Walker* v *Boyle*. [75] The vendor misled his purchaser by stating that there was no current boundary dispute affecting the property. In fact there was a dispute with a neighbour over the position of a fence. The sale was subject to the National Conditions of Sale (19th ed.), condition 17 of which was similar to the current condition 17, except that it stated that damages were only available for a misrepresentation made in writing which materially affected the description or value of the property. Dillon J., giving judgement for the purchaser, held that (the old) condition 17 did not meet the requirements of fairness and reasonableness contained in section 11 of the Unfair Contract Terms Act 1977. The fact that the condition had been in use for many years and that both parties were independently advised did not "entitle it to the automatic accolade of fairness and reasonableness." Dillon J. also commented unfavourably on the fact that the condition purported to exclude compensation for any oral mistatement, fraudulent or otherwise, no matter how serious it might be. It was this *obiter* comment which prompted the inclusion of the present sub-condition(2).

As redrafted, condition 17 now only attempts to exclude the purchaser's remedies for misrepresentation (whether oral or written) in cases where it is not material or substantial in its effect and is not made recklessly or fraudulently. Whether the condition as redrafted will satisfy the requirements of section 3 of the Misrepresentation Act remains to be seen.

Law Society general condition 7, like National condition 17, entitles the purchaser to rescind the contract for a misrepresentation which results in him getting property "differing substantially ... from the property agreed to be sold." This result is achieved by reading sub-condition (1) with sub-condition (4). Compensation is given to the purchaser if the misrepresentation is shown to be material. In *Re Fawcett and*

Re Fawcett and   *Holmes' Contract* [76] the vendor agreed to sell a house, builder's
Holmes' Contract   yard and stables. He stated that the area of the property was 1,372 square yards. The true figure should have been 1,033 square yards. When the purchaser sought rescission it was held that the misrepresentation was material not substantial and therefore only entitled him to compensation. No compensation is payable for misstatements relating to matters of which the purchaser is deemed to have knowledge by condition 5(2) (state and condition, easements and so on). Similarly a misrepresentation as to matters within the scope of condition 6(3) (rent lawfully recoverable from a tenant and so on) does not carry a right to compensation. [77]

Oral   Law Society condition 7(5) attempts to prevent the
misrepresentations   purchaser from obtaining relief on the basis of any oral misrepresentation made by the vendor before contract. The courts have shown a willingness to go behind statements like this and enquire whether a representation was relied on. [78] If so the exclusion will be ineffective, unless it passes the "reasonableness"

---

[75] [1982] 1 W.L.R. 495.
[76] (1889) 42 Ch. D. 150.
[77] For a fuller discussion of LSC5 (2) and LSC6 (3) see Annand & Whish, *Conveyancing Solutions 2: The Contract* (1987).
[78] *Lowe* v. *Lombank Ltd.* [1960] 1 W.L.R. 196.

test. Despite this and despite Dillon J.'s criticism in *Walker* v. *Boyle* of the former and similarly drafted National condition 17, no change to Law Society condition 7 was recommended in 1984. Presumably it was not thought profitable to try and predict what the courts would find reasonable in any particular case. As drafted the clause seems "to put a duty on a purchaser's solicitor to find out from his client what representations have been made to him and either warn his client not to rely on them or insist that the vendor puts them into writing."[79] Finally, it should be noted that the condition does not expressly give a purchaser the right to rescind for a fraudulent mis-statement unless it is substantial.

Case-example

McGrath v. Shah   The recent case of *McGrath* v. *Shah* [80] provides a good example of the way in which vendors of property may be able to exclude or restrict their liability in the event of some misrepresentation or misdescription relating to the property. It also shows how the contractual provisions which are designed to limit or restrict liability impact upon the other provisions in the contract such as those which allow the vendor to serve a notice to complete.

The facts of the case are as follows. The plaintiffs were registered proprietors of the property which they had agreed to sell to the defendants for £345,000. Contracts were exchanged on June 18 1987. Special condition 9 of the contract was in the following terms:

> "this contract constitutes the entire contract between the parties, and may be varied (by way of collateral contract or otherwise) only in writing under the hands of the parties or their solicitors. The purchaser hereby admits that saving in respect of such written statements of the vendor's solicitors prior to the date hereof as were not capable of independent verification (whether by inspection or by search or enquiry of any local or any other public authority, whether or not such inspection, search or enquiry has been made, or otherwise) no representation, whether oral or written, has been made to him by or on behalf of the vendor concerning the property on which he has relied or which has influenced, induced or persuaded him to enter into this contract."

The National conditions applied to the contract unless expressly varied by the parties.

The contractual completion date passed and the vendors' solicitors served a notice to complete upon the purchasers under National condition 22. The purchasers' solicitors registered a caution at the land registry to protect their clients' position after the vendors had served formal notice to rescind the contract and forfeit the deposit.

The vendors brought an action by way of notice of motion to have the caution vacated. The court could only do this if it was satisfied that there was no serious argument on behalf of the defendants which substantiated the claim protected by the caution.

The purchasers argued that prior to exchange of contracts

---

[79] H.W.Wilkinson [1980] Conv. 404.
[80] *The Times*, October 22, 1987.

**Misrepresentation
and notices to
complete**

serious misrepresentations were made by the vendors and that
these entitled them to rescind the contract before completion.
The argument ran that because the purchasers were entitled to
rescind the contract prior to completion the vendors were not
entitled to serve a notice to complete. J. Chadwick Q.C, (sitting
as a Deputy High Court Judge) dealt very shortly with this
argument. He held that under National condition 22 a vendor is
entitled to serve a notice to complete, provided, at the time the
notice is served, the contract has not been rescinded by the
purchaser. This was without prejudice to a purchaser's right to
rescind the contract if he had ground for so doing after the notice
to complete had been served. In this case the purchasers did not
want to rescind the contract as evidenced by their registration of
the caution.

Contractual term?

The second argument put forward by the purchasers was
that certain statements made before exchange of contracts had
become contractual terms even though they were not expressly
referred to in the written contract exchanged on June 18. The
argument ran that the vendors were not able and willing to
comply with those terms and therefore were not in a position to
fulfill their outstanding obligations under the contract and to
serve notice under National condition 22. The two alleged
contractual terms were that there would be a playroom in the
attic of the property and that the kitchen would be fitted with an
oven and hob. It was common ground that if these were
contractual terms the vendor could not comply with them. The
judge held that Special condition 9 placed an "inseparable
hurdle" which the defendants could not overcome. He held that
the provision which stated that the contracts exchanged on June
18 constituted the entire contract between the parties and could
only be varied in writing, was effective to prevent the defendants'
argument from succeeding. The defendants submitted that this
provision was a provision which excluded or restricted liability
and so was subject to the test of reasonableness set out in section
11 of the Unfair Contract Terms act 1977. The judge stated that

> "[Section 3 of the Misrepresentation Act 1967], which is in
> terms directed to the exclusion or restriction of liability for
> misrepresentation, or of remedies arising by reason of
> misrepresentation, is not apt to cover a contractual provision
> which seeks to define where the contractual terms are
> actually to be found. But if I am wrong in that, then it seems
> to me that far from it being fair or unreasonable for the
> parties to include in that contract a term in the form of the
> first sentence of Special condition 9, it is eminently fair and
> reasonable that they should do so where the contract is a
> contract relating to the sale of land."

The judge went on to state that in the event that the pre-
June 18 representations effectively formed a collateral contract
this would not affect the liability of the vendor to serve a notice to
complete. He was quite able, ready and willing to fulfil the
outstanding obligations under the contract of which National
condition 22 formed the part. The default under some collateral
contract would not prevent him from serving a notice to complete
under the principal contract.

The third and final argument advanced on behalf of the

Estate agents' particulars
purchaser was to the effect that the estate agents' particulars which referred to a playroom in the attic and oven and hob formed part of the contractual arrangement between the parties. The estate agents' particulars contained the following clause "these particulars do not constitute, or constitute any part, of an offer or contract . . . . the vendors or lessors do not make or give, and neither do (the estate agents) nor any person in their employment have any authority to make or give, any representation or warranty whatever in relation to this property."

The judge held that these terms were effective to prevent the purchaser from relying on the particulars in his claim against the vendor.

Misdescription

Misdescription is merely a form of misrepresentation. It is a statement of fact, relating to the description of the property, contained in the contract. The particulars of sale form part of the contract and if the vendor cannot convey the property therein described he will be in breach of contract.

The misdescription may relate to the physical extent of the property, the nature of the interest sold or the quality of the land. Under an open contract the parties rights depend on whether the error is trivial, material or substantial. The standard conditions mainly reflect the common law position but do make changes in places.

Types of misdescription

Trivial errors
Falling within the category of trivial errors would be cases where the purchaser obtains almost exactly that for which he paid. For example in *Vartoukian* v. *Daejan Properties Ltd.*[81] a number of flats were sold. The contract described them as being held on long leases. In fact one of the tenants held under a short lease. Soon after the contract was made the vendor remedied the position by granting that tenant a long lease. It was held that the purchaser, having obtained substantially all he agreed to buy, could only recover nominal damages. Trivial errors do not allow a purchaser to rescind the contract.

Standard conditions
The standard conditions of sale contain provisions dealing with the parties' rights in the event of a slight misdescription. National condition 17(1) provides that no compensation or damages shall be payable for an error, which does not materially affect the description or value of the property.[82] This exclusion does not apply to slight errors if they are made recklessly or fraudulently: National condition 17 (2).

Law Society condition 7 (3) precludes either party from claiming compensation for "immaterial" errors.

Material errors
The category of material errors comprises those cases where the purchaser receives a different property from that which he bargained for, but not drastically different. In *Belsworth* v. *Hassell*[83] there was an agreement to assign "the unexpired term

---

[81] (1969) 113 S.J. 646.
[82] *Pagebar Properties Ltd.* v. *Derby Investment Holdings Ltd.* [1972] 1 W.L.R. 1500.
[83] (1815) 4 Camp. 410.

of eight years" remaining under a lease. The remainder of the term was actually seven years and seven months. Lord Ellenborough decided that the purchaser was obliged to complete since he received more or less that which he had agreed to pay for. A misdescription relating to the physical extent of the property would be dealt with in the same way.[84]

A material error will generally not allow a purchaser to rescind the contract; only to claim damages[85] However, he is entitled to seek specific performance of the contract with an abatement of the purchase price. Where the price of property is reached not on the basis of area, but on its value for some other reason, for example, it gives the purchaser access to previously isolated property, this can be of considerable advantage to the purchaser. By being given an abatement he is in effect being allowed to pay a lower price for something he thought more valuable.[86]

The purchaser will not be able specifically to enforce the contract with an abatement in the price if the error cannot fairly be assessed in monetary terms. In these circumstances he is given the right to rescind. In *Rudd* v. *Lascelles*[87] L. agreed to sell some property to R. for £3,500. The land, unknown to R. when he contracted, was subject to restrictive covenants limiting the uses to which it could be put. R. claimed specific performance with an abatement in the price of £1,000. The action was dismissed on the ground, *inter alia*, that compensation for such an error could not be assessed. R. was left to his remedies for breach of contract and he rescinded.

Standard conditions The National and Law Society conditions reflect the common law, giving the purchaser a right to compensation in respect of any misdescription shown to be material. Law Society general condition 7 (4) also takes into account the decision in *Rudd* v. *Lascelles* by giving the purchaser the opportunity to rescind where compensation cannot be assessed. The National conditions leave the common law to apply.

Under an open contract the purchaser has to claim compensation for a material misdescription before completion.[88]
After conveyance After completion the contract merges into the conveyance and no action can be brought on it. The purchaser can sue on the implied covenants for title but only if the misdescription is repeated in the conveyance. However, if on the construction of a contract for the sale of land any of its provisions are intended to be effective after a formal conveyance has been executed, those provisions "survive" the conveyance and remain operative. This is the case where the contract contains a term giving a right to compensation for any misdescription. National condition 17 and Law Society condition 7 are examples of such provisions and will allow the purchaser to claim compensation even after completion has taken place.

Law Society condition 7 (2) provides that no compensation can be claimed by the purchaser for matters falling within the

---

[84] *Watson* v. *Burton* [1957] 1 W.L.R. 19.
[85] *Dyer* v. *Hargrave* (1805) 10 Ves. 505.
[86] *Hill* v. *Buckley* (1811) 17 Ves. 394.
[87] [1900] 1 Ch.815.
[88] *Joliffe* v. *Baker* (1883) 11 Q.B.D. 255.

ambit of condition 5 (2) (state and condition, easements and so on) or condition 6 (3) (matters affecting a subsisting tenancy subject to which the property is sold).

Vendor's position

A vendor who innocently misdescribes his property is able specifically to enforce the contract, subject to giving the purchaser proper compensation for the deficiency. Equity looks to the substance of the transaction rather than the form and will not permit a purchaser to avoid a contract because of some insubstantial error which would not have altered his decision to buy.[89]

Extreme hardship

The misdescription may be to the prejudice of the vendor, for example where he contracts to sell more property than he intended to. At common law he has no implied right to increase the price. It is the vendor's responsibility to ensure that he describes the property accurately. However if the misdescription means that the vendor will suffer extreme hardship, as where the acreage of land contracted to be sold is far in excess of the intended acreage, the court may refuse specific performance and order a purchaser to pursue his remedies for breach of contract.[90] In *Manser* v. *Back*[91] property was put up for sale at auction. The particulars omitted to reserve the vendor a right of way. Although the auctioneer subsequently amended the particulars the purchaser signed an agreement which through some oversight, again omitted to reserve the right of way. The purchaser claimed specific performance of the contract for sale free from the right of way. The court held that to grant the decree would cause great hardship to the vendor. They therefore, gave the purchaser a choice; specific performance subject to a right of way and proper compensation, or damages for breach of contract.

Standard conditions

Both the National and Law Society conditions greatly improve the position of the vendor. National condition 17 (1) and Law Society general condition 7 (2) give the vendor a right to compensation for material or substantial errors.

Substantial errors
Flight v. _Booth_

Whether the sale is under an open contract or the standard contracts of sale a vendor cannot force on the purchaser property which differs substantially from that which he has agreed to buy. The rule at common law was developed in *Flight* v. *Booth*.[92] A purchaser bought a market stall in Covent Garden at an auction. The particulars gave details of restrictive covenants preventing use of the premises for any offensive trade, the business of a working hatter or as a coffee shop. The contract contained a term saying that errors should not vitiate the sale, but that there should be an allowance in price to either party in the event of a misdescription. After the auction the purchaser discovered other covenants preventing use for various trades including, *inter alia*, butcher, tripe seller, distiller, dyer, dealer in old iron and fruiterer. In view of the location of the property, the purchaser objected. He was allowed to rescind and recover his deposit despite the clause in the contract forbidding him to do so. In the course of his judgment Tindal C. J. said that a purchaser can rescind despite a contractual clause to the contrary if the

---

[89] *Bowyer* v. *Bright* (1824) 13 Price 698.
[90] *Rudd* v. *Lascelles* [1900] 1 Ch.815.
[91] (1848) 6 Hare 443.
[92] (1834) 1 Bing. N.C. 370; *Re Belcham and Gawley's Contract* [1930] 1 Ch.56.

misdescription, "although not proceeding from fraud was in a material and substantial point, so far affecting the subject matter of the contract that it may be reasonably supposed, that, but for such misdescription, the purchaser might never have entered into the contract at all." The vendor is not given the option of specific performance even if he is willing to pay the purchaser compensation.

Examples of substantial misdescriptions

The following have been held to be substantial misdescriptions allowing the purchaser to rescind: describing a factory as having an area of 3,920 square yards when it only had 2,360 square yards[93]; describing a house as 58 Pall Mall when it had no frontage to Pall Mall[94]; stating that a property is connected to a mains water supply and that water rates are payable when water is supplied by a private company and is paid for annually according to their scale of charges[95]; and describing a freehold house as sold with "entire vacant possession" when part of the first floor is completelty blocked off and rented as a storeroom by the owners of adjoining property.[96]

Whether a misdescription is substantial is a question of fact to be decided by the court in every case. No general rule can be stated other than the quote of Tindal C.J. given above. However, the more particularity with which the property is described the smaller the margin of error allowed to a vendor before the purchaser is allowed to rescind.

The purchaser does not have to rescind. He is given the choice of enforcing the contract and taking the vendor's property as it is with compensation. As with material errors, the purchaser's right to compensation and specific performance is limited to cases where the loss is assessable and the grant of a decree would not cause the vendor undue hardship. Again under an open contract the purchaser must pursue his remedies before completion.

Standard conditions

The rule in *Flight* v. *Booth* is expressly incorporated into the current editions of both forms of standard conditions. National condition 17 (1) provides that "no error ... in the sale plan or the Special conditions, shall annul the sale." This is subject to condition 17 (2) which goes on to state that 17 (1) shall not apply if the misdescription is made "recklessly or fraudulently ... or to any matter ... by which the purchaser is prevented from getting substantially what he contracted to buy." Law Society general condition 7 (1) read with 7 (4) is of similar effect. However, the Law Society condition adds that a party seeking rescission must be prejudiced by the error even it if is substantial. It is arguable that this requirement is in conflict with the rule in *Flight* v. *Booth* where there is no need for a purchaser to prove the prejudicial effect of a substantial error. Despite this, the requirement in the condition was accepted without question in *Watson* v. *Burton*.[97] In practice, a purchaser receiving property fundamentally different from that described in the contract would almost certainly be prejudiced in some respect.

---

[93] *Watson* v. *Burton* [1957] 1 W.L.R. 19.
[94] *Stanton* v. *Tattersall* (1853) 15 M. & Griff. 529.
[95] *Fisher* v. *Andrews* [1955] J.P.L. 452.
[96] *Mustafa* v. *Baptist Union Corp. Ltd.* (1983) 266 E.G. 812.
[97] [1957] 1 W.L.R. 19.

Non-Disclosure

Remedies

A purchaser's remedies for non-disclosure of a latent defect in title are exactly the same as those available to him where the vendor has misdescribed the property in the contract. Under an open contract a substantial non-disclosure will entitle a purchaser either to rescind the contract or specifically to enforce it with an abatement in the purchase price. A material non-disclosure will entitle the purchaser to compensation only. The vendor will be able to enforce the contract subject to giving the purchaser property compensation. A trivial non-disclosure does not entitle the purchaser to relief.

Standard conditions

National condition 17 and Law Society general condition 7 apply to non-disclosure ("omissions") in the same way as they apply to misdescription and misrepresentation.

6 DAMAGES FOR BREACH OF CONTRACT

Introduction

This chapter is concerned only with the remedy of damages for breach of a contract for the sale of land. It normally assumes that the contract has not been completed. This is because once completion has taken place, the contract and any remedies under it become merged in the conveyance. Some contractual conditions, however, do survive the conveyance. The vendor's contractual obligation (if any) to give vacant possession is perhaps the most common example.

The principles governing the recovery of damages *by a vendor* in conveyancing are those which apply to the law of contract generally. The same principles apply in the converse situation, *i.e.* where a purchaser sues a defaulting vendor, with the exception of the qualification imposed by the rule in *Bain* v. *Fothergill*[1] under which a purchaser cannot obtain damages from the vendor for loss of bargain where the vendor is unable, through no fault of his own, to provide a good title to the land sold.

It is proposed to discuss briefly the general principles and then to deal with the rights of the vendor and purchaser separately. The particular issues of damages for misdescription and non-disclosure are discussed in the previous chapter.

General principles

Starting point

The general principle and starting point in the consideration of the assessment of contractual damages, is that the injured party (in the present context, the vendor or purchaser) is to be placed in the same situation, so far as money can achieve this, as if the contract had been performed.[2]

Remoteness
Hadley v.
Baxendale

This general principle is, however, limited by the "rule" in *Hadley* v. *Baxendale*.[3] The judgment of Alderson B. contains the following, now famous, statement of law:

> "Now we think the proper rule in such a case as the present is this: Where two parties have made a contract which one of them has broken, the damages which the other party ought to receive in respect of such breach of contract should be such as may fairly and reasonably be considered either arising naturally, *i.e.*, according to the usual course of

[1] (1874) L.R. 7 H.L. 158.
[2] *Robinson* v. *Harman* (1848) 1 Ex. 850 at 855, *per* Parke B.
[3] (1854) 156 E.R. 145 at 151.

things, from such breach of contract itself, or such as may reasonably be supposed to have been in the contemplation of both parties, at the time they made the contract, as the probable result of the breach of it. Now, if the special circumstances under which the contract was actually made were communicated by the plaintiffs to the defendants, and thus known to both parties, the damages resulting from the breach of such a contract, which they would reasonably contemplate, would be the amount of injury which would ordinarily follow from a breach of contract under these special circumstances so known and communicated. But, on the other hand, if these special circumstances were wholly unknown to the party breaking the contract, he, at the most, could only be supposed to have had in his contemplation the amount of injury which would arise generally, and in the great multitude of cases not affected by any special circumstances, from such a breach of contract. For, had the special circumstances been known, the parties might have specially provided for the breach of contract by special terms as to the damages in that case; and of this advantage it would be very unjust to deprive them. Now the above principles are those by which we think the jury ought to be guided in estimating the damages arising out of any breach of contract."

Modern interpretation of the rule

Although Alderson B. stated the "proper rule" in one sentence (at the beginning of the passage) it has been interpreted as containing two limbs. In the words of Lord Upjohn in *Koufos v. Czarnikow Ltd.*,[4] they are:

Two limbs

"(1) Damages should be such as may naturally and normally arise from the breach, or
    (2) Damages should be such as in the special circumstances of the case known to both parties may be reasonably supposed to have been in the contemplation of the parties, as the result of a breach, assuming the parties to have applied their minds to the contingency of there being such a breach."

Lord Reid in the same case, discussing *Hadley* v. *Baxendale*, said that it was not enough that in fact the plaintiff's loss was directly caused by the defendant's breach of contract:

"The crucial question is whether, on the information available to the defendant when the contract was made, he should, or the reasonable man in his position would, have realised that such loss was sufficiently likely to result from the breach of contract to make it proper to hold that the loss flowed naturally from the breach or that loss of that kind should have been within his contemplation."[5]

The modern version of the rule in *Hadley* v. *Baxendale* dates back to 1949. In *Victoria Laundry (Windsor) Ltd.* v. *Newman*

---

[4] [1969] 1 A.C. 350 at 421.
[5] *Ibid.* at 385.

Victoria Laundry (Windsor) Ltd. v. Newman Industries Ltd.

Six propositions

Industries Ltd.[6] the Court of Appeal discussed at length the decision in *Hadley* v. *Baxendale* and concluded that a number of propositions emanated from that and later decisions. The propositions are most relevant to the second "limb" of the rule, and are [7]:

"(1) It is well settled that the governing purpose of damages is to put the party whose rights have been violated in the same position, so far as money can do, as if his rights had been observed. . . . This purpose, if relentlessly pursued, would provide him with a complete indemnity for all loss de facto resulting from a particular breach, however improbable, however unpredictable. This in contract at least, is recognised as too harsh a rule. Hence,

(2) In cases of breach of contract the aggrieved party is only entitled to recover such part of the loss actually resulting as was at the time of the contract reasonably forseeable as likely to result from the breach.

(3) What was at that time reasonably so forseeable depends on the knowledge then possessed by the parties or, at all events, by the party who later commits the breach.

(4) For this purpose, knowledge 'possessed' is of two kinds; one imputed, the other actual. Everyone, as a reasonable person, is taken to know the 'ordinary course of things' and consequently what loss is liable to result from a breach of contract in that ordinary course. This is the subject matter of the 'first rule' in *Hadley* v. *Baxendale*. But to this knowledge, which a contract-breaker is assumed to possess whether he actually possesses it or not, there may have to be added in a particular case knowledge which he actually possesses of special circumstances outside the 'ordinary course of things,' of such a kind that a breach in those special circumstances would be liable to cause more loss. Such a case attracts the operation of the 'second rule' so as to make additional loss also recoverable.

(5) In order to make the contract-breaker liable under either rule it is not necessary that he should actually have asked himself what loss is liable to result from a breach. As has often been pointed out, parties at the time of contracting contemplate not the breach of contract, but its performance. It suffices that, if he had considered the question, he would as a reasonable man have concluded that the loss in question was liable to result. . . .

(6) Nor, finally, to make a particular loss recoverable need it be proved that upon a given state of knowledge the defendant could, as a reasonable man, forsee that a breach must necessarily result in that loss. It is enough if he could forsee it was likely so to result. It is indeed enough . . . if the loss (or some factor without which it would not have occurred) is a 'serious possibility' or a 'real danger.' For short, we have used the word 'liable' to result. Possibly

---

[6] [1949] 2 K.B. 528.
[7] *Ibid.* at 539, *per* Asquith L.J.

the colloquialism on the cards—indicates the shade of meaning with some approach to accuracy."

Tests of recoverability

The House of Lords in *Koufos* v. *C. Czarnikow Ltd.*[8] doubted the efficacy of the "on the cards" test of recoverability, but were unable to agree on an alternative test. Suggestions included: ought the defendant to have realised that the loss was "not unlikely to occur?"[9]; was the loss "one that was liable to result or at least was not unlikely to result?"[10]; or was the loss a "real danger" or a "serious possibility?"[11]

In the later case of *H. Parsons* v. *Uttley Ingham & Co.*[12] the Court of Appeal said that the test is whether the consequences were of such a kind that a reasonable man, at the time of making the contract, would contemplate them as being "of a very substantial degree of probability,"[13] or, "given the situation of the parties at the time of contract, was the loss . . . a serious possibility, something that would have been in their minds had they contemplated breach."[14]

The application of the rule in the conveyancing context is illustrated by two contrasting decisions, concerning the recoverability of lost profits. In *Diamond* v. *Campbell-Jones*[15]

Diamond v. Campbell-Jones

there was a contract for the sale of a leasehold house in Mayfair. The property was ripe for conversion and the purchaser was a well-known property developer. He stated in his affidavit that his purpose in acquiring the property was to develop it by sub-dividing it, but he failed to recover damages for the loss of profits that he would have gained by converting the property. Buckley J. held that the vendor did not know that the purchaser was in fact going to convert the property himself (as opposed to selling it unconverted). Nor should such knowledge be imputed to him:

"The vendor of a shop equipped for use as a butcher's shop would not, in my judgment, be justified by that circumstance alone in assuming, and ought not to be treated as knowing, that the purchaser would intend to use it for the business of a butcher rather than that of a baker or candlestick-maker. . . . Special circumstances are necessary to justify imputing to a vendor of land a knowledge that the purchaser intends to use it in any particular manner."[16]

"Special circumstances"

"Special circumstances" were found to exist and damages for lost profits recovered by the disappointed purchaser in *Cottrill* v. *Steyning & Littlehampton Building Society*.[17] The vendors knew, at the time of the contract, that the purchaser had a specific plan[18] in mind to develop the land profitably.

[8] [1969] 1 A.C. 350.
[9] *Ibid.* at 383, *per* Lord Reid.
[10] *Ibid.* at 406, *per* Lord Morris of Borth-y-Gest.
[11] *Ibid.* at 425, *per* Lord Upjohn.
[12] [1978] Q.B. 791 at 801.
[13] *Ibid.* at 531, *per* Lord Denning M.R.
[14] *Ibid.* at 813, *per* Scarman L.J.
[15] [1961] 1 Ch. 22.
[16] *Ibid.* at 36.
[17] [1966] 1 W.L.R. 753.
[18] To convert the hotel into flats, and erect six new houses in the grounds. See also *Cochrane (Decorators) Ltd.* v. *Sarabandi* (1983) 133 New L.J. 558.

Quantum of damage need not be forseeable
A plaintiff invoking the second limb of *Hadley* v. *Baxendale*, "need show only a contemplation of circumstances which embrace the head or type of damage in question, and need not demonstrate a contemplation of the quantum of damages under that head or type."[19] Thus in *Wroth* v. *Tyler*,[20] where the purchaser sued the vendor for failure to complete the sale of a dwelling house, it was within the parties' contemplation that house prices would rise in the future, but not that those prices would almost double in 18 months. Megarry J. held that the defaulting vendor was liable for the full quantum of the damages.

Date for assessment of damages
One of the main issues in *Wroth* v. *Tyler* was the date at which damages ought to be assessed. The contract price of the house in that case was £6,000. At the date when completion was to take place the house was worth £7,500, but by the date of the hearing it had risen to £11,500. The traditional practice at common law is to assess damages at the date of breach, which would have entitled the purchaser to only £1,500. Megarry J. instead awarded damages in lieu of specific performance under section 2 of the Chancery Amendment Act 1858,[21] so that he could assess them at the date of the hearing.

The approach taken by Megarry J. in *Wroth* v. *Tyler* now appears to be unnecessary. The House of Lords, in *Johnson* v. *Agnew*,[22] made it clear that although the compensatory principle normally led, as in sale of goods, to assessment of damages at the date of breach:

> " . . . this is not an absolute rule: if to follow it would give rise to injustice, the court has power to fix such other date as may be appropriate in the circumstances.

"Contract lost" approach
> In cases where a breach of contract for sale has occurred, and the innocent party reasonably continues to try and have the contract completed, it would appear to me more logical and just rather than tie him to the date of the original breach, to assess damages as at the date when (otherwise than by his default) the contract is lost."[23]

In *Johnson* v. *Agnew* itself, the vendors had obtained an order for specific performance, which subsequently became impossible to enforce because their mortgagees stepped in and sold the property. It was held that the vendors were entitled in substitution, to an order for damages at common law, to be assessed at the date when the mortgagees first contracted to sell the property.

Domb v. Isoz
The "contract lost" approach was applied to an assessment of the purchasers' damages in *Domb* v. *Isoz*.[24] The purchasers had at first claimed specific performance of a contract to sell a house to them, but before the appeal was heard they bought another house to live in. At the hearing of the appeal they successfully elected to have damages instead of specific performance; the date for the assessment of damages to be the date of their election.

[19] *Wroth* v. *Tyler* [1974] Ch. 30, *per* Megarry J. at 61.
[20] [1974] Ch. 30.
[21] See now the Supreme Court Act 1981, s.50.
[22] [1980] A.C. 367.
[23] *Ibid.* at 401, *per* Lord Wilberforce.
[24] [1980] Ch. 548.

In *Malhotra* v. *Choudhury*,[25] a case of a vendor's failure to complete the sale of a house and surgery, the correct date for the assessment of damages was taken to be the date of judgment, but the date for valuing the property was moved back by one year to take account of the purchaser's delay in pursuing his claim.

Duty to mitigate loss—vendor

A party claiming damages for breach of contract is under the duty imposed generally by the common law to mitigate the loss he has suffered.[26] This principle applies equally to both vendor and purchaser although in practical terms, it is more likely to affect the quantum of damages obtained by the vendor.[27] *Techno Land Improvements Ltd.* v. *British Leyland (U.K.) Ltd.*[28] concerned the breach in 1975 of an agreement to take a 35 year lease of two industrial units at an annual rent of £61,286. The vendor originally sought specific performance of the agreement but in 1976 found short-term licensees for the units and elected to proceed for damages only. In 1977 the vendor managed to re-let the units for a term of 25 years at an annual rent of £52,266. The vendor claimed that damages should be assessed at the date the agreement was "lost," that is, in the year 1976 when the licences were granted. However it was held that the vendor had been under a continuing duty to take reasonable steps to mitigate its loss and had done so by re-letting the property: the purchaser was entitled to rely on that successful mitigation and have damages assessed in the year 1977. Goulding J. added, that given an unstable financial climate, it might be necessary in the future to reconsider and qualify the principle upon which he had assessed damages in this case. He gave the following example:[29]

> "Suppose that a vendor sells a house for £20,000 at a time when experts would put on it a market value of only £18,000 and that he loses his good bargain by the purchaser's refusal to complete. Suppose further that it takes him a year to find a new purchaser and that then he gets £20,500; but £20,500 is then no more than bare market value through the continuing corruption of the currency, which has raised the price of everything by about 15 per cent. It might seem hard to say in such circumstances that the vendor has suffered no capital loss, but it might be argued on the other hand that he will be sufficiently compensated by the damages recoverable in respect of the year's delay, rates of interest being notoriously high in inflationary times . . . ."

Duty to mitigate loss—purchaser

In *Strutt* v. *Whitnell*[30] the defendants contracted to sell a house to the plaintiff with vacant possession. At the time of conveyance, however, the house was occupied by a Rent Act protected tenant. The plaintiff sued for damages for breach of contract, but the defendants contended that they had immediately offered to buy back the house at the contract price, so that the plaintiff's damages, had he accepted, would have been nil. The Court of Appeal held that the plaintiff had been under

[25] [1980] Ch. 52.
[26] *Payzn Ltd.* v. *Saunders* [1919] 2 K.B. 581.
[27] But see purchaser's duty to mitigate his loss in cases of delay: *Raineri* v. *Miles* [1981] A.C. 1050 at 1064, *per* Templeman L.J.
[28] (1979) 252 E.G. 805.
[29] *Ibid.* at 809.
[30] [1975] 1 W.L.R. 870.

no duty to mitigate his damages by reconveying the property to the defendants; rather he was entitled to retain the property and recover as damages the difference between the value of the house with and without vacant possession.

Physical inconvenience and mental distress

In formulating a claim for damages, it may be necessary to distinguish any physical inconvenience suffered from mental distress (disappointment, vexation etc.). Damages for physical inconvenience have been recoverable for a long time,[31] but it was thought that the decision in *Addis* v. *Gramophone Co. Ltd.*[32] precluded any award of contract damages for mental distress. In *Jarvis* v. *Swans Tours Ltd.*,[33] however, the plaintiff was compensated—for his disappointment at not getting as good a holiday as he had contracted for. Damages of £125 were awarded on a holiday costing just over £60. *Jarvis'* case was regarded as exceptional, in that the purpose of the contract was to provide enjoyment, but later decisions[34] have suggested that damages for mental distress can be recovered where the loss is contemplated and unavoidable. Recently, however, in *Bliss* v. *South East Thames Regional Health Authority*,[35] the Court of Appeal disallowed an award of damages for mental distress to a surgeon suspended on the unfounded ground that he was mentally unfit for his job; *Addis* was reaffirmed. The law is thus in some doubt.

Bliss v. S.E.T.R.H.A.

In the present context, physical inconvenience is more likely to affect the purchaser than the vendor, whereas mental distress may affect either party.

Specific heads of damage

With these general principles firmly in mind, we now turn to the specific heads of damages which fall for consideration in litigation between vendor and purchaser.

Damages recoverable by vendor

(1) On termination of the contract for the purchaser's breach

Difference between contract price and market value

As a starting point the vendor is entitled to damages equal to the difference (if any) between the contract price and the market value of the land at the date of the breach of contract[36] or at a later date where appropriate.[37] In *Keck* v. *Faber*[38] the vendor terminated the contract for the purchaser's persistent failure to complete. The contract price was £251,700 but at the time of the breach of contract the value of the land had fallen to £231,882. The vendor was held entitled to damages for the difference between the two sums (after giving credit for the deposit).[39]

If, at the time when damages are assessed, the contract price

[31] *Hobbs* v. *L.S.W.R.* (1875) L.R. 10 Q.B. 111.
[32] [1909] A.C. 488.
[33] [1973] Q.B. 233.
[34] See *e.g. Jackson* v. *Chrysler Acceptances* [1978] R.T.R. 474.
[35] [1985] I.R.L.R. 308.
[36] *Laird* v. *Pym* (1841) 7 M. & W. 474 at 478; 151 E.R. 852; *Noble* v. *Edwardes* (1877) 5 Ch.D. 378 at 385, 388; *Jamal* v. *Moolla, Dawood, Sons & Co.* [1916] A.C. 175.
[37] *Johnson* v. *Agnew* [1980] A.C. 367, and see p. 83 above.
[38] (1915) 60 S.J. 253.
[39] See p. 88 below.

is below the market price (whether because it was originally below the market price or because it has since been overtaken by a rising market) nothing is payable to the vendor under this head.

Resale price   Where the vendor has resold the land following the purchaser's breach, the resale price will be taken as prima facie but not conclusive evidence of its market value.[40]

Expenses of abortive sale   It is doubtful whether the vendor can recover from a defaulting purchaser the expenses necessarily incurred in the abortive sale, at least where the vendor has received substantial damages for loss of bargain. The matter has not been judicially considered in any case involving a vendor's claim for damages for the purchaser's breach of contract of sale of land, but a similar rule has been applied in cases where purchasers have been awarded substantial damages for loss of bargain against defaulting vendors.[41] The reasoning is the same in both situations:

> "[W]here a party (whether as vendor or purchaser) to a contract for the sale of land is entitled to substantial damages for the loss of his bargain, he cannot recover his expenses either of entering into the contract of sale, or of proving or investigating the title. For . . . the principle on which he is to be so compensated is that he is to be placed, as far as money can do it, in as good a position as if the contract had been carried out. But had the sale been completed, each party would have had to bear his own expenses of entering into the contract and proving or investigating the title. If, therefore, he were allowed to recover these expenses as damages, and compensation for loss of his bargain *as well*, he would be placed, not in the same position as, but in *a better position* than if the contract had been carried out."[42]

Cost of enforcing or terminating the contract   This rule does not prevent the vendor from recovering as damages legal costs incurred in connection with enforcing or terminating the contract[43]; he would not have had to pay these had the contract been fulfilled.

Wasted expenses   Nor, it seems, does the restriction upon the vendor's right to recover the expenses incurred in the abortive sale apply where there is no substantial difference between the market value of the land and the contract price, that is, where the vendor is not entitled to damages for loss of bargain. Indeed, purchasers have been awarded damages for wasted expenses where substantial damages for loss of bargain have not been available[44] and by analogy, the same should apply where vendors are seeking damages for costs and expenses wasted as a result of the purchaser's default. The vendor must however, elect to claim *either* wasted expenses *or* damages for loss of bargain; he cannot

---

[40] *Engell* v. *Fitch* (1869) L.R. 4 Q.B. 659; *Day* v. *Singleton* [1899] 2 Ch. 320 at 335; *Ridley* v. *De Geerts* [1945] 2 All E.R. 654.

[41] *Day* v. *Singleton* (1899) 2 Ch. 320; *Re Daniel* [1917] 2 Ch. 405 at 412. But *cf. Ridley* v. *De Geerts* [1945] 2 All E.R. 654.

[42] T.C. Williams, (1916) 60 S.J. 303. This view is shared by Barnsley, *Conveyancing Law and Practice* (2nd ed.), p. 586 and Farrand, *Contract and Conveyance* (4th ed.), p. 213.

[43] *Griffiths* v. *Vezey* [1906] 1 Ch. 796.

[44] *Wallington* v. *Townsend* [1939] Ch. 588; *Lloyd* v. *Stanbury* [1971] 1 Q.B. 60.

claim both.[45] "Wasted expenses" includes pre-contract expenses.[46]

Loss of income

The vendor can recover any loss of income from the land attributable to the purchaser's breach of contract. Thus in *Keck* v. *Faber*,[47] besides damages for loss of bargain the vendor was held entitled to damages for:

(1) loss of rent sustained as a result of discharge of tenants at the purchaser's request;
(2) compensation paid to outgoing tenants; and
(3) the costs of re-letting the premises.

Resale expenses

If the vendor resells the property at a lower figure, he can claim the expenses of the resale in addition to the difference in price. (The resale must, of course, take place sufficiently soon after the purchaser's breach of contract for the loss to be attributable to the breach). In *Bruce* v. *Waziri*,[48] under this head of damage, the vendor was able to recover the costs of maintenance of the property pending resale.

Interest

In the absence of a provision in the contract, express or implied, the vendor cannot claim interest on the unpaid purchase price as damages.[49] There are, however, two exceptions to this general rule.

A.J.A. 1982, s.15

First, section 15 of the Administration of Justice Act 1982 and the first Schedule thereto gives the court a wide discretion to award interest on contract debts and damages if the money was outstanding at the time proceedings were commenced. The rate of interest likely to be obtained under the Act is the rate which the plaintiff would have had to pay on borrowing the money.[50]

Wadsworth v. Lydall

Secondly, in *Wadsworth* v. *Lydall*[51] the Court of Appeal allowed the vendor to recover what were in effect sums of interest as part of the computation of special damages. In this case, a purchaser of land had agreed to pay a purchase price of £10,000 on an agreed date, when knowing that the vendor was going to use the £10,000 to make a down payment on a piece of land that he in turn was buying. The purchaser paid only £7,200 and the vendor was forced to take out a second mortgage of £2,800 in order to complete his purchase on time. The Court of Appeal held that this loss (that is, the interest on the £2,800 and the arrangement fee on the second mortgage) was within the contemplation of the parties at the time of the contract and was recoverable by the vendor.

President of India v. Pintada Cia. Navegacion S.A.

The decision in *Wadsworth* v. *Lydall* was enthusiastically approved by the House of Lords in *President of India* v. *La Pintada Cia. Navegacion S.A.*[52] Lord Brandon explained it as turning on the distinction between the first and second limb of

---

[45] *Anglia* v. *Television Ltd.* v. *Reed* [1972] 1 Q.B. 60.
[46] *Lloyd* v. *Stanbury* [1971] 1 W.L.R. 535; *Anglia Television Ltd.* v. *Reed* [1972] 1 Q.B. 60.
[47] (1915) 60 S.J. 253.
[48] (1983) 46 P. & C.R. 81; and see [1984] Conv. 82.
[49] *London Chatham and Dover Railway* v. *S.E. Railway* [1893] A.C. 429, reaffd. by the House of Lords in *President of India* v. *La Pintada Cia. Navegacion S.A.* [1985] 2 A.C. 104.
[50] *Tate & Lyle Food and Distribution* v. *G.L.C.* [1982] 1 W.L.R. 149.
[51] [1981] 1 W.L.R. 598. See also *Bruce* v. *Waziri* (1982) 46 P. & C.R. 81.
[52] [1985] A.C. 104.

the rule in *Hadley* v. *Baxendale,* that is, turning on the existence of special facts known to both parties at the time of contracting, which made the loss one which could be contemplated as not unlikely to arise from non-payment.

Set-offs   In assessing the damages payable to the vendor on termination of the contract for the purchaser's breach, credit must be given for the amount of the forfeited deposit (if any).[53-54] If the amount of damages exceeds the amount of the deposit, the vendor may recover only the difference. If on the other hand, the amount of the deposit exceeds the amount of damages, the vendor may recover the whole of the deposit (subject to the court's discretion to order its return).[55]

Although there is no direct authority on the point, the purchaser is probably entitled to insist that any excess in value of the land at the date for assessment of damages over the contract price be brought into account in determining the extent of his liability to pay damages. Any other rule would offend against the compensatory principle of contractual damages.

(2) On the purchaser's delay in completing

Damages for delay   It has been finally established in *Raineri* v. *Miles*[56] that any delay past the date fixed for completion (time not being of the essence) is a breach of contract giving rise to liability in damages at the instance of the other party (whether vendor or purchaser). The damages most likely to be suffered by a vendor where the purchaser fails to complete on time are the interest costs of borrowing money to complete the purchase of a new property. However, as we have seen,[57] in the absence of a provision in the contract, such damages are not payable by the purchaser unless they can be brought under the second limb of the rule in *Hadley* v. *Baxendale.*[58] Furthermore if the vendor fails to take action before the purchase is actually completed, he loses the right to make a claim for interest under the Administration of Justice Act 1982.[59]

Damages recoverable by purchaser

(1) On termination of the contract due to vendor's breach, other than failure to give good title

Deposit   First, the purchaser is entitled to return of his deposit, with interest for its use.[60]

[53-54] *Ockenden* v. *Henly* (1858) E.B. & E. 485 at 492; 120 E.R. 590 at 593; *Howe* v. *Smith* (1884) 27 Ch.D. 89 at 100; *Shuttleworth* v. *Clews* [1910] 1 Ch. 176; *Keck* v. *Faber* (1915) 60 S.J. 253.
[55] See pp. 48–50 above.
[56] [1981] A.C. 1050.
[57] See pp. 80–83 above.
[58] (1854) 156 E.R. 145.
[59] See p. 87 above.
[60] *Engell* v. *Fitch* (1869) L.R. 4 Q.B. 659; *Jones* v. *Gardiner* [1902] 1 Ch. 191.

Difference between contract price and market price—loss of bargain

Secondly, he may recover as damages the difference (if any) between the contract price of the property and its market value at the date of breach or at a later date where appropriate.[61] For example, in *Re Daniel*[62] the purchaser terminated the contract for the vendor's wrongful refusal to complete. The contract price was £1,000 but at the time of the breach of contract the value of the property had risen to £1,125. The purchaser was held entitled to damages of £125.

Obviously, this principle will result in an award of damages only where the market price exceeds the contract price at the time when damages are to be assessed. If, at the time when damages are to be assessed the market price is below the contract price (whether because it was originally below the contract price or because property prices have fallen) nothing is payable to the purchaser under this head.

Resale price

If the property is resold at an increased price, then the resale price is taken as prima facie evidence of the market value.[63]

Loss of profit

Where the purchaser intended to use or develop the property for profit, he may recover from the defaulting vendor an amount in respect of such loss of profit as can fairly be attributed to the default. However, this head of damage must be brought within the second limb of the rule in *Hadley* v. *Baxendale,* so that the purchasers specific intention must have been within the contemplation of the parties at the date of entry into the (abortive) contract.[64]

Costs incurred in the abortive transaction

The purchaser cannot recover from a defaulting vendor both substantial damages for loss of bargain/profit and the expenses necessarily incurred in the abortive transaction.[65] The reason is that in an action against the vendor for breach of contract the purchaser is entitled to be put in as good a position as if the contract had been performed, but he is not entitled to be placed in a better position; had the property been conveyed to the purchaser, he would have had to pay his conveyancing expenses. In *Ridley* v. *De Geerts*[66] the vendor claimed there should be deducted from the purchaser's damages the costs (including stamp duty) that the purchaser would have paid had the transaction been completed. The Court of Appeal accepted that this might be an appropriate deduction in some cases, but disallowed it on the particular facts.

Additional legal costs may of course be incurred by the purchaser in enforcing or terminating the contract. Presumably, such costs can be recovered from a defaulting vendor in addition to substantial damages for loss of bargain/profit.[67]

Wasted expenditure

The purchaser is not precluded from obtaining damages for costs and expenses thrown away as a reason of the vendor's default, where substantial damages for loss of bargain/profit are

---

[61] *Johnson* v. *Agnew* [1980] A.C. 367 and see p. 83 above.
[62] [1917] 2 Ch. 405.
[63] *Engell* v. *Fitch* (1869) L.R. 4 Q.B. 659.
[64] *Diamond* v. *Campbell-Jones* [1961] Ch. 22; *Cottrill* v. *Steyning & Littlehampton Building Society* [1966] 1 W.L.R. 753; *Cochrane (Decorators) Ltd.* v. *Sarabandi* (1983) 133 New L.J. 558.
[65] *Re Daniel* [1917] 2 Ch. 405.
[66] [1945] 2 All E.R. 654.
[67] *Keck* v. *Faber* (1915) 60 S.J. 253.

unavailable.[68] In *Lloyd* v. *Stanbury*,[69] Brightman J. said that the damages which such a purchaser is entitled to recover include:

" . . . expenditure incurred prior to the contract representing (1) legal costs of approving and executing of the contract and (2) costs of performing an act required to be done by the contract notwithstanding that the act is performed in anticipation of the execution of the contract."[70]

The learned judge added that, on general principles, the purchaser is entitled to damages for any other loss which ought to be regarded as within the contemplation of the parties, but subject to one important limitation:

Improvements

"If the buyer is let into possession prior to completion and sees fit to improve the property after the date of the contract I do not think that the expenses which he incurs can in any normal case be recovered, for two reasons. In the first place it is not . . . usually to be regarded as in the contemplation of the parties that a buyer will spend money on improving the property before it has been conveyed to him. Secondly, if the buyer treats the contract as repudiated he is not . . . entitled to recover an expense which he only incurred because he was at that time keeping his option open to sue for specific performance. If he decides to claim damages such expenditure is the very reverse of mitigation of damages; it increases them. In other words, a purchaser cannot keep his options open at the expense of the vendor and then elect to treat the contract as repudiated and recover his intermediate expenditure."[71]

Election

The decision in *Lloyd* v. *Stanbury* was approved by the Court of Appeal in *Anglia Television Ltd.* v. *Reed.*[72] In this case, Lord Denning M.R. made it clear that suing for damages for wasted expenditure and suing for damages for loss of bargain/profit are alternative courses of action: the purchaser "can either claim for loss of profits; or he can claim for his wasted expenditure. But he must elect between them. He cannot claim both."[73]

(2) On termination of the contract, where the vendor is in breach of his duty to show good title

The rule in *Bain* v. *Fothergill*

The purchaser's right to damages in this situation is severely restricted by the rule in *Bain* v. *Fothergill*.[74] The rule in that case, which arose out of the inherent complexity of title under the old system of land law, exempts a vendor from liability for the purchaser's loss of bargain/profit where, despite all reasonable efforts on his part, the vendor is unable to give a good title to the subject property.

[68] *Re Daniel* [1917] 2 Ch. 405.
[69] [1971] 2 All E.R. 267.
[70] *Ibid.* at 275.
[71] *Ibid.*
[72] [1972] 1 Q.B. 60.
[73] *Ibid.* at 63–64, *per* Lord Denning M.R.
[74] (1874) L.R. 7 H.L. 158. See generally A. Sydenham (1977) 41 Conv. (N.S.); C. Harpum [1983] Conv. 435; M.P. Thompson (1985) 82 L.S.Gaz. 2402; C.T. Emery [1978] Conv. 338.

Cases where the rule has been applied

The rule has been applied on numerous occasions: where one partner contracted "in perfect good faith" to sell partnership land without first securing his co-partner's consent, which was later refused[75]; where a vendor could not make title because his mortgagee had failed to exercise due care in the custody and preservation of the title deeds[76]; where a vendor could not carry out his contract to grant a lease because of restrictive covenants affecting the user of the land[77]; where a vendor of a mining lease failed to obtain the required consent to assign, despite all reasonable efforts on his part; and where a vendor could not convey because of a dispute about the extent of the land which the vendor had previously sold off.[78]

Wasted expenditure

In cases where the rule in *Bain* v. *Fothergill* is applied, the purchaser is limited to recovering his deposit with interest and the expenses of such matters as investigating title. Since the rule excludes him from obtaining substantial damages for loss of bargain/profit, it seems to follow that the purchaser should be entitled to claim in full for expenses incurred in reliance on the contract. However, the authorities[79] suggest that this is not the case and that the purchaser cannot recover pre-contract expenditure, such as survey fees.

Matter of title or matter of conveyance

The rule is only applied where the vendor fails to complete because of a matter of title, rather than a matter of conveyance.[80] In *Engell* v. *Fitch*,[81] vendor–mortgagees were held liable to pay damages for loss of bargain to the purchaser, because their failure to give vacant possession, as required by the contract, resulted from their unwillingness to incur expense in evicting the mortgagor. Similarly in *Re Daniel*,[82] there was a contract to sell a house which was in mortgage with other land. The mortgagees refused to release the house, because the vendor had insufficient funds to pay off the whole mortgage. The purchaser was held entitled to substantial damages for loss of bargain.

Vendor must use his best endeavours to perfect his title

The vendor must have used his best endeavours to make a good title, if he is to enjoy the protection of the rule. In *Day* v. *Singleton*,[83] a vendor contracted to assign the lease of a hotel. He died before the required consent could be obtained. The purchaser brought an action against the vendor's personal representatives for specific performance of the contract. The personal representatives wished to free the estate from the action and, to this end, persuaded the lessor to refuse his consent to assign. The purchaser was held entitled to damages for loss of bargain. More recently in *Malhotra* v. *Choudhury*,[84] one joint tenant failed to attempt to gain the other's consent to the sale, and it was held that the purchaser's damages were not limited by

---

[75] *Keen* v. *Mear* [1920] 2 Ch. 574.
[76] *Browning* v. *Handiland Group Ltd.* (1976) 35 P. & C.R. 345.
[77] *J.W. Cafes Ltd.* v. *Brownlow Trust Ltd.* [1950] W.N. 191.
[78] *Ray* v. *Druce* [1985] Ch. 437.
[79] *Jones* v. *Gardiner* [1902] 1 Ch. 191 and see C. Harpum [1983] Conv. 435.
[80] The distinction between matters of conveyance and matters of title was discussed at pp. 14–16 above.
[81] (1869) L.R. 4 Q.B. 659.
[82] [1917] 2 Ch. 405.
[83] [1899] 2 Ch. 320.
[84] [1980] Ch. 52.

Sharneyford
Supplies Ltd. v.
Edge

the rule. In *Sharneyford Supplies Ltd.* v. *Edge*,[85] the vendor was unable to give vacant possession of a maggot farm because it was occupied by business tenants protected under Part II of the Landlord and Tenant Act 1954. The vendor could not rely on the rule because he had not served notice on the tenants (even though such an attempt to clear the farm would probably have failed). Balcombe L.J. thought that a vendor's duty to perfect his title did not extend to buying out an adverse right whereas Parker L.J. thought it did. Kerr L.J. expressed no view on this point.

Class F.
registration

Megarry J. held in *Wroth* v. *Tyler*[86] that a Matrimonial Homes Act 1967 (now 1983) charge was not within the spirit and intendment of the rule in *Bain* v. *Fothergill*, and so a vendor who could not procure, the cancellation of his wife's registration was made to pay substantial damages for loss of bargain to the disappointed purchaser.[87]

Fraud

The fact that the vendor, at the time of contracting, knows that he has not got a good title nor any means of acquiring it will not make the rule inapplicable.[88] But if the vendor fraudulently misrepresents to the purchaser that he can make good title, then the bar on the purchaser recovering full contractual damages is lifted.[89] Negligent and innocent misrepresentation do not have the same effect.[90] At one time it was thought that a way round the rule in *Bain* v. *Fothergill* had been found in *Watts* v. *Spence*.[91] In that case, a husband contracted to sell the matrimonial home without the consent of his wife, who was the joint owner. She refused consent, and the husband was unable to give good title. As no fraud or bad faith was alleged, the rule in *Bain's* case operated to limit the purchaser's damages for breach of contract. Graham J. held that the husband had, by his conduct, negligently misrepresented to the purchaser that he was the owner of the house and able to sell on his own and awarded damages for loss of bargain under section 2(1) of the Misrepresentation Act 1967.[92]

Avoiding *Bain* v.
Fothergill.—Watts
v. *Spence*

Watts v. *Spence* was not followed in *Sharneyford Supplies Ltd.* v. *Edge*,[93] where Mervyn-Davies J. said:

Damages for
misrepresentation
to be assessed on
tortious basis, *i.e.*
no loss of bargain

"An action on the new statutory right [s.2(1) of the Misrepresentation Act 1967] is an action in which damages will be measured as in tort, not contract; and in tort, as I understand, loss of bargain damages may not, in every case be recoverable."[94]

Residential
conveyancing

It has been suggested[95] that tortious damages for non-fraudulent misrepresentation could include an element for loss of bargain in residential conveyancing. Suppose a purchaser contracts to buy a house for £90,000. The vendor is unable to

---

[85] [1987] 1 All E.R. 588.
[86] [1974] Ch. 30.
[87] The charge is imposed by statute and has nothing to do with pre-1925 land law.
[88] *Bain* v. *Fothergill* (1874) L.R. 7 H.L. 158 at 207; *J.W. Cafes Ltd.* v. *Brownlow Trust Ltd.* [1950] 1 All E.R. 894 at 897.
[89] *Bain* v. *Fothergill* (1874) L.R. 7 H.L. 158; *Sharneyford Supplies Ltd.* v. *Edge* [1985] 3 W.L.R. 1; *Sharneyford Supplies Ltd.* v. *Edge; Barrington Black & Co. (Third Party)* [1986] 1 Ch. 128.
[90] *Sharneyford Supplies Ltd.* v. *Edge* [1985] 3 W.L.R. 1.
[91] [1976] Ch. 165; J.T. Farrand (1975) 39 Conv. (N.S.) 381.
[92] Criticised in *McGregor on Damages* (14th ed.), p. 497.
[93] [1985] 3 W.L.R. 1; *Sharneyford Supplies Ltd.* v. *Edge; Barrington Black & Co. (Third Party)* [1986] 1 Ch. 128.
[94] *Sharneyford Supplies Ltd.* v. *Edge* [1985] 3 W.L.R. 1 at 15.
[95] M.P. Thompson [1985] Conv. 137.

make a good title and is found liable of negligent misrepresentation under section 2(1) of the 1967 Act. The tort method of assessing damages is to put the purchaser in the position he would have been in had the misrepresentation not been made. His position was having the purchasing power to buy the vendor's type of house for £90,000. If there has been an increase in prices and an equivalent house would now cost £100,000, then the purchaser's damages should be £10,000.

(3) Where the vendor delays in completing for reasons other than a defect in title

Whether time is of the essence of the contract or not, the vendor is in breach of contract and liable to the purchaser for loss or damage suffered thereby.

Phillips v. Lamdin

In *Phillips* v. *Lamdin*,[96] a purchaser contracted to buy leasehold premises for residential and business use. The vendor delayed two months in completing. The purchaser was held entitled to damages for additional removal expenses, furniture storage expenses, advertising expenses (wasted through inability to carry on business), loss of business profits, and staff wages (wasted through inability to carry on business).

Raineri v. Miles

Phillips v. *Lamdin* was approved by the House of Lords in *Raineri* v. *Miles*.[97] There, completion was arranged for July 12, but due to a delay on the vendor's purchase of a new property, did not take place until August 11. The purchaser was awarded damages covering temporary accommodation expenses incurred as a result of the delay.

Can damages for delay be claimed after completion?

In *Phillips* v. *Lamdin*, the purchaser's action was commenced *after* actual completion. Croom-Johnson J. was unimpressed with the vendor's argument that the contract had merged with the conveyance and that therefore damages were unavailable. The learned judge considered there was no difference in this respect between contracts for the sale of land and contracts for the sale of goods (where damages for delay are available after completion). However, he professed to follow *Jones* v. *Gardiner*,[98] and in that case the writ was issued *before* actual completion and, without prejudice to the purchaser's rights. The question of merger did not arise in *Raineri* v. *Miles*; the writ was issued claiming specific performance and damages on the day of completion.

(4) Where completion delayed because the vendor is unable, through no fault of his own, to make good title

Bain v. Fothergill

The purchaser's damages for breach of contract for delay are limited by the rule in *Bain* v. *Fothergill*,[99] but it is unclear as to what extent. If the true effect of the rule is to preclude only the recovery of damages for loss of bargain/profit, then in cases where completion is delayed owing to a defect in title damages may still be substantial, if, for example, the purchaser has to move into

---

[96] [1949] 2 K.B. 33.
[97] [1981] A.C. 1050; see also *Cochrane (Decorators) Ltd.* v. *Sarabandi* (1983) 133 New L.J. 558.
[98] [1902] 1 Ch. 191.
[99] (1874) L.R. 7 H.L. 158.

temporary accommodation. However, in *Raineri* v. *Miles*[1] views were expressed that the rule would prevent the purchaser from obtaining anything but additional conveyancing expenses in the event of delayed completion.

(5) On the vendor's failure to give vacant possession

The purchaser is entitled to damages for breach of the obligation to give vacant possession.[2] These damages may be claimed after completion as a contractual stipulation that vacant possession will be given does not merge on completion.[3] The right to damages is determined by normal contractual principles. So, for example, in *Beard* v. *Porter*,[4] the vendor could not give vacant possession in accordance with the contract, because of the presence of a sitting tenant. The purchaser was entitled to damages for the difference in value between the purchase price and the value of the house subject to the tenancy, conveyancing costs and stamp duty incurred in purchasing another house in which to live, and temporary accommodation expenses.

Beard v. *Porter*

The right to vacant possession includes freedom from any "physical impediment which substantially prevents or interferes with the enjoyment of the right of possession of a substantial part of the property."[5] Thus, in *Cumberland Consolidated Holdings Ltd.* v. *Ireland*,[6] where the breach lay in the vendor's act in leaving on the premises large quantities of rubbish (hardened cement and empty drums), the purchaser was entitled to damages covering the cost of its removal.

No rubbish

The rule in *Bain* v. *Fothergill* does *not* apply to protect a vendor from the consequences of breach of contract in failing to give vacant possession as promised.[7]

Rule in *Bain* v. *Fothergill*

Effect of the standard conditions on contractual damages

(1) On failure to comply with a completion notice

National condition 22(3)

"(3) In case the purchaser refuses or fails to complete in conformity with this condition, then (without prejudice to any other right or remedy available to the vendor) the purchaser's deposit may be forfeited (unless the court otherwise directs) and, if the vendor resells the property within twelve months of the expiration of the said period of 16 working days, he shall be entitled (upon crediting the deposit) to recover from the purchaser hereunder the

---

[1] [1981] A.C. 1050.
[2] For purchaser's duty to mitigate damage, see *Strutt* v. *Whitnell* [1975] 1 W.L.R. 870.
[3] *Cumberland Consolidated Holdings Ltd.* v. *Ireland* [1946] K.B. 264; *Hissett* v. *Reading Roofing Co. Ltd.* [1969] 1 W.L.R. 1757.
[4] [1946] 1 K.B. 321.
[5] *Cumberland Consolidated Holdings Ltd.* v. *Ireland* [1946] K.B. 264 at 277, *per* Lord Greene.
[6] [1946] K.B. 264.
[7] *Engell* v. *Fitch* (1869) L.R. 4 Q.B. 659.

amount of any loss occasioned to the vendor by expenses of
or incidental to such resale, or by diminution in the price."

**Law Society
general condition
23(4)–(6)**

"(4) If the purchaser does not comply with a completion
notice—
   (*a*) the purchaser shall forthwith return all documents
delivered to him by the vendor and at his own expense
procure the cancellation of any entry relating to the contract
in any register
   (*b*) without prejudice to any other rights or remedies
available to him, the vendor may—
      (i) forfeit and retain any deposit paid and/or
      (ii) re-sell the property by auction, tender or private
         treaty.
   (5) If on any such re-sale contracted within one year after
contractual completion date the vendor incurs a loss and so
elects by notice to the purchaser within one month after the
contract for such re-sale, the purchaser shall pay to the
vendor liquidated damages. The amount payable shall be the
aggregate of such loss, all costs and expenses reasonably
incurred in any such re-sale and any attempted re-sale and
interest at the contract rate on such part of the purchase
money as is from time to time outstanding (giving credit for
all sums received under any re-sale contract on account of
the re-sale price) after contractual completion date.
   (6) If the vendor does not comply with a completion
notice, the purchaser, without prejudice to any other rights
or remedies available to him, may give notice to the vendor
forthwith to pay to the purchaser any sums paid by way of
deposit or otherwise under the contract and interest on such
sums at the contract rate from four working days after
service of the notice until payment. On compliance with
such notice the purchaser shall not be entitled to specific
performance of the contract, but shall forthwith return all
documents delivered to him by the vendor and at the
expense of the vendor procure the cancellation of any entry
relating to the contract in any register."

As we have seen,[8] at common law a vendor who has (validly)
terminated the contract for the purchaser's breach may resell the
property, because the termination puts an end to the purchaser's
interest in the property, but the deficiency (if any) on resale is not
necessarily the measure of the vendor's damages for loss of

**Purpose of the
conditions**

bargain. It is therefore in the vendor's interest for the contract to
provide expressly for recovery of any deficiency as liquidated
damages. This, generally speaking, is the purpose of National
condition 22(3) and Law Society general condition 23(4)(*b*)–(6).[9]
It is important to note that the conditions operate *only* where an
effective notice to complete has been served under the
conditions.

**Law Society
general condition
23(4)(*b*)**

Law Society condition 23(4)(*b*) states that if the purchaser
does not comply with a completion notice the vendor may forfeit
the deposit and/or resell the property. The rights conferred by
23(4)(*b*) are *not* alternative to the rights conferred at common law

---

[8] See pp. 85–86 above.
[9] The conditions are also discussed at pp. 41–47.

if the purchaser fails to comply with a completion notice, because 23(4)(b) is expressly "without prejudice to any other rights or remedies available to [the vendor]". In other words, the rights conferred by 23(4)(b) are cumulative upon, rather than in substitution for, the vendor's ordinary rights at common law. Accordingly the vendor is not required to elect between the exercise of his common law rights and the rights conferred by condition 23(4)(b).

Law Society general condition 23(5)—vendor to make election

It will be necessary, however, for the vendor to make an election if he resells the property within 1 year of contractual completion date.[10] In this event he must elect between—(i) suing for damages for breach of contract; and (ii) claiming the liquidated damages specified in sub-condition 23(5)—namely, the deficiency (if any) arising on resale, the costs and expenses of the resale and any attempted resale, and interest at the contract rate on the outstanding purchase price (giving credit for sums received under any resale contract) at contractual completion date. Having elected to pursue one right, the vendor cannot later change his mind and choose the other if it transpires that he has elected the least advantageous course.

National condition 22(3)

The effect of the first limb of National condition 22(3) (up to, " . . . the purchaser's deposit may be forfeited (unless the court otherwise directs)") is the same as Law Society general condition 23(4)(b). However, recent cases[11] indicate that insufficient attention was given, in the drafting of the rest of National condition 22(3), to the distinction between a vendor's common law right to resell and his contractual right to resell. For this reason it is unclear whether 22(3) does provide for recovery of liquidated damages on a resale within one year and, *a fortiori*, whether the vendor is required to elect between the exercise of his common law rights and his rights under 22(3).

Recovery of liquidated damages on resale?
Bruce v. Waziri

In *Bruce v. Waziri*,[12] it was held that National condition 22(3) was *not* a liquidated damages provision and that a vendor could recover, as special damages, items of expenditure not mentioned in that condition.

Wallace-Turner v. Cole

However in *Wallace-Turner v. Cole*,[13] it was held that National condition 22(3) *was* a liquidated damages provision and that a vendor who had elected to sue for damages for breach of contract could not later resile from his election to claim the liquidated damages specified in that condition.

Purchaser's position where vendor in default

National condition 22(3) deals only with a vendor's rights in the event of the purchaser's non-compliance with a completion notice; a purchaser in the converse situation is left with his remedies at common law. By way of contrast, Law Society condition 23(6) states that if it is the vendor in default, the purchaser may serve notice requiring the return of the deposit and any other sums paid under the contract. The vendor then becomes liable to pay interest at the contract rate, if he does not return the money within four working days of receiving the purchaser's notice. The sub-condition does not affect the

[10] *Talley v. Wolsey-Neech* (1978) 38 P. & C.R. 45.
[11] *Bruce v. Waziri* (1983) 46 P. & C.R. 81; *Sakkas v. Donford Ltd.* (1983) 46 P. & C.R. 290; *Wallace-Turner v. Cole* (1983) 46 P. & C.R. 164.
[12] (1983) 46 P. & C.R. 81.
[13] (1983) 46 P. & C.R. 164.

purchaser's right at common law to sue for damages for breach of contract.

(2) On delay in completion

National condition 7

"7. Interest

(1) If the purchase shall not be completed on the completion date then (subject to the provisions of paragraph (2) of this condition) the purchaser shall pay interest on the remainder of his purchase money at the prescribed rate from that date until the purchase shall actually be completed Provided nevertheless—

(i) That (without prejudice to the operation of proviso (ii) to this paragraph) the vendor may by notice in writing before actual completion elect to take the income of the property (less outgoings) up to the date of actual completion instead of interest as aforesaid

(ii) That, if the delay arises from any cause other than the neglect or default of the purchaser, and if the purchaser (not being in occupation of the property in circumstances to which condition 8 applies) places the remainder of his purchase money (at his own risk) at interest on a deposit account in England or Wales with any designated bank, and gives written notice thereof to the vendor or his solicitor, then in lieu of the interest or income payable to or receivable by the vendor as aforesaid, the vendor shall from the time of such notice be entitled to such interest only as is produced by such deposit

(iii) That the vendor shall in no case be or become entitled in respect of the same period of time both to be paid interest and to enjoy income of the property, or to be paid interest more than once on the same sum of money

(2) The purchaser shall not be liable to pay interest under paragraph (1) of this condition—

(i) so long as, or to the extent that, delay in completion is attributable to any act or default of the vendor or his mortgagee or Settled Land Act trustees

(ii) in case the property is to be constructed or converted by the vendor, so long as the construction or conversion is unfinished."

Law Society general condition 22

"22 COMPENSATION FOR LATE COMPLETION

(1) For the purposes of this condition—

(a) "delay" means failure to perform or lateness in performing any obligation of the contract which causes or contributes to lateness in completion

(b) a party is "in default" if and to the extent that the period, or the aggregate of the periods, of his delay exceeds the period, or the aggregate of the periods, of delay of the other party

(c) "the period of default" means the length of the excess defined in paragraph (b) or, if shorter, the period from contractual completion date to the date of actual completion.

(2) If the sale shall be completed after contractual completion date, the party in default (if any) shall be

liable to compensate the other for loss occasioned to him by reason of that default.

(3) Before actual completion, or within five working days thereafter (as to which period time shall be of the essence), the party entitled to compensation may, by notice to the other party, opt to be paid or allowed a sum calculated at the contract rate on the amount of the purchase money (less any deposit paid) for the period of default as liquidated damages in settlement of his claim for compensation.

(4) If the vendor is entitled to compensation, he may, before actual completion, by notice to the purchaser, opt to take the net income of the property for the period of default in lieu of such compensation.

(5) The right to recover any compensation under this condition shall not be prejudiced by completion of the sale, whether before or after the commencement of proceedings."

National condition 7(1)—purchaser must pay interest for delay

By National condition 7(1) the purchaser is obliged to pay interest on the unpaid purchase price in most cases of delayed completion. Interest is charged at the prescribed rate,[14] for the period from contractual completion date to actual completion. The period of delay is not calculated in working days, so that the purchaser must pay interest for each day of delay.

National condition 7(1)(i)—vendor may elect to take actual income

By condition 7(1)(i) the vendor may elect by notice in writing before actual completion to take the income of the property (less outgoings) instead of interest, for the period of the delay. He will of course, opt to take the income of the property only where it exceeds the amount of interest, and may do so only if he would otherwise be entitled to interest. In *Re Hewitt's Contract*,[15] completion was delayed because the vendors, former shareholders of a company in voluntary liquidation, were tardy in registering certain transfers of their title to the bank which was acting on their behalf in the sale of the property to the purchaser.[16] The vendors failed in their attempt to claim the income of the property for the period of the delay. The delay was the vendors' fault; they had no right to interest and therefore no right to take income instead.

National condition 7(1)(ii)—purchaser may place money on deposit if not the delayor

If the delay in completion is not attributable to the purchaser's default, he may lodge the unpaid purchase price in a deposit account in a designated bank[17] and on giving the vendor notice, need only pay to the vendor the interest actually earned on the deposit, rather than interest at the prescribed rate (7(1)(ii)). In this case the vendor is not entitled to elect to take the income of the property under condition 7(1)(i).

Purchaser in occupation pending completion

A purchaser who goes into occupation of the property under National condition 8 (that is, not as a lessee or tenant of the vendor) has to pay interest at the prescribed rate from the date of his going into occupation until actual completion,[18] even if the

---

[14] Defined by construction condition (4).
[15] [1963] 1 W.L.R. 1298.
[16] The sale was governed by National Conditions of Sale, (17th ed).
[17] Defined by construction condition (7). The definition will need to be amended to take account of the Building Societies Act 1986.
[18] National condition 8(1)(ii).

delay is caused by the vendor. Such a purchaser cannot avoid paying interest at the prescribed rate by depositing the unpaid purchase price.[19] No double charge to interest arises under conditions 7 and 8; that is, the purchaser cannot be made to pay interest for occupation pending actual completion and interest for delay (7(1)(iii)).

National condition 7(2)—vendor in default

The purchaser need not pay interest where the delay in completion is attributable to the default of the vendor or his mortgagee or Settled Land Act trustees (7(2)(i)). The vendor will be in default:

> "If [he] knows the material facts—knows that there are difficulties which it is his duty to overcome—knows that he may not be able to overcome them by the time fixed for completion, and he fails to overcome them by that time, although no fresh unforeseen occurrence prevents him from doing so . . . ."[20]

The "default" in question must be the reason for the delay[21]; if not, the purchaser must still pay interest.

Unfinished works

Condition 7(2)(ii) further relieves the purchaser from liability for interest where the subject property is undergoing construction or conversion and the works are unfinished.

Damages for delay

National condition 7 does not affect the vendor's right to sue a defaulting purchaser for damages for breach of contract for delay.[22]

Law Society general condition 22—concept of comparative default

Condition 22 approaches the problem of delay in a different manner, combining the decision in *Raineri* v. *Miles* with the provisions for payment of interest. The general principle behind the condition is one of comparative default: the party in default in completing should be liable to compensate the other for loss caused by the default (22(2)). By 22(1)(b) a party is in default to the extent that the period of his delay exceeds the delay (if any) of the other, and the period of default is the excess (or the delay in completion if shorter) (22(1)(c)). A party has delayed if he has failed or has been late in performing an obligation of the contract which has caused or contributed to lateness in completion (22(1)(a)). Such delay is calculated by reference to ordinary days, and not to working days.

Alternative remedies available

By 22(3), a party entitled to compensation has the choice of either (i) suing for damages for breach of contract for delay; or (ii) claiming, as liquidated damages, interest at the contract rate[23] on the purchase price (less the deposit) for the period of default. An election to take liquidated damages must be notified to the other party before actual completion or within five working days thereafter (as to which period, time is of the essence).

Vendor's choice of three remedies

Where it is the purchaser who is in default, the vendor may elect by notice before actual completion to take the net income of the property for the period of default in lieu of such compensation (22(4)). A vendor thus has the choice of three alternative remedies.

---

[19] *Re Priestley's Contract* [1947] Ch. 469.
[20] *Re Hetling and Merton's Contract* [1893] 3 Ch. 269, *per* Lindley L.J. at 281; followed by Wilberforce J. in *Re Hewitt's Contract* [1963] 1 W.L.R. 1298.
[21] *Re Mayor of London and Tubb's Contract* [1894] 2 Ch. 524.
[22] *Raineri* v. *Miles* [1981] A.C. 1050.
[23] Defined by Law Society general condition 1(b).

Purchaser in occupation before completion

Law Society general condition 22 does not relieve a purchaser who goes into occupation before completion under condition 18 from his liability to pay interest at the contract rate on the purchase price (less the deposit), from the time of his going into occupation until actual completion.[24] Such a purchaser who is also in default in completing may have to pay interest twice: once under condition 18 and again under condition 22. Purchasers' conveyancers desirous of avoiding this harsh possibility should seek to amend the contract as follows:

> "Interest payable by the purchaser under condition 18 for any period after contractual completion date shall be allowed as a deduction from any compensation payable by him under condition 22."

No merger

It is expressly stated that condition 22 shall not merge with the conveyance, 22(5), which means that the remedies given by the condition are available after completion.

Note

A party having made an election under either National condition 7 or Law Society general condition 22 will be prevented from later resiling from his election to seek another remedy under the condition.[25]

Reform?

Law Commission Report No. 166 (1987) recommends the abolition of the rule in *Bain* v. *Fothergill*. The parties should, however, continue to be able by express agreement to limit the damages payable by the vendor should his title prove to be defective. A copy of the Report and draft Bill to implement the recommendation is included at Appendix E.

Law Commission Report No. 166

---

[24] *Re Priestley's Contract* [1947] Ch. 469.
[25] *Talley* v. *Wolsey-Neech* (1978) 38 P. & C.R. 45.

7 SPECIFIC PERFORMANCE

Introduction

A plaintiff's primary remedy if he establishes that the defendant has failed to perform his part of the contract is to seek damages for his loss of bargain. The availability of damages in the context for breach of a conveyancing contract has already been discussed.[1] However, an award of damages will not always ensure that justice is served where there has been breach of a contract for the sale of a property. In equity the plaintiff may be able to obtain a decree of specific performance. Specific performance is a discretionary remedy. It is not available to a plaintiff as of right. It is, however, now accepted that specific performance is a remedy which will normally be available to a plaintiff where the contract which has been breached concerns the disposition of an interest in land.[2]

Discretionary remedy

The attractiveness of the availability of the remedy of specific performance is best illustrated where the vendor is bankrupt, or, in the case of a company, insolvent. In *Freevale Ltd.* v. *Metrostore (Holdings) Ltd.*[3] the defendant company contracted to sell certain property to the plaintiff. After exchange of contracts but prior to completion of the sale the defendant company was placed into receivership. The defendant company, acting through the agency of its receiver, refused to complete the contract and the plaintiff brought an action against it for the specific performance of the contract. It was argued that the company having had a receiver appointed over it prior to completion was a defence to the plaintiff's claim for specific performance of the contract and that therefore the action must fail. If the defence had succeeded the plaintiff would have been left to its remedy in damages—a remedy which in practice may have been virtually worthless to the plaintiff purchaser. The court rejected this argument and stated that the mere fact that a receiver had been appointed could not destroy the purchaser's equitable interest in the land. The plaintiff was entitled to a decree of specific performance notwithstanding the receivership. There is similar case law authority which shows that the remedy of specific performance is available as against a vendor's trustee in bankruptcy.[4]

Bankruptcy

Although the remedy is available only at the discretion of the courts they will in practice exercise that discretion in accordance with a body of fixed rules which have developed over the years.[5] Furthermore, an award of specific performance may be given along with damages if this is necessary to achieve substantial

Fixed rules

---

[1] See Chap. 6.
[2] *Hexter* v. *Pearce* [1900] 1 Ch. 341.
[3] [1984] Ch. 199.
[4] *Pearce* v. *Bastable's Trustee in Bankruptcy* [1901] 2 Ch. 122.
[5] *Holliday* v. *Lockwood* [1917] 2 Ch. 47; *Lamare* v. *Dixon* (1873) L.R. 6 H.L. 414.

justice to the parties concerned.[6] This gives the courts a great deal of flexibility which is, obviously, desirable.

Contempt

When a decree of specific performance is given, the party against whom the order is made is compelled to perform the contract in accordance with the terms of the order. If that party refuses to so perform the contract he will be in contempt of court. If necessary the court will ensure that its order is complied with even if this necessitates the instrument of conveyance being executed by one of the court's own officers.

Conditions of grant

The following are some of the conditions which must be satisfied before a court will exercise its discretion and award a plaintiff a decree of specific performance of a contract. These conditions apply to all types of contract, not simply to those involving the sale or other disposition of an interest in land.

Existence of a binding contract

Section 40 must be complied with

For a plaintiff to succeed he must first establish that there is a binding contract for the sale of property which the court can enforce. Thus, the remedy is not available to a plaintiff against a defendant who has not signed a memorandum of a contract for the sale of an interest in land (rendering the contract unenforceable against him under section 40 of the Law of Property Act 1925).[7] All of the other necessary elements of a binding contract will need to be established, such as consideration and an intention by the parties to create legally binding obligations. The court will be particularly reluctant to grant an order for specific performance of a contract when its terms are not clearly defined. The reason for this reluctance is the court's unwillingness to compel a defendant to perform obligations without it being clearly established that he had agreed to them in the first place.

Conditional contract

It has also been held that where a contract for the sale of a property is conditional and that condition has not been satisfied, specific performance will not be granted.[8] In such a case it may be prejudicial to the defendant to order specific performance of a contract which was always subject to some contingency which has not been fulfilled.

Inadequacy of damages

Generally speaking a court will only grant specific performance of a contract if the plaintiff's remedy in damages is not adequate for some reason. The position as stated in *Chitty on Contracts* is: "the question is not simply whether damages are an adequate remedy, but whether specific performance will do more perfect and complete justice than an award of damages."[9]

---

[6] See ss.49 and 50 of the Supreme Court Act 1981.
[7] *Seton* v. *Slade* (1802) 7 Ves. 265.
[8] *Beech Properties Ltd.* v. *G.E. Wallis & Sons Ltd.* (1976) 241 E.G. 685.
[9] (25th ed.), p. 979, para. 1763, citing *Tito* v. *Waddell (No. 2)* [1977] Ch. 106.

Land is unique

In the case of contracts for the sale of an interest in land the court recognises the unique character of each parcel of land, and unless there are compelling reasons not to do so will usually give the plaintiff a decree of specific performance. Whilst this general acceptance of the unique character of each piece of land and the implicit recognition that damages may not be sufficient is understandable in the case of a plaintiff purchaser, who may be attracted to a particular property for a host of reasons, it is less understandable in the case of a plaintiff vendor. If a vendor is able to sell the property to a third party why should he not be left to his remedy in damages for loss suffered as against the defendant purchaser? However, it seems to be trite law that the vendor of land can obtain a decree of specific performance against his recalcitrant purchaser even where the property is capable of being sold elsewhere in a buoyant property market.[10]

Special factors rendering damages unascertainable

Damages may also prove to be an inadequate remedy where they are not readily capable of being ascertained. While it will be unusual for there to be a difficulty in ascertaining the plaintiff's damages in a conveyancing contract, because a property will usually be readily capable of valuation, there may be special factors operating which would make the quantum of damage suffered by the plaintiff difficult to calculate. In such cases the courts may be minded to require the defendant to perform the contract rather than take a "guess" as to the level of damages to award the plaintiff.

Mutuality

It was formerly thought that if the court could not order specific performance of the contract at the instance of both parties, the remedy was not available to either.[11] The rationale behind the rule was that in the absence of the court being able to ensure specific performance of both parties' obligations under the contract, it would be unfair to impose specific performance of the contract on the defendant (leaving the possibility that the plaintiff might leave some part of his obligations unperformed). Furthermore the requirement of mutuality had to be satisfied when the contract was concluded.

Price v. Strange

However, in *Price* v. *Strange*[12] the Court of Appeal held that the requirement that the remedy of specific performance be mutually available to both plaintiff and defendant was to be considered in relation to the facts and circumstances existing at the time of the hearing and not the date of the contract. The case concerned a plaintiff who was the tenant of a maisonette. After the expiry of her underlease she continued to occupy the property. The defendant was the head lessee of the property. An oral agreement was concluded between the plaintiff and the defendant that the plaintiff should execute certain works of repair in return for a new underlease at an increased rent. The plaintiff completed the bulk of the work. There was a dispute and the defendant refused to allow the plaintiff to finish the agreed works. After the defendant had purported to terminate the oral

---

[10] *Clifford* v. *Turrell* (1841) 1 Y. & C.C.C. 138; (1845) 1 L.J.Ch. 390; see also *Hillingdon Estates Co.* v. *Stonefield Estates Ltd.* [1952] Ch. 627.
[11] *Lumley* v. *Ravenscroft* [1895] 1 Q.B. 683; *Flight* v. *Bolland* (1828) 4 Russ. 298.
[12] [1978] Ch. 337.

agreement, rent was tendered by the plaintiff and accepted by the defendant at the rate which had been orally agreed. The plaintiff asked the court to grant specific performance of the agreement to grant an underlease. At first instance the judge decided that at the time the oral contract was concluded specific performance could not have been granted against the plaintiff had the defendant requested it, because the obligations of the plaintiff were in the nature of services and such an order could not have been made by the court because of the difficulty in policing it.

The Court of Appeal decided that since at the date of the hearing the plaintiff had carried out the work, she was entitled to specific performance of the defendant's obligation to grant a new underlease. The fact that at the date of the oral agreement there was an absence of mutuality was not a bar to the plaintiff's request. The court went on to say that lack of mutuality would not always result in the court refusing to exercise its discretion and grant specific performance but was merely one (albeit an important one) of the factors to be taken into account.[13]

Defendant's own acts or default

Where the requirement of mutuality is not satisfied at the date of the hearing in consequence of the defendant's own acts or default this will not stop a plaintiff from obtaining a decree. For example, where the defendant has signed the memorandum for the purposes of section 40 but the plaintiff has not, it is not open to the defendant to rely upon the lack of mutuality as an answer to the plaintiffs claim.[14]

Absence of consideration

"Equity will not assist a volunteer"

One of the principles of equity is that "equity will not assist a volunteer." In order to obtain specific performance of an agreement the plaintiff must show that he gave consideration.[15] This is only likely to affect a plaintiff whose claim arises out of a promise made under seal by a defendant which is not otherwise supported by consideration. For example, a court would not require a donor of land under a deed of gift specifically to perform his obligations under the deed if there was no element of consideration.

The plaintiff's conduct

Effect of the plaintiff's misconduct

The court may refuse to exercise its discretion to award the plaintiff specific performance if his conduct is in some way questionable or the contract is oppressive or unfair.[16] So, if the plaintiff had failed to disclose material facts even where such disclosure was not required at law the court may refuse to award specific performance of the contract.[17] The court will also take into account the relationship which existed between the parties at the time the contract was made in deciding whether or not to exercise its discretion. If the defendant can establish that the relationship which existed was such as to make it inequitable for

[13] See also *Lavery* v. *Pursell* (1888) 39 Ch.D. 508.
[14] *C.H. Giles & Co. Ltd.* v. *Morris* [1972] 1 W.L.R. 307.
[15] The court will not investigate the adequacy of the consideration; see *Mountford* v. *Scott* [1975] Ch. 258.
[16] *Rees* v. *Marquis of Bute* [1916] 2 Ch. 64.
[17] *Lamare* v. *Dixon* (1873) L.R. 6 H.L. 414; *Beyfus* v. *Lodge* [1925] Ch. 350.

the remedy to be granted, for example, if the plaintiff had pressurised the defendant into entering into an agreement (without allowing the defendant time to obtain relevant advice), the court will sometimes refuse to enforce the contract by way of specific performance and leave the plaintiff to his remedy in damages.[18]

Sang Lee Investment Co. Ltd. v. Wing Kwai Investment Co. Ltd.

In the recent Privy Council case *Sang Lee Investment Co. Ltd.* v. *Wing Kwai Investment Co. Ltd.*[19] Lord Brightman stated that where there was an allegation that specific performance should be denied on the basis of the plaintiff's misconduct there were two elements which had to be proved. First, the alleged want of probity or misconduct had to arise in connexion with the transaction forming the basis of the plaintiff's claim. Misconduct which had no relation to that transaction was not relevant. Secondly, where there were allegations of improper conduct on both sides it was not for the courts to perform a "balancing act." The court had to decide whether there had been some "want of faith, honesty or righteous dealing on the part of the person seeking relief and then decide whether as a matter of discretion and in all the circumstances, which might include any relevant misconduct on the part of the person resisting, if it was right to grant or refuse specific performance."

Bars to specific performance

Supervision

The court will not grant an order for specific performance if in so doing it would have constantly to supervise the actions of the parties concerned. For example, the court has refused specifically to enforce an agreement whereby a landlord agreed to provide a housekeeper.[20]

Building contracts

Recent trend

This aspect of the remedy is most commonly encountered in contracts concerning building work.[21] The difficulty which the court faces in these circumstances is defining in the order exactly what the defendant has to do in order to comply with it. The recent trend has been to regard the degree to which the supervision of the parties is necessary as a subsidiary issue and not on its own a reason for refusing to grant a decree where this is otherwise the only way to ensure justice is done between the parties.[22] Thus, providing that the terms of the subject agreement are sufficiently clear and the defendant's obligations are capable of definition, specific performance will be available.

In the case of contracts for the sale of property where no element of continuing obligations is present, it will not normally be necessary for the court to supervise the parties to a large degree.

---

[18] *Helsham* v. *Langley* (1841) 1 Y. & C.Ch.Cas. 175; this is not to say that the remedy will be denied if the defendant did not have the benefit of legal advice.
[19] (1983) 127 S.J. 410.
[20] *Barnes* v. *City of London Real Property Co.* [1918] 2 Ch. 18.
[21] *Hill* v. *Barclay* (1810) 16 Ves. 402.
[22] *Hounslow London Borough Council* v. *Twickenham Garden Developments Ltd.* [1971] Ch. 233.

Delay

Laches

The remedy of specific performance may be available to the plaintiff in an action even though, strictly speaking, the six year limitation period usually applicable to claims in contract has expired.[23] However, it would be extremely unusual for the court to enforce a contract by way of specific performance after a six year period had elapsed. A plaintiff wishing to bring an action for specific performance of a contract for the sale of land will have to bear in mind that any delay in prosecuting his claim will be taken into account by the court in considering whether or not to exercise its discretion in his favour. Equity insists that a plaintiff acts diligently and if the plaintiff is guilty of laches the court may refuse to grant relief to him.[24] The modern approach taken by the courts in cases where the question of the plaintiff's delay is in issue was illustrated in *Lazard Brothers & Co. Ltd.* v. *Fairfield*

Lazard Bros. & Co. Ltd. v. Fairfield Props. Co. (Mayfair) Ltd.

Properties Co. (Mayfair) Ltd.[25] In this case the contract was concluded by an exchange of letters passing between the plaintiff and defendant on March 12, 1975. Between March 1975 and January 1977 the parties (who had instructed solicitors to prepare a formal contract which was intended to take the place of the contract concluded by the exchange of letters) corresponded on the terms of the formal contract. Unfortunately, problems occurred and eventually, on January 7, 1977, the plaintiff's solicitors wrote to the defendant's solicitors stating that they intended to enforce the contract concluded in the March 1975 correspondence and requiring an undertaking that the defendants would complete by February 28. Nothing happened and finally, on May 14, 1977 a writ was issued in which the plaintiff claimed specific performance of the contract. Megarry V.C. stated:

Modern approach to delay

"[T]he classic phrase of Sir Richard Arden M.R. in *Milward* v. *Earl of Thanet*[26] was that a plaintiff seeking specific performance has to show himself 'ready, desirous, prompt and eager.' If specific performance was to be regarded as a prize, to be awarded by equity to the diligent and denied to the indolent, the plaintiff should fail. But whatever might have been the position over a century ago that was the wrong approach today. If between the plaintiff and the defendant it was just that the plaintiff should obtain the remedy, the court ought not to withhold it merely because the plaintiff had been guilty of delay."

Gross or prejudicial delay

The court granted the order and specifically enforced the contract. The case clearly indicates that unless the delay has in some way prejudiced the defendant, or has been so gross as to render it inequitable to enforce the contract, the court will only regard a failure on the part of the plaintiff to prosecute his claim in a timely manner as another factor to be taken into account in deciding whether or not justice requires the contract to be specifically enforced at the instance of the plaintiff.

Sometimes when there has been a difficulty in completing a sale, the vendor will allow his purchaser to go into occupation of

[23] *Talmash* v. *Mugleston* (1826) 4 L.J. (O.S.) Ch. 200.
[24] *Lloyd* v. *Collett* (1793) 4 Bro. C.C. 469; *Rich* v. *Gale* (1871) 24 L.T. 745.
[25] (1977) 121 S.J. 793.
[26] (1801) 5 Ves. 720.

Purchaser in occupation pending completion
the premises. He may do this informally (which is a course of action not recommended in the light of the problems which may arise if the vendor has to regain possession) or under the provisions contained in the standard conditions of sale.[27] Allowing the purchaser into occupation is usually regarded as the best means of ensuring that the minimum amount of dislocation takes place as a result of completion of a sale being delayed. It would obviously be undesirable for this practice to be inhibited in any way by a vendor or purchaser worrying that he may forego his right to obtain specific performance of the contract if the period of the purchaser's occupation were to drag on. It has now been held that where a purchaser goes into occupation for a lengthy period pending completion of the contract with the consent of the vendor, this will not provide the defendant with a defence to a claim for specific performance on the grounds of delay.[28]

Where delay has occurred the defendant must be careful that he does not waive his right to defend the claim on the basis of the plaintiff's delay and so give up a potential defence to the plaintiff's claim for specific performance.[29]

Impossibility

The court will not order specific performance of a contract where it is impossible for the defendant to comply with the order.[30] For example, the court has refused to grant specific performance of a contract for the sale of land against a defendant who does not own the land and so is not in a position to convey the legal title to the plaintiff.[31]

Similarly, the court will not enforce a contract by way of specific performance where this would result in the defendant **Third parties** being in breach of a contract with a third party. In *Warmington* v. *Miller*[32] the defendant had agreed to create an underlease of premises occupied by him in favour of the plaintiff. The defendant was himself a tenant of a superior lessor. In the lease under which the defendant held the premises there was a covenant against, *inter alia*, underletting without the consent of the superior lessor. At the time the agreement to underlease was made, the consent of the superior lessor had not been obtained; nor was it forthcoming. The plaintiff sought to enforce the contract by way of specific performance. It was held that the court would not exercise its discretionary power to grant specific performance where to do so would result in a defendant being put in the position of having to break a contract with a third party to comply with the court order. In this case the order could not be made in the plaintiff's favour because by requiring the defendant to execute an underlease it would immediately result in a breach

---

[27] L.S.C. 18; N.C. 8.
[28] *Williams* v. *Greatrex* [1957] 1 W.L.R. 31; see also *McMurray* v. *Spicer* (1868) L.R. 5 Eq. 527.
[29] *Lord Darnley* v. *London Chatham & Dover Railway Co.* (1863) 1 De G.J. & Slm. 204.
[30] *Green* v. *Smith* (1738) 1 Atk. 572 at 573; *Ferguson* v. *Wilson* (1866) 2 Ch.App. 77.
[31] *Castle* v. *Wilkinson* (1870) L.R. 5 Ch.App. 534; *Wroth* v. *Tyler* [1974] Ch. 30.
[32] [1973] 1 Q.B. 877; see also *Harnett* v. *Yielding* (1805) 2 Sch. & Lef. 549.

of the covenant contained in the head lease with the superior lessor. The plaintiff was left to his remedy in damages.

Time for impossibility

The court will look at the question of whether performance of the contract is impossible on the part of the defendant, not at the time the contract was concluded, but at the time when the defendant is properly required to carry out his obligations under the contract. For example, at the date the defendant contracts to sell certain property to the plaintiff he may not have title to that land. However, prior to completion of the sale it is quite possible that the vendor may acquire title to the property either by buying it in or by some other method. In this case it is quite proper for the defendant to be ordered to convey the property in accordance with his contract with the plaintiff.[33]

Jones v. Lipman

An unusual example of a case in which the court has ordered specific performance against a defendant vendor who was not legally entitled to the property occurred in *Jones* v. *Lipman*.[34] The defendant agreed to sell to the plaintiff certain freehold land. After exchange of contracts the defendant transferred the subject land to a company which was under his sole control. The plaintiff asked for an order of specific performance against the defendant. The defendant argued that he was no longer the legal owner of the land and so could not possibly comply with any order for specific performance. The court found that the company had been created as a "creature of the defendant" to mask and avoid recognition by the eye of equity and that accordingly in those circumstances a decree of specific performance would be granted against him despite the fact that he no longer had title to the property concerned.

Illegality

There is general principle of contract law that contracts which are illegal will not be held to be enforceable. It follows that a contract which is illegal will not be enforced by the court by granting an order for specific performance. Sometimes, however, it is possible for the court to grant an order for specific performance, but make it a term of the order that any illegal element of the **Severance** contract is severed in order to ensure that the defendant does not commit an illegal act in complying with the order.[35]

Ultra vires contract

In transactions which involve companies, a defence to a claim for specific performance might consist of the fact that the contract entered into was *ultra vires*. The plaintiff may be able to rely upon section 35 of the Companies Act 1985 where he deals with the directors of the company in good faith. However, if this is not the case it is possible that specific performance would be denied.[36]

Defendant's hardship

A court will not grant specific performance if in so doing it would cause great hardship to the defendant. In deciding whether hardship would be caused, the facts and circumstances as they

[33] *Holroyd* v. *Marshall* (1862) 10 H.L.Cas. 191.
[34] [1962] 1 W.L.R. 832.
[35] *Briggs* v. *Parsloe* [1937] 3 All E.R. 831; *Ailion* v. *Spiekermann* [1976] Ch. 158.
[36] *Halsbury's Laws of England*, Vol. 44, para. 465 and the cases there cited.

exist at the time of the contract may be taken into account.[37] Occasionally, the court will take into account hardship arising after the date of the contract or hardship which would be caused not only to the defendant but to third parties such as members of the defendants family.[38]

Two recent cases illustrate the approach adopted by the court.

Francis v. Cowcliff Ltd.

In *Francis* v. *Cowcliff Ltd.*[39] the defendant landlords argued that specific performance of an agreement to put a lift into a block of flats should not be granted on the basis that it would cause them great financial hardship and inevitably lead to a winding-up of the company. The court held that the fact that the property market had collapsed after the contract had been entered into was irrelevant. At the time of the contract there was no hardship which would have been suffered by the defendant. Even though the company had suffered as a result of the collapse of the property market after the contract had been made, and would endure severe financial hardship and possibly liquidation, the court would still make the Order.

Patel v. Ali

The second case is *Patel* v. *Ali.*[40] In July 1979 Mrs Ali contracted to sell her house. Her husband had been adjudicated bankrupt two months prior to the contract being entered into. Shortly after the contract was exchanged the husband's trustee in bankruptcy obtained an injunction restraining completion of the sale. The injunction was not lifted until a year later. In July 1983 the plaintiffs applied for an order for specific performance of the contract of sale. By this time Mrs Ali's husband was in prison and she had given birth to three children. Unfortunately, she had also suffered a serious illness which had led to the amputation of one of her legs. It was clear that she was heavily dependant upon the support of friends and relatives who lived locally to enable her to keep her children at home with her and run her home. Additional evidence was adduced at the trial to show that in the event that an award of damages was made in the plaintiff's favour, there were friends of Mrs Ali within the Asian community who would put funds up to meet that claim. There was enough evidence before the court to show it was obvious that in all probability any judgment for damages would be met. The court held that this was a case in which it should exercise its discretion and not grant specific performance of the contract. Goulding J. stated that:

> "the court's discretion is wide enough, in an otherwise proper case, to refuse specific performance on the ground of hardship subsequent to the contract and not caused by the plaintiff."

Plaintiff's delay

It is clear that in this case a factor which weighed heavily in favour of Mrs Ali and against the plaintiff was that the considerable delay which had taken place was not due to any fault on Mrs Ali's part. The Judge went on to say that if specific performance were granted:

> "she can say she is being asked to do what she never

---

[37] *Webb* v. *Direct London & Portsmouth Railway Co.* (1852) 1 De G.M. & G. 521.
[38] *Wroth* v. *Tyler* [1974] Ch. 30.
[39] (1976) 120 S.J. 353.
[40] [1984] Ch. 283.

bargained for, namely to complete the sale after more than four years, after all the unforeseeable changes that such a period entailed. I think that in this way she can fairly assert that specific performance would inflict upon her 'a hardship amounting to injustice.' "[41]

Uncertainties surrounding the title

Under an open contract for the sale of land the common law implies a term into the contract that the vendor is selling the fee simple in the land free from incumbrances.[42] Where there is uncertainty surrounding the title which the vendor is selling the court will be reluctant to force upon the purchaser a doubtful title by ordering specific performance of the contract.[43] The law is concisely stated in *Halsburys Laws of England*[44] as follows:

Doubtful title

"A particular instance in which non-performance of a condition by the plaintiff is a bar to his action is where he is a vendor of land suing for specific performance of the contract, but is unable to prove a good title. Although the rule, established in the early part of the 18th century, that specific performance will be refused if the court, although not actually pronouncing a title to be bad, considers it too doubtful to be forced on a purchaser is still in force, the defence that a title is too doubtful to be forced on a purchaser has in modern times found little favour with the court, and the general rule now is that it is the courts duty, unless there are exceptional circumstances to decide the rights between vendor and purchaser and to ascertain and determine as best it may be what the law is."

Effect on third party

Unfortunately, if the court does decide the issues as between the vendor and purchaser this will not bind any third party. This may give the purchaser who is forced to take the land difficulties when he comes to sell the land himself. It is also not beyond the bounds of possibility that the purchaser would find himself subject to further litigation which might even result in him being forced to spend substantial sums of money in legal costs and/or meeting an award of damages.[45]

Court will attempt to resolve ambiguity

Thus, the court will attempt to resolve any ambiguity in any document upon which the vendor's title is dependant.[46] If the doubts surrounding the vendor's title arise out of facts rather than the construction of a document and the court does not have all the evidence before it, the plaintiff will be refused specific performance of the contract.[47] In *Re Handman and Wilcox's Contract*[48] a tenant for life of settled land agreed to grant a building lease to a third party. Under section 7(2) of the Settled Land Act 1882 the lease would have been impeachable if it was not at the best rent reasonably obtainable. There was some

---

[41] See also *Webb* v. *Direct London & Portsmouth Railway Co.* (1852) 1 De G.M. & G. 521; *Denne* v. *Light* (1857) 8 D.M. & G. 774.
[42] *Purvis* v. *Rayer* (1821) 9 Price 488.
[43] *Mullings* v. *Trinder* (1870) L.R. 10 E. 449.
[44] Vol. 44, para. 481.
[45] *M.E.P.C. Ltd.* v. *Christian-Edwards* [1981] A.C. 205.
[46] *Radford* v. *Willis* (1871) 7 Ch.App. 7; *Alexander* v. *Mills* (1870) 6 Ch.App. 124.
[47] *Warde* v. *Dixon* (1858) 28 L.J. Ch. 315.
[48] [1902] 1 Ch. 599.

evidence that the rent payable under the lease as between the original lessor and lessee had been reduced in consideration of a waiver by the lessee of a claim for damages against the lessor. The vendor had purchased the lease from the original lessee and had taken without notice of the arrangements concluded between the original lessor and lessee as to reduction of the rent. The vendor agreed to sell the lease to the purchaser who raised the objection that it was not clear that the vendor could give good title. In the circumstances the court thought that the title was sufficiently doubtful and refused to grant specific performance of the contract.

APPENDICES

Appendices B, C and D reproduced by kind permission of the Solicitors' Law Stationery Society plc.

Appendix E is Crown Copyright and is reproduced with permission of the Controller of Her Majesty's Stationery Office.

Appendix A

Law of Property Act 1925 (15 & 16 Geo. 5, c. 20)

Provisions as to contracts

42.—(1) A stipulation that a purchaser of a legal estate in land shall accept a title made with the concurrence of any person entitled to an equitable interest shall be void, if a title can be made discharged from the equitable interest without such concurrence—

(*a*) under a trust for sale; or
(*b*) under this Act, or the Settled Land Act 1925, or any other statute.

(2) A stipulation that a purchaser of a legal estate in land shall pay or contribute towards the costs of or incidental to—

(*a*) obtaining a vesting order, or the appointment of trustees of a settlement, or the appointment of trustees of a conveyance on trust for sale; or
(*b*) the preparation stamping or execution of a conveyance on trust for sale, or of a vesting instrument for bringing into force the provisions of the Settled Land Act 1925;

shall be void.

(3) A stipulation contained in any contract for the sale or exchange of land made after the commencement of this Act, to the effect that an outstanding legal estate is to be traced or got in by or at the expense of a purchaser or that no objection is to be taken on account of an outstanding legal estate, shall be void.

(4) If the subject matter of any contract for the sale or exchange of land—

(i) is a mortgage term and the vendor has power to convey the fee simple in the land, or, in the case of a mortgage of a term of years absolute, the leasehold reversion affected by the mortgage, the contract shall be deemed to extend to the fee simple in the land or such leasehold reversion;
(ii) is an equitable interest capable of subsisting as a legal estate, and the vendor has power to vest such legal estate in himself or in the purchaser or to require the same to be so vested, the contract shall be deemed to extend to such legal estate;
(iii) is an entailed interest in possession and the vendor has power to vest in himself or in the purchaser the fee simple in the land, (or, if the entailed interest is an interest in a term of years absolute, such term,) or to require the same to be so vested, the contract shall be deemed to extend to the fee simple in the land or the term of years absolute.

(5) This section does not affect the right of a mortgagee of leasehold land to sell his mortgage term only if he is unable to convey or vest the leasehold reversion expectant thereon.

(6) Any contract to convey an undivided share in land made before or after the commencement of this Act, shall be deemed to

be sufficiently complied with by the conveyance of a corresponding share in the proceeds of sale of the land in like manner as if the contract had been to convey that corresponding share.

(7) Where a purchaser has power to acquire land compulsorily, and a contract, whether by virtue of a notice to treat or otherwise, is subsisting under which title can be made without payment of the compensation money into court, title shall be made in that way unless the purchaser, to avoid expense or delay or for any special reason, considers it expedient that the money should be paid into court.

(8) A vendor shall not have any power to rescind a contract by reason only of the enforcement of any right under this section.

(9) This section only applies in favour of a purchaser for money or money's worth.

Section 42(7) saved by Compulsory Purchase Act 1965 (c. 56) s. 2 Sched. 1, para. 1

★ ★ ★ ★ ★

Other statutory conditions of sale

45.—(1) A purchaser of any property shall not—

(*a*) require the production, or any abstract or copy, of any deed, will, or other document, dated or made before the time prescribed by law, or stipulated, for the commencement of the title, even though the same creates a power subsequently exercised by an instrument abstracted in the abstract furnished to the purchaser; or

(*b*) require any information, or make any requisition, objection, or inquiry, with respect to any such deed, will, or document, or the title prior to that time, notwithstanding that any such deed, will, or other document, or that prior title, is recited, agreed to be produced, or noticed;

and he shall assume, unless the contrary appears, that the recitals, contained in the abstract instruments, of any deed, will, or other document, forming part of that prior title, are correct, and given all the material contents of the deed, will, or other document so recited, and that every document so recited was duly executed by all necessary parties, and perfected, if and as required, by fine, recovery, acknowledgment, inrolment, or otherwise:

Provided that this subsection shall not deprive a purchaser of the right to require the production, or an abstract or copy of—

(i) any power of attorney under which any abstracted document is executed; or

(ii) any document creating or disposing of an interest, power or obligation which is not shown to have ceased or expired, and subject to which any part of the property is disposed of by an abstracted document; or

(iii) any document creating any limitation or trust by reference to which any part of the property is disposed of by an abstracted document.

(2) Where land sold is held by lease (other than an under-lease), the purchaser shall assume, unless the contrary appears, that the lease was duly granted; and, on production of the receipt for the last payment due for rent under the lease before the date of actual completion of the purchase, he shall assume, unless the contrary appears, that all the convenants and provisions of the lease have been duly performed and observed up to the date of actual completion of the purchase.

(3) Where land sold is held by under-lease, the purchaser shall assume, unless the contrary appears, that the under-lease and every superior lease were duly granted; and, on production of the receipt for the last payment due for rent under the under-lease before the date of actual completion of the purchase, he shall assume, unless the contrary appears, that all the covenants and provisions of the under-lease have been duly performed and observed up to the date of actual completion of the purchase, and further that all rents due under every superior lease, and all the covenants and provisions of every superior lease, have been paid and duly performed and observed up to that date.

(4) On a sale of any property, the following expenses shall be borne by the purchaser where he requires them to be incurred for the purpose of verifying the abstract or any other purpose, that is to say—

(*a*) the expenses of the production and inspection of all Acts of Parliament, inclosure awards, records, proceedings of courts, court rolls, deeds, wills, probates, letters of administration, and other documents, not in the possession of the vendor or his mortgagee or trustee, and the expenses of all journeys incidental to such production or inspection; and

(*b*) the expenses of searching for, procuring, making, verifying, and producing all certificates, declarations, evidences, and information not in the possession of the vendor or his mortgagee or trustee, and all attested, stamped, office, or other copies or abstracts of, or extracts from, any Acts of Parliament or other documents aforesaid, not in the possession of the vendor or his mortgagee or trustee;

and where the vendor or his mortgagee or trustee retains possession of any document, the expenses of making any copy thereof, attested or unattested, which a purchaser requires to be delivered to him, shall be borne by that purchaser.

(5) On a sale of any property in lots, a purchaser of two or more lots, held wholly or partly under the same title, shall not have a right to more than one abstract of the common title, except at his own expense.

(6) Recitals, statements, and descriptions of facts, matters, and parties contained in deeds, instruments, Acts of Parliament, or statutory declarations, twenty years old at the date of the contract, shall, unless and except so far as they may be proved to be inaccurate, be taken to be sufficient evidence of the truth of such facts, matters, and descriptions.

(7) The inability of a vendor to furnish a purchaser with an acknowledgment of his right to production and delivery of copies of documents of title or with a legal covenant to produce and

furnish copies of documents of title shall not be an objection to
title in case the purchaser will, on the completion of the contract,
have an equitable right to the production of such documents.

(8) Such acknowledgments of the right of production or
covenants for production and such undertakings or covenants for
safe custody of documents as the purchaser can and does require
shall be furnished or made at his expense, and the vendor shall
bear the expense of perusal and execution on behalf of and by
himself, and on behalf of and by necessary parties other than the
purchaser.

(9) A vendor shall be entitled to retain documents of title
where—

    (*a*) he retains any part of the land to which the documents
           relate; or

    (*b*) the document consists of a trust instrument or other
           instrument creating a trust which is still subsisting, or an
           instrument relating to the appointment or discharge of a
           trustee of a subsisting trust.

(10) This section applies to contracts for sale made before or
after the commencement of this Act, and applies to contracts for
exchange in like manner as to contracts for sale, except that it
applies only to contracts for exchange made after such
commencement;

    Provided that this section shall apply subject to any
stipulation or contrary intention expressed in the contract.

(11) Nothing in this section shall be construed as binding a
purchaser to complete his purchase in any case where, on a
contract made independently of this section, and containing
stipulations similar to the provisions of this section, or any of
them, specific performance of the contract would not be enforced
against him by the court.

    *Section 45(6) applied by Welsh Church (Burial Grounds) Act 1945 (c. 27), s.
1(4)(b)*

★   ★   ★   ★   ★

125.—(1) ....

(2) Notwithstanding any stipulation to the contrary, a
purchaser of any interest in or charge upon land (not being land
or a charge registered [¹under the Land Registration Act 1925])
shall be entitled to have any instrument creating a power of
attorney which affects his title, or [²a copy] thereof or of the
material portions thereof delivered to him free of expense.

(3) This section only applies to instruments executed after the
commencement of this Act, and no right to rescind a contract
shall arise by reason of the enforcement of the provisions of this
section.

¹ *Words substituted by Powers of Attorney Act 1971 (c. 27), s. 11(3).*
¹ *Words substituted by Law of Property (Amendment) Act 1926 (c. 11), Sch.*

Appendix B

The Law Society's General Conditions of Sale (1984 Revision)

1 DEFINITIONS
In these conditions—
(a) "completion notice" means a notice served under condition 23 (2)
(b) "the contract rate" means the rate specified in a special condition or, if none is so specified, the rate prescribed from time to time under section 32 of the Land Compensation Act 1961 for interest payable thereunder
(c) "contractual completion date" has the meaning given in condition 21
(d) "conveyance" includes an assignment and a transfer under the Land Registration Acts
(e) "lease" includes underlease
(f) "normal deposit" means the sum which, together with any preliminary deposit paid by the purchaser, amounts to ten per centum of the purchase money (excluding any separate price to be paid for any chattels, fixtures or fittings)
(g) "working day" means any day from Monday to Friday (inclusive) other than—
  (i) Christmas Day, Good Friday and any statutory bank holiday, and
  (ii) any other day specified in a special condition as not a working day
(h) a reference to a statute includes any amendment or re-enactment thereof.

2 SERVICE AND DELIVERY
(1) Section 196 of the Law of Property Act 1925 applies to any notice served under the contract, save that—
(a) a notice shall also be sufficiently served on a party if served on that party's solicitors
(b) a reference to a registered letter shall include a prepaid first class ordinary letter
(c) if the time at which a letter containing a notice would in the ordinary course be delivered is not on a working day, the notice shall be deemed to be served on the next following working day
(d) a notice shall also be sufficiently served if—
  (i) sent by telex or by telegraphic facsimile transmission to the party to be served, and that service shall be deemed to be made on the day of transmission if transmitted before 4 p.m. on a working day, but otherwise on the next following working day
  (ii) when the addressee is a member of a document exchange (as to which the inclusion of a reference thereto in the solicitors' letterhead shall be conclusive evidence) delivered to that or any other affiliated exchange, and that service shall be deemed to have been made on the first working day after that on which the document would, in the ordinary course, be available for collection by the addressee.
(2) Sub-condition (1) applies to the delivery of documents as it applies to the service of notices.

3 MATTERS AFFECTING THE PROPERTY
(1) In this condition—
(a) "competent authority" means a local authority or other body exercising powers under statute or Royal Charter
(b) "requirement" includes (whether or not subject to confirmation) any notice, order or proposal
(c) "relevant matter" means any matter specified in sub-condition (2) whenever arising.
(2) The property is sold subject to—
(a) all matters registrable by any competent authority pursuant to statute
(b) all requirements of any competent authority
(c) all matters disclosed or reasonably to be expected to be disclosed by searches and as a result of enquiries formal or informal, and whether made in person, by writing or orally by or for the purchaser or which a prudent purchaser ought to make
(d) all notices served by or on behalf of a reversioner, a tenant or sub-tenant, or the owner or occupier of any adjoining or neighbouring property.
(3) (a) Notwithstanding sub-condition (2), the vendor warrants that he has informed the purchaser of the contents of any written communication received by, or known to, the vendor on or before the working day preceding the date of the contract relating to any relevant matter. Failure to give such information before the contract is made shall be deemed to be an omission in a statement in the course of the negotiations leading to the contract, but shall give rise to no right to compensation to the extent that the purchaser has a claim for damages against a competent authority
(b) In the event of any conflict or variation between information in fact received from any competent authority relating to any relevant matter and any statement made by the vendor in respect of the same matter, the purchaser shall rely on the information received from the competent authority to the exclusion of that given by the vendor
(c) The vendor shall forthwith inform the purchaser of the contents of any written communication received by him after the working day preceding the date of the contract and before the day of actual completion which if received on or before the former day would have fallen within paragraph (a).
(4) The purchaser (subject to any right or remedy arising under sub-condition (3)) will indemnify the vendor in respect of any liability under any requirement of a competent authority (whether made before or after the date of the contract), including the reasonable cost to the vendor of compliance after reasonable notice to the purchaser of the vendor's intention to comply, such sum to be payable on demand. The provisions of this sub-condition shall prevail in the event of conflict with any other condition.

4 OPPORTUNITY TO RESCIND
(1) This condition only applies if a special condition so provides.
(2) Within such period as is specified in a special condition or, if none is so specified, within twenty working days from the date of the contract (as to which, in either case, time shall be of the essence), the purchaser shall be entitled, notwithstanding condition 3 (2), to rescind the contract by service of notice on the vendor specifying a matter to which this condition applies affecting the property.
(3) This condition applies to any of the following matters of which the purchaser had no knowledge on or before the working day preceding the date of the contract—
(a) a financial charge which the vendor cannot or has not at the purchaser's written request agreed to discharge on or before actual completion

(*b*) a statutory provision prohibiting, restricting or imposing adverse conditions upon the use or the continued use of the property for such purpose as is specified in a special condition or, if none is so specified, the purpose for which the vendor used it immediately before the date of the contract

(*c*) a matter which is likely materially to reduce the price which a willing purchaser could otherwise reasonably be expected to pay for the relevant interest in the property in the open market at the date of the contract.

(4) For the purposes of this condition, the purchaser's knowledge—

(*a*) includes everything in writing received in the course of the transaction leading to the contract by a person acting on his behalf from the vendor, a person acting on the vendor's behalf, or a competent authority (as defined in condition 3 (1) (*a*))

(*b*) does not include anything solely because a statute deems that registration of a matter constitutes actual notice of it.

5   EASEMENTS, RESERVATIONS, RIGHTS AND LIABILITIES

(1) The vendor warrants that he has disclosed to the purchaser the existence of all easements, rights, privileges and liabilities affecting the property, of which the vendor knows or ought to know, other than the existence of those known to the purchaser at the date of the contract, or which a prudent purchaser would have discovered by that date.

(2) Without prejudice to the generality of sub-condition (1)—

(*a*) the purchaser shall purchase with full notice of the actual state and condition of the property and shall take it as it stands, save where it is to be constructed or converted by the vendor

(*b*) the property is sold, and will if the vendor so requires be conveyed, subject to all rights of way, water, light, drainage and other easements, rights, privileges and liabilities affecting the same.

(3) (*a*) In this sub-condition "the retained land" means land retained by the vendor—

   (i) adjoining the property, or

   (ii) near to the property and designated as retained land in a special condition.

(*b*) The conveyance of the property shall contain such reservations in favour of the retained land and the grant of such rights over the retained land as would have been implied had the vendor conveyed both the property and the retained land by simultaneous conveyances to different purchasers.

6   TENANCIES

(1) This condition applies if the property is sold subject to any lease or tenancy and shall have effect notwithstanding any partial, incomplete or inaccurate reference to any lease or tenancy in the special conditions or the particulars of the property.

(2) Copies or full particulars of all leases or tenancies not vested in the purchaser having been furnished to him, he shall be deemed to purchase with full knowledge thereof and shall take the property subject to the rights of the tenants thereunder or by reason thereof. The purchaser shall indemnify the vendor against all claims, demands and liability in respect of such rights, notwithstanding that they may be void against a purchaser for want of registration.

(3) The vendor gives no warranty as to the amount of rent lawfully recoverable from any tenant, as to the effect of any legislation in relation to any lease or tenancy or as to the compliance with any legislation affecting the same.

(4) The vendor shall inform the purchaser of any change in the disclosed terms and conditions of any lease or tenancy.

(5) If a lease or tenancy subject to which the property is sold terminates for any reason, the vendor shall inform the purchaser and, on being indemnified by the purchaser against all consequential loss, expenditure or liability, shall act as the purchaser may direct.

7   ERRORS, OMISSIONS AND MISSTATEMENTS

(1) No error, omission or misstatement herein or in any plan furnished or any statement made in the course of the negotiations leading to the contract shall annul the sale or entitle the purchaser to be discharged from the purchase.

(2) Any such error, omission or misstatement shown to be material shall entitle the purchaser or the vendor, as the case may be, to proper compensation, provided that the purchaser shall not in any event be entitled to compensation for matters falling within conditions 5 (2) or 6 (3).

(3) No immaterial error, omission or misstatement (including a mistake in any plan furnished for identification only) shall entitle either party to compensation.

(4) Sub-condition (1) shall not apply where compensation for any error, omission or misstatement shown to be material cannot be assessed nor enable either party to compel the other to accept or convey property differing substantially (in quantity, quality tenure or otherwise) from the property agreed to be sold if the other party would be prejudiced by the difference.

(5) The purchaser acknowledges that in making the contract he has not relied on any statement made to him save one made or confirmed in writing.

8   LEASEHOLDS

(1) This condition applies if the property is leasehold.

(2) In all cases the immediate title to the property shall begin with the lease. Where the lease, unless registered with absolute title, is dated not more than fifteen years before the date of the contract and was granted for a term exceeding twenty-one years, the freehold title and all other titles superior to the lease shall be deduced for a period beginning not less than fifteen years prior to the date of the contract and ending on the date of the lease.

(3) A copy of the lease and a copy of, sufficient extract from, or abstract of, all superior leases, the contents of which are known to the vendor, having been supplied or made available to the purchaser, he shall be deemed to purchase with full notice of the contents thereof, whether or not he has inspected the same.

(4) Where any consent to assign is necessary—

(*a*) the vendor shall forthwith at his own cost apply for and use his best endeavours to obtain such consent

(*b*) the purchaser shall forthwith supply such information and references as may reasonably be required by the reversioner before granting such consent

(*c*) if any such consent is not granted at least five working days before contractual completion date, or is subject to any condition to which the purchaser reasonably objects, either party may rescind the contract by notice to the other.

(5) Any statutory implied covenant on the part of the vendor shall not extend to any breach of the terms of the lease as to the state and condition of the property and the assignment shall so provide. This sub-condition applies notwithstanding that a special condition provides for the vendor to convey as beneficial owner.

(6) Where the property is sold subject to an apportioned rent specified as such in a special condition, the purchaser shall not require the consent of the reversioner to be obtained, or the rent to be otherwise legally apportioned.

(7) The purchaser shall assume that any receipt for the last payment due for rent under the lease before actual completion was given by the person then entitled to such rent or his duly authorised agent.

9 DEPOSIT

(1) The purchaser shall on or before the date of the contract pay by way of deposit to the vendor's solicitors as stakeholders the normal deposit, or such lesser sum as the vendor shall have agreed in writing. On a sale by private treaty, payment shall be made by banker's draft or by cheque drawn on a solicitors' bank account.

(2) Upon service by the vendor of a completion notice, the purchaser shall pay to the vendor any difference between the normal deposit and any amount actually paid (if less).

(3) If any draft, cheque or other instrument tendered in or towards payment of any sum payable under this condition is dishonoured when first presented the vendor shall have the right by notice to the purchaser within seven working days thereafter to treat the contract as repudiated.

10 OPTIONAL METHODS OF EXCHANGE

(1) Exchange of contracts may be effected by a method authorised by condition 2 for the service of notices. If so effected, the contract shall be made when the last part is, as the case may be, posted or delivered to a document exchange.

(2) Where contracts have not been exchanged, the parties' solicitors may agree by telephone or telex that the contract be immediately effective and thereupon the solicitors holding a part of the contract signed by their client shall hold it irrevocably to the order of the other party.

11 INSURANCE

(1) If the property is destroyed or damaged prior to actual completion and the proceeds of any insurance policy effected by or for the purchaser are reduced by reason of the existence of any policy effected by or for the vendor, the purchase price shall be abated by the amount of such reduction.

(2) Sub-condition (1) shall not apply where the proceeds of the vendor's policy are applied towards the reinstatement of the property pursuant to any statutory or contractual obligation.

(3) This condition takes effect in substitution for section 47 of the Law of Property Act 1925.

(4) The vendor shall be under no duty to the purchaser to maintain any insurance on the property, save where the property is leasehold and the vendor has an obligation to insure.

12 ABSTRACT OF TITLE

(1) Forthwith upon exchange of contracts the vendor shall deliver to the purchaser—

(a) where the title is not registered, an abstract of the title to the property or an epitome of the title together with photocopies of the relevant documents

(b) where the title is registered—

    (i) the documents, particulars and information specified in sub-sections (1) and (2) of section 110 of the Land Registration Act 1925, save that copies of the entries on the register, the filed plan and any documents noted on the register and filed in the registry shall be office copies, and

    (ii) such additional authorities to inspect the register as the purchaser shall reasonably require for any sub-purchaser or prospective mortgagee or lessee.

(2) Where the title is not registered, the vendor shall at his own expense produce the relevant documents of title or an abstract, epitome of title or copy thereof (bearing in each case original markings of examination of all relevant documents of title or of examined abstracts thereof).

(3) Where before the date of the contract any abstract, epitome or document has been delivered to the purchaser, he shall not, save as provided by conditions 6 (2) or 8 (3), be deemed to have had notice before the date of the contract of any matter of title thereby disclosed.

13 IDENTITY AND BOUNDARIES

(1) The vendor shall produce such evidence as may be reasonably necessary to establish the identity and extent of the property, but shall not be required to define exact boundaries, or the ownership of fences, ditches, hedges or walls, nor, beyond the evidence afforded by the information in his possession, separately to identify parts of the property held under different titles.

(2) If reasonably required by the purchaser because of the insufficiency of the evidence produced under sub-condition (1), the vendor shall at his own expense provide and hand over on completion a statutory declaration as to the relevant facts, in a form agreed by the purchaser, such agreement not to be unreasonably withheld.

14 MORTGAGES IN FAVOUR OF FRIENDLY AND OTHER SOCIETIES

Where the title includes a mortgage or legal charge in favour of trustees on behalf of a friendly society, a building society or a society registered under the Industrial and Provident Societies Acts, the purchaser shall assume that any receipt given on the discharge of any such mortgage or legal charge and apparently duly executed was in fact duly executed by all proper persons and is valid.

15 REQUISITIONS

(1) In this condition "abstract" means all the documents, particulars and information required to be delivered by the vendor under condition 12.

(2) Subject to sub-condition (4), the purchaser shall deliver any requisitions or objections relating to the title, evidence of title or the abstract, in writing within six working days of receipt of the abstract (or, in the case of an abstract delivered before the date of the contract, within six working days of the date of contract). Within four working days of such delivery the vendor shall deliver his replies in writing.

(3) The purchaser shall deliver any observations on any of the vendor's replies in writing within four working days of their receipt.

(4) Where some but not all parts of the abstract have been delivered, and defects in title are not disclosed by such parts of the abstract as have been delivered, then in respect only of the undelivered parts or undisclosed defects (as the case may be) the abstract shall be deemed to be received for the purpose of sub-condition (2) at the time or respective times when any previously undelivered part is delivered.

(5) Time shall be of the essence for the purposes of this condition.

16 RESCISSION

(1) If the vendor is unable, or on some reasonable ground unwilling, to satisfy any requisition or objection made by the purchaser, the vendor may give the purchaser notice (specifying the reason for his inability or the ground of his unwillingness) to withdraw the same. If the purchaser does not withdraw the same within seven working days of service, either party may thereafter, notwithstanding any intermediate negotiation or litigation, rescind the contract by notice to the other.

(2) Upon rescission under any power given by these conditions or any special condition—
(a) the vendor shall repay to the purchaser any sums paid by way of deposit or otherwise under the contract, with interest on such sums at the contract rate from four working days after rescission until payment
(b) the purchaser shall forthwith return all documents delivered to him by the vendor and at his own expense procure the cancellation of any entry relating to the contract in any register.

17 PREPARATION OF CONVEYANCE

(1) The purchaser shall deliver the draft conveyance at least twelve working days before contractual completion date, and within four working days of such delivery the vendor shall deliver it back approved or revised.

(2) The purchaser shall deliver the engrossment of the conveyance (first executed by him, where requisite) at least five working days before contractual completion date.

(3) The purchaser shall not, by delivering the draft conveyance or the engrossment, be deemed to accept the vendor's title or to waive any right to raise or maintain requisitions.

(4) Save to the extent that a covenant for indemnity will be implied by statute, the purchaser shall in the conveyance covenant to indemnify the vendor and his estate (and any estate of which the vendor is personal representative or trustee) against all actions, claims and liability for any breach of any covenant, stipulation, provision or other matter subject to which the property is sold and in respect of which the vendor or any such estate will remain liable after completion.

(5) The vendor shall give an acknowledgment for production and, unless in a fiduciary capacity, an undertaking for safe custody of documents of title retained by him. Where any such document is retained by a mortgagee, trustee or personal representative, the vendor shall procure that such person shall give an acknowledgment for production, and the vendor, unless in a fiduciary capacity, shall covenant that if and when he receives any such document he will, at the cost of the person requiring it, give an undertaking for safe custody.

(6) The vendor shall be entitled on reasonable grounds to decline to convey the property to any person other than the purchaser, by more than one conveyance, at more than the contract price or at a price divided between different parts of the property.

18 OCCUPATION BEFORE COMPLETION

(1) This condition applies if the vendor authorises the purchaser to occupy the property before actual completion, except—
(a) where the purchaser already lawfully occupies any part of the property, or
(b) where the property is a dwellinghouse and the authority for the occupation is only for the purpose of effecting works of decoration, repair or improvement agreed by the vendor.

(2) The purchaser occupies the property as licensee and not as tenant. The purchaser may not transfer his licence or authorise any other person save members of his immediate family to occupy any part of the property.

(3) The purchaser shall not, by taking such occupation, be deemed to accept the vendor's title or to waive any right to raise or maintain requisitions.

(4) While the purchaser is in occupation of the whole or any part of the property under this condition, he shall—
(a) pay and indemnify the vendor against all outgoings and any other expenses in respect of the property and pay to the vendor in respect of such occupation a sum calculated at the contract rate on the amount of the purchase money (less any deposit paid)
(b) be entitled to receive any rents and profits from any part of the property not occupied by him
(c) insure the property in a sum not less than the purchase price against all risks in respect of which premises of the like nature are normally insured.

(5) The purchaser's licence to occupy the property shall end—
(a) on contractual completion date, or
(b) upon termination of the contract, or
(c) upon the expiry of five working days' notice given by either party to the other,
and thereupon the purchaser shall give up occupation of the property and leave the same in as good repair as it was in when he went into occupation.

(6) If the purchaser, after his licence has ended under sub-condition 5(a), remains in occupation with the express or implied consent of the vendor, he shall thereafter occupy on the other terms of this condition and on the further term that the vendor's rights under condition 22 shall not thereby be affected.

19 APPORTIONMENTS

(1) In this condition—
(a) "the apportionment day" means—
(i) if the property is sold with vacant possession of the whole, the date of actual completion
(ii) in any other case, contractual completion date
(b) "payment period" means one of the periods for which a sum payable periodically is payable, whether or not such periods are of equal length.

(2) This condition shall not apply to any sum if—
(a) the purchaser cannot, by virtue only of becoming the owner of the property, either enforce payment of it or be obliged to pay it, or
(b) it is an outgoing paid in advance, unless the vendor cannot obtain repayment and the purchaser benefits therefrom or is given credit therefor against a sum that would otherwise be his liability.

(3) On completion the income and outgoings of the property shall, subject to sub-condition (2) and conditions 3 and 22(4) and to any adjustment required by condition 18(4), be apportioned as at the apportionment day.

(4) For the purposes of apportionment only, it shall be assumed—
(a) that the vendor remains owner of the property until the end of the apportionment day, and
(b) that the sum to be apportioned—
(i) accrues from day to day
(ii) is payable throughout the relevant period at the same rate as on the apportionment day.

(5) Sums payable periodically shall be apportioned by charging or allowing—
(a) for any payment period entirely attributable to one party, the whole of the instalment payable therefor
(b) for any part of a payment period, a proportion on an annual basis.
(6) (a) This sub-condition applies to any sum payable in respect of any period falling wholly or partly prior to the apportionment day, the amount of which is not notified to either party before actual completion
(b) A provisional apportionment shall be made on the best estimate available. Upon the amount being notified, a final apportionment shall be made and one party shall thereupon make to the other the appropriate balancing payment.

20 ENDORSEMENT OF MEMORANDUM

Where the vendor does not hand over all the documents of his title, he shall at completion endorse a memorandum of the sale to the purchaser on the last such document in each relevant title and thereupon produce the endorsed documents for inspection.

21 COMPLETION

(1) Contractual completion date shall be as stated in the special conditions but if not so stated shall be the twenty-fifth working day after the date of the contract. Completion shall take place in England or Wales either at the office of the vendor's solicitors or, if required by the vendor at least five working days prior to actual completion, at the office of the vendor's mortgagee or his solicitors.
(2) The vendor shall not be obliged to accept payment of the money due on completion otherwise than by one or more of the following methods—
(a) legal tender
(b) a banker's draft drawn by and upon a settlement bank for the purposes of the Clearing House Automated Payments System or any other bank specified in a special condition
(c) an unconditional authority to release any deposit held by a stakeholder
(d) otherwise as the vendor shall have agreed before actual completion.
(3) If completion is effected otherwise than by personal attendance the time for completion is when on a working day
(a) the money due on completion is paid to the vendor or his solicitors, and
(b) the vendor's solicitors hold to the order of the purchaser all the documents to which he is entitled on completion.
(4) For the purposes of this condition money is paid when the vendor receives payment by a method specified in sub-condition (2). Where the parties have agreed upon a direct credit to a bank account at a named branch, payment is made when that branch receives the credit.
(5) (a) This sub-condition applies if the money due on completion is not paid by 2.30 p.m. on the day of actual completion or by such other time on that day as is specified in a special condition
(b) For the purposes of condition 22 only, completion shall be deemed to be postponed by reason of the purchaser's delay from the day of actual completion until the next working day
(c) The purchaser shall not as a result of the deemed postponement of completion be liable to make any payment to the vendor unless the vendor claims such payment by giving notice at completion or within five working days thereafter (as to which period time shall be of the essence). Payment shall be due five working days after receipt of such notice.

22 COMPENSATION FOR LATE COMPLETION

(1) For the purposes of this condition—
(a) "delay" means failure to perform or lateness in performing any obligation of the contract which causes or contributes to lateness in completion
(b) a party is "in default" if and to the extent that the period, or the aggregate of the periods, of his delay exceeds the period, or the aggregate of the periods, of delay of the other party
(c) "the period of default" means the length of the excess defined in paragraph (b) or, if shorter, the period from contractual completion date to the date of actual completion.
(2) If the sale shall be completed after contractual completion date, the party in default (if any) shall be liable to compensate the other for loss occasioned to him by reason of that default.
(3) Before actual completion, or within five working days thereafter (as to which period time shall be of the essence), the party entitled to compensation may, by notice to the other party, opt to be paid or allowed a sum calculated at the contract rate on the amount of the purchase money (less any deposit paid) for the period of default as liquidated damages in settlement of his claim for compensation.
(4) If the vendor is entitled to compensation, he may, before actual completion, by notice to the purchaser, opt to take the net income of the property for the period of default in lieu of such compensation.
(5) The right to recover any compensation under this condition shall not be prejudiced by completion of the sale, whether before or after the commencement of proceedings.

23 COMPLETION NOTICE

(1) This condition applies unless a special condition provides that time is of the essence in respect of contractual completion date.
(2) If the sale shall not be completed on contractual completion date, either party, being then himself ready able and willing to complete, may after that date serve on the other party notice to complete the transaction in accordance with this condition. A party shall be deemed to be ready, able and willing to complete—
(a) if he could be so but for some default or omission of the other party
(b) notwithstanding that any mortgage on the property is unredeemed when the completion notice is served if the aggregate of all sums necessary to redeem all such mortgages (to the extent that they relate to the property) does not exceed the sum payable on completion.
(3) Upon service of a completion notice it shall become a term of the contract that the transaction shall be completed within fifteen working days of service and in respect of such period time shall be of the essence.
(4) If the purchaser does not comply with a completion notice—
(a) the purchaser shall forthwith return all documents delivered to him by the vendor and at his own expense procure the cancellation of any entry relating to the contract in any register
(b) without prejudice to any other rights or remedies available to him, the vendor may—
(i) forfeit and retain any deposit paid and/or
(ii) re-sell the property by auction, tender or private treaty.
(5) If on any such re-sale contracted within one year after contractual completion date the vendor incurs a loss and so elects by notice to the purchaser within one month after the contract for such re-sale, the purchaser shall pay to the vendor liquidated damages. The amount payable shall be the aggregate of such loss, all costs and expenses reasonably incurred in any such re-sale and any attempted re-sale and interest at the contract rate on such part of the purchase money as is from time to time outstanding (giving credit for all sums received under any re-sale contract on account of the re-sale price) after contractual completion date.

(6) If the vendor does not comply with a completion notice, the purchaser, without prejudice to any other rights or remedies available to him, may give notice to the vendor forthwith to pay to the purchaser any sums paid by way of deposit or otherwise under the contract and interest on such sums at the contract rate from four working days after service of the notice until payment. On compliance with such notice the purchaser shall not be entitled to specific performance of the contract, but shall forthwith return all documents delivered to him by the vendor and at the expense of the vendor procure the cancellation of any entry relating to the contract in any register.

(7) Where after service of a completion notice the time for completion shall have been extended by agreement or implication, either party may again invoke the provisions of this condition which shall then take effect with the substitution of "seven working days" for "fifteen working days" in sub-condition (3).

24 CHATTELS

The property in any chattels agreed to be sold shall pass to the purchaser on actual completion.

25 AUCTIONS

(1) This condition applies if the property is sold by auction.

(2) The sale is subject to a reserve price for the property and, when the property is sold in lots, for each lot.

(3) The vendor reserves the right—

(a) to divide the property into lots and to sub-divide, re-arrange or consolidate any lots

(b) to bid personally or by his agent up to any reserve price

(c) without disclosing any reserve price, to withdraw from the sale any property or lot at any time before it has been sold, whether or not the sale has begun.

(4) The auctioneer may—

(a) refuse to accept a bid

(b) in the case of a dispute as to any bid, forthwith determine the dispute or again put up the property or lot at the last undisputed bid.

(5) The purchaser shall forthwith complete and sign the contract and pay, but not necessarily by the means specified in condition 9(1), the normal deposit.

Appendix C

The National Conditions of Sale (20th Edition)

Construction of the conditions

In these conditions, where the context admits—
(1) The "vendor" and the "purchaser" include the persons deriving title under them respectively
(2) "Purchase money" includes any sum to be paid for chattels, fittings or other separate items
(3) References to the "Special Conditions" include references to the particulars of sale and to the provisions of the contract which is made by reference to the conditions
(4) The "prescribed rate" means the agreed rate of interest or, if none, then the rate of interest prescribed from time to time under Land Compensation Act 1961, s. 32
(5) "Solicitor" includes a barrister who is employed by a corporate body to carry out conveyancing on its behalf and is acting in the course of his employment
(6) "Working day" means a day on which clearing banks in the City of London are (or would be but for a strike, lock-out, or other stoppage, affecting particular banks or banks generally) open during banking hours Except in condition 19(4), in which "working day" means a day when the Land Registry is open to the public
(7) "Clearing bank" means a bank which is a member of CHAPS and Town Clearing Company Limited
(8) The "Planning Acts" means the enactments from time to time in force relating to town and country planning
(9) On a sale by private treaty references to the "auctioneer" shall be read as references to the vendor's agent
(10) On a sale in lots, the conditions apply to each lot
(11) "Abstract of title" means in relation to registered land such documents as the vendor is required by Land Registration Act 1925, s. 110, to furnish.

The conditions

1. The Sale: by Auction: by Private Treaty
(1) Paragraphs (2) to (5) of this condition apply on a sale by auction and paragraphs (6) and (7) on a sale by private treaty
(2) Unless otherwise provided in the Special Conditions, the sale of the property and of each lot is subject to a reserve price and to a right for the vendor or any one person on behalf of the vendor to bid up to that price
(3) The auctioneer may refuse any bid and no person shall at any bid advance less than the amount fixed for that purpose by the auctioneer
(4) If any dispute arises respecting a bid, the auctioneer may determine the dispute or the property may, at the vendor's option, either be put up again at the last undisputed bid, or be withdrawn
(5) Subject to the foregoing provisions of this condition, the highest bidder shall be the purchaser and shall forthwith complete and sign the contract, the date of which shall be the date of the auction
(6) Where there is a draft contract, or an arrangement subject to contract, or a negotiation in which there are one or more outstanding items or suspensory matters (which prevent there being yet a concluded agreement of a contractual nature), a solicitor, who holds a document signed by his client in the form of a contract or such in writing and embodying this condition, shall (unless the other party or his solicitor is informed to the contrary) have the authority of his client to conclude, by formal exchange of contracts, or by post, or by telex or other telegraphic means, or by telephone, and in any case with or without involving solicitors' undertakings, a binding contract in the terms of the document which his client has signed
(7) The date of the contract shall be—
    (i) the date, if any, which is agreed and put on the contract, but if none, then
    (ii) on an exchange of contracts by post (unless the parties' solicitors otherwise agree), the date on which the last part of the contract is posted, or
    (iii) in any other case, the date on which, consistently with this condition, a binding contract is concluded.

2. Deposit
(1) Unless the Special Conditions otherwise provide, the purchaser shall on the date of the contract pay a deposit of 10 per cent. of the purchase price, on a sale by auction, to the auctioneer, or on a sale by private treaty, to the vendor's solicitor and, in either case, as stakeholder
(2) In case a cheque taken for the deposit (having been presented, and whether or not it has been re-presented) has not been honoured, then and on that account the vendor may elect—
either   (i) to treat the contract as discharged by breach thereof on the purchaser's part
or   (ii) to enforce payment of the deposit as a deposit, by suing on the cheque or otherwise.

3. Purchaser's short right to rescind
(1) This condition shall have effect if the Special Conditions so provide, but not otherwise
(2) If the property is affected by any matter to which this condition applies, then the purchaser may by notice in writing (hereinafter referred to as a "Condition 3 Notice") given to the vendor or his solicitor and expressly referring to this condition and the matter in question, and notwithstanding any intermediate negotiation, rescind the contract on the same terms as if the purchaser had persisted in an objection to the title which the vendor was unable to remove
(3) A Condition 3 Notice shall not be given after the expiration of 16 working days from the date of the contract, time being of the essence of this condition
(4) This condition applies to any matter materially affecting the value of the property, other than—
    (i) a matter which was not yet in existence or subsisting at the date of the contract
    (ii) a specific matter to which the sale was expressly made subject, or
    (iii) a matter of which the purchaser had at the date of the contract express notice or

actual knowledge, not being notice or knowledge imputed to the purchaser by statute solely by reason of a registration of such matter, or notice or knowledge which the purchaser is only deemed to have had by the conditions

(5) This condition and condition 15 are additional to each other.

4. Chattels, etc., and separate items

If the sale includes chattels, fittings or other separate items, the vendor warrants that he is entitled to sell the same free from any charge, lien, burden, or adverse claim.

5. Date and manner of completion

(1) The completion date shall be the date specified for the purpose in the contract or, if none, the 26th working day after the date of the contract or the date of delivery of the abstract of title, whichever be the later

(2) Unless the Special Conditions otherwise provide, in respect of the completion date time shall not be of the essence of the contract, but this provision shall operate subject and without prejudice to—

(i) the provisions of condition 22 and

(ii) the rights of either party to recover from the other damages for delay in fulfilling his obligations under the contract

(3) The purchaser's obligations to pay money due on completion shall be discharged by one or more of the following methods—

(i) authorisation in writing to release a deposit held for the purposes of the contract by a stakeholder

(ii) banker's draft issued by a clearing bank

(iii) cheque drawn on and guaranteed by a clearing bank

(iv) telegraphic or other direct transfer (as requested or agreed to by the vendor's solicitor) to a particular bank or branch for the credit of a specified account

(v) legal tender

(vi) any other method requested or agreed to by the vendor's solicitor

(4) Completion shall be carried out, either formally at such office or place as the vendor's solicitor shall reasonably require, or (if the parties' solicitors so arrange) by post, or by means of solicitors' undertaking concerning the holding of documents or otherwise Provided that on a sale with vacant possession of the whole or part of the property, if the conveyance or transfer will not, by overreaching or otherwise, discharge the property from interests (if any) of persons in, or who may be in, actual occupation of the property or such part of it, then (subject always to the rights of the purchaser under Law of Property Act 1925, s. 42 (1)), the purchaser may, by giving reasonable notice, require that on, or immediately before the time of, completion possession of the property or part be handed over to the purchaser or his representative at the property

(5) The date of actual completion shall be the day on which, the contract being completed in other respects the purchaser has discharged consistently with the provisions of this condition the obligations of the purchaser to pay the money due on completion Provided that—

(i) for the purposes only of conditions 6, 7 and 8, if but for this proviso the date of actual completion would be the last working day of a week (starting on Sunday) and the purchaser is unable or unwilling to complete before 2.15 p.m. on that day, then the date of actual completion shall be taken to be the first working day thereafter

(ii) a remittance sent by post or delivered by hand shall be treated as being made on the day on which it reaches the vendor's solicitor's office, unless that day is not a working day in which case the remittance shall be treated as being made on the first working day thereafter.

6. Rents, outgoings and apportionments

The purchase being completed (whether on the completion date or subsequently), the income and outgoings shall be apportioned as follows (the day itself in each case being apportioned to the vendor):—

(1) In a case to which proviso (i) to condition 7 (1) applies apportionment shall be made as at the date of actual completion

(2) In a case in which the purchaser is in possession of the whole of the property as lessee or tenant at a rent apportionment shall be made as at the date of actual completion unless proviso (ii) to condition 7 (1) applies, when apportionment shall be made as at the date of the purchaser's notice under that proviso

(3) In any other case apportionment shall be made as from the completion date Provided nevertheless that, if delay is attributable to the vendor's failure to obtain the reversioner's licence, where necessary, or if the vendor remains in beneficial occupation of the property after the completion date, the purchaser may by notice in writing before actual completion elect that apportionment shall be made as at the date of actual completion

(4) Rates shall be apportioned according to the period for which they are intended to provide and rents (whether payable in advance or in arrear) according to the period in respect of which they have been paid or are payable; and apportionment of yearly items (whether or not the same are payable by equal quarterly, monthly or other instalments) shall be according to the relevant number of days relatively to the number of days in the full year

(5) Service charges under leases, in the absence of known or readily ascertainable amounts, shall be apportioned according to the best estimate available at the time of completion and, unless otherwise agreed, the vendor and the purchaser shall be and remain mutually bound after completion to account for and pay or allow to each other, within 15 working days after being informed of the actual amounts as ascertained, any balances or excesses due.

7. Interest

(1) If the purchase shall not be completed on the completion date then (subject to the provisions of paragraph (2) of this condition) the purchaser shall pay interest on the remainder of his purchase money at the prescribed rate from that date until the purchase shall actually be completed Provided nevertheless—

(i) That (without prejudice to the operation of proviso (ii) to this paragraph) the vendor may by notice in writing before actual completion elect to take the income of the property (less outgoings) up to the date of actual completion instead of interest as aforesaid

(ii) That, if the delay arises from any cause other than the neglect or default of the purchaser, and if the purchaser (not being in occupation of the property in circumstances to which condition 8 applies) places the remainder of his purchase money (at his own risk) at interest on a deposit account in England or Wales with any clearing bank, and gives written notice thereof to the vendor or his solicitor, then in lieu of the interest or income payable to or receivable by the vendor as aforesaid, the vendor shall from the time of such notice be entitled to such interest only as is produced by such deposit

(iii) That the vendor shall in no case be or become entitled in respect of the same period of time both to be paid interest and to enjoy income of the property, or to be paid interest more than once on the same sum of money

(2) The purchaser shall not be liable to pay interest under paragraph (1) of this condition—

(i) so long as, or to the extent that, delay in completion is attributable to any act or default of the vendor or his mortgagee or Settled Land Act trustees

(ii) in case the property is to be constructed or converted by the vendor, so long as the construction or conversion is unfinished.

8. Occupation pending completion

(1) If the purchaser (not being already in occupation as lessee or tenant at a rent) is let into occupation of the property before the actual completion of the purchase, then, as from the date of his going into occupation and until actual completion, or until upon discharge or rescission of the contract he ceases to occupy the property, the purchaser shall—

(i) be the licensee and not the tenant of the vendor

(ii) pay interest on the remainder of the purchase money at the prescribed rate

(iii) keep the property in as good repair and condition as it was in when he went into occupation

(iv) pay, or otherwise indemnify the vendor against, all outgoings and expenses (including the cost of insurance) in respect of the property, the purchaser at the same time taking or being credited with the income of the property (if any)

(v) not carry out any development within the meaning of the Planning Acts

(2) Upon discharge or rescission of the contract, or upon the expiration of 7 working days' or longer notice given by the vendor or his solicitor to the purchaser or his solicitor in that behalf, the purchaser shall forthwith give up the property in such repair and condition as aforesaid

(3) A purchaser going into occupation before completion shall not be deemed thereby to have accepted the vendor's title

(4) Where the purchaser is allowed access to the property for the purpose only of carrying out works or installations, the purchaser shall not be treated as being let into occupation within the meaning of this condition.

9. Abstract, requisitions and observations

(1) The vendor shall deliver the abstract of title not later than 11 working days after the date of the contract but, subject and without prejudice as mentioned in condition 5 (2), that time limit shall not be of the essence of the contract

(2) Subject always to the rights of the purchaser under Law of Property Act 1925, s. 42 (1), the vendor may be required by the purchaser to deal with requisitions and observations concerning persons who are or may be in occupation or actual occupation of the property, so as to satisfy the purchaser that the title is not, and that the purchaser will not be, prejudicially affected by any interests or claims of such persons.

(3) The purchaser shall deliver in writing his requisitions within 11 working days after delivery of the abstract, and his observations on the replies to the requisitions within 6 working days after delivery of the replies

(4) In respect of the delivery of requisitions and observations, time shall be of the essence of the contract, notwithstanding that the abstract may not have been delivered within due time

(5) The purchaser shall deliver his requisitions and observations on the abstract as delivered, whether it is a perfect or an imperfect abstract, but for the purposes of any requisitions or observations which could not be raised or made on the information contained in an imperfect abstract, time under paragraph (3) of this condition shall not start to run against the purchaser, until the vendor has delivered the further abstract or information on which the requisition or observations arise

(6) Subject to his requisitions and observations, the purchaser shall be deemed to have accepted the title.

10. Vendor's right to rescind

(1) If the purchaser shall persist in any objection to the title which the vendor shall be unable or unwilling, on reasonable grounds, to remove, and shall not withdraw the same within 10 working days of being required so to do, the vendor may, subject to the purchaser's rights under Law of Property Act 1925, ss. 42 and 125, by notice in writing to the purchaser or his solicitor, and notwithstanding any intermediate negotiation or litigation, rescind the contract

(2) Upon such rescission the vendor shall return the deposit, but without interest, costs of investigating title or other compensation or payment, and the purchaser shall return the abstract and other papers furnished to him.

11. Existing leaseholds

(1) Where the interest sold is leasehold for the residue of an existing term the following provisions of this conditon shall apply

(2) The lease or underlease or a copy thereof having been made available, the purchaser (whether he has inspected the same or not) shall be deemed to have bought with full notice of the contents thereof

(3) On production of a receipt for the last payment due for rent under the lease or underlease, the purchaser shall assume without proof that the person giving the receipt, though not the original lessor, is the reversioner expectant on the said lease or underlease or his duly authorised agent

(4) No objection shall be taken on account of the covenants in an underlease not corresponding with the covenants in any superior lease

(5) The sale is subject to the reversioner's licence being obtained, where necessary. The purchaser supplying such information and references, if any, as may reasonably be required of him, the vendor will use his best endeavours to obtain such licence and will pay the fee for the same. But if the licence cannot be obtained, the vendor may rescind the contract on the same terms as if the purchaser had persisted in an objection to the title which the vendor was unable to remove

(6) Where the property comprises part only of the property comprised in a lease or underlease, the rent, covenants and conditions shall, if the purchaser so requires, be legally apportioned at his expense, but completion shall not be delayed on that account and in the meantime the apportionment by the auctioneer shall be accepted, or the property may at the option of the vendor be sub-demised for the residue of the term, less one day, at a rent apportioned by the auctioneer and subject to the purchaser executing a counterpart containing covenants and provisions corresponding to those contained in the lease or underlease aforesaid

(7) Any statutory covenant to be implied in the conveyance on the part of a vendor shall be so limited as not to affect him with liability for a subsisting breach of any covenant or condition concerning the state or condition of the property, of which state and condition the purchaser is by paragraph (3) of condition 13 deemed to have full notice, and where Land Registration Act 1925, s. 24, applies the purchaser, if required, will join in requesting that an appropriate entry be made in the register.

12. Vendor's duty to produce documents

(1) If an abstracted document refers to any plan material to the description of the property, or to any covenants contained in a document earlier in date than the document with which the title commences, and such plan or earlier document is in the possession or power of the vendor or his trustees or mortgagee, the vendor shall supply a copy thereof with the abstract

(2) If the property is sold subject to restrictive covenants, the deed imposing those covenants or a copy thereof having been made available, the purchaser (whether he has inspected the same or not) shall be deemed to have purchased with full knowledge thereof

(3) The vendor shall not be required to procure the production of any document not in his possession or not in the possession of his mortgagee or trustees, and of which the vendor cannot obtain production, or to trace or state who has the possession of the same.

13. Identity: boundaries: condition of property

(1) The purchaser shall admit the identity of the property with that comprised in the muniments offered by the vendor as the title thereto upon the evidence afforded by the descriptions contained in such muniments, and of a statutory declaration, to be made (if required) at the purchaser's expense, that the property has been enjoyed according to the title for at least twelve years

(2) The vendor shall not be bound to show any title to boundaries, fences, ditches, hedges or walls, or to distinguish parts of the property held under different titles further than he may be able to do from information in his possession

(3) The purchaser shall be deemed to buy with full notice in all respects of the actual state and condition of the property and, save where it is to be constructed or converted by the vendor, shall take the property as it is.

14. Property sold subject to easements, etc.

Without prejudice to the duty of the vendor to disclose all latent easements and latent liabilities known to the vendor to affect the property, the property is sold subject to any rights of way and water, rights of common, and other rights, easements, quasi-easements, liabilities and public rights affecting the same.

15. Town and Country Planning

(1) In this condition, where the context admits, references to "authorised use" are references to "established use", or to use for which permission has been granted under the Planning Acts, or to use for which permission is not required under those Acts, as the case may be

(2) The purchaser shall be entitled to deliver, with his requisitions in respect of the title, requisitions concerning the authorised use of the property for the purposes of the Planning Acts. The vendor in reply shall give all such relevant information as may be in his possession or power

(3) Where the property is in the Special Conditions expressed to be sold on the footing of an authorised use which is specified, then if it appears before actual completion of the purchase that the specified use is not an authorised use of the property for the purposes of the Planning Acts, the purchaser may by notice in writing rescind the contract, and thereupon paragraph (2) of condition 10 shall apply. But, subject to the foregoing provisions of this condition, the purchaser shall be deemed to have accepted that the specified use is an authorised use of the property for the purposes of the Planning Acts

(4) Save as mentioned in the Special Conditions, the property is not to the knowledge of the vendor subject to any charge, notice, order, restriction, agreement or other matter arising under the Planning Acts, but (without prejudice to any right of the purchaser to rescind the contract under paragraph (3) of this condition) the property is sold subject to any such charges, notices, orders, restrictions, agreements and matters affecting the interest sold

(5) Subject as hereinbefore provided, and without prejudice to the obligations of the vendor to supply information as aforesaid, the purchaser shall be deemed to buy with knowledge in all respects of the authorised use of the property for the purposes of the Planning Acts.

16. Requirements by local authority

(1) If after the date of the contract any requirement in respect of the property be made against the vendor by any local authority, the purchaser shall comply with the same at his own expense, and indemnify the vendor in respect thereof: in so far as the purchaser shall fail to comply with such requirement, the vendor may comply with the same wholly or in part and any money so expended by the vendor shall be repaid by the purchaser on completion

(2) The vendor shall upon receiving notice of any such requirement forthwith inform the purchaser thereof.

17. Errors, mis-statements or omissions

(1) Without prejudice to any express right of either party, or to any right of the purchaser in reliance on Law of Property Act 1969, s. 24, to rescind the contract before completion and subject to the provisions of paragraph (2) of this condition, no error, mis-statement or omission in any preliminary answer concerning the property, or in the sale plan or the Special Conditions shall annul the sale, nor (save where the error, mis-statement or omission relates to a matter materially affecting the description or value of the property) shall any damages be payable, or compensation allowed by either party, in respect thereof

(2) Paragraph (1) of this condition shall not apply to any error, mis-statement or omission which is recklessly or fraudulently made, or to any matter or thing by which the purchaser is prevented from getting substantially what he contracted to buy

(3) In this condition a "preliminary answer" means and includes any statement made by or on behalf of the vendor to the purchaser or his agents or advisers, whether in answer to formal preliminary enquiries or otherwise, before the purchaser entered into the contract.

18. Leases and tenancies

(1) Abstracts or copies of the leases or agreements (if in writing) under which the tenants hold having been made available, the purchaser (whether he has inspected the same or not)

shall be deemed to have notice of and shall take subject to the terms of all the existing tenancies and the rights of the tenants, whether arising during the continuance or after the expiration thereof, and such notice shall not be affected by any partial or incomplete statement in the Special Conditions with reference to the tenancies, and no objection shall be taken on account of there not being an agreement in writing with any tenant

(2) Where a lease or tenancy affects the property sold and other property, the property sold will be conveyed with the benefit of the apportioned rent (if any) mentioned in the Special Conditions or (if not so mentioned) fixed by the auctioneer, and no objection shall be taken on the ground that the consent of the tenant has not been obtained to the apportionment and the purchaser shall not require the rent to be legally apportioned

(3) The purchaser shall keep the vendor indemnified against all claims by the tenant for compensation or otherwise, except in respect of a tenancy which expires or is determined on or before the completion date or in respect of an obligation which ought to have been discharged before the date of the contract

(4) Land in the occupation of the vendor is sold subject to the right (hereby reserved to him) to be paid a fair price for tillages, off-going and other allowances as, if he were an outgoing tenant who had entered into occupation of the land after 1st March 1948, and as if the purchaser were the landlord, and in case of dispute such price shall be fixed by the valuation of a valuer, to be nominated in case the parties differ by the President of the Royal Institution of Chartered Surveyors.

19. Preparation of conveyance: priority notices: indemnities

(1) Where the interest sold is leasehold for a term of years to be granted by the vendor, the lease or underlease and counterpart shall be prepared by the vendor's solicitor in accordance (as nearly as the circumstances admit) with a form or draft annexed to the contract or otherwise sufficiently identified by the signatures of the parties or their solicitors

(2) In any other case the conveyance shall be prepared by the purchaser or his solicitor and the following provisions of this condition shall apply

(3) The draft conveyance shall be delivered at the office of the vendor's solicitor at least 6 working days before the completion date and the engrossment for execution by the vendor and other necessary parties (if any) shall be left at the said office within 3 working days after the draft has been returned to the purchaser approved on behalf of the vendor and other necessary parties (if any)

(4) Where the property is unregistered land not in an area of compulsory registration and the conveyance is to contain restrictive covenants, and the purchaser intends contemporaneously with the conveyance to execute a mortgage or conveyance to a third party, he shall inform the vendor of his intention and, if necessary, allow the vendor to give a priority notice for the registration of the intended covenants at least 15 working days before the contract is completed

(5) Where the property is sold subject to legal incumbrances, the purchaser shall covenant to indemnify the vendor against actions and claims in respect of them; and the purchaser will not make any claim on account of increased expense caused by the concurrence of any legal incumbrancer

(6) Where the property is sold subject to stipulations, or restrictive or other covenants, and breach thereof would expose the vendor to liability, the purchaser shall covenant to observe and perform the same and to indemnify the vendor against actions and claims in respect thereof

(7) Paragraphs (5) and (6) of this condition shall have effect without prejudice to the provisions of Law of Property Act 1925, s. 77, and Land Registration Act 1925, s. 24, where such provisions respectively are applicable, and in respect of matters covered by a covenant implied under either of those sections no express covenant shall be required.

20. Severance of properties formerly in common ownership

Where the property and any adjacent or neighbouring property have hitherto been in common ownership, the purchaser shall not become entitled to any right to light or air over or in respect of any adjacent or neighbouring property which is retained by the vendor and the conveyance shall, if the vendor so requires, reserve to him such easements and rights as would become appurtenant to such last-mentioned property by implication of law, if the vendor had sold it to another purchaser at the same time as he has sold the property to the purchaser.

21. Insurance

(1) With respect to any policy of insurance maintained by the vendor in respect of damage to or destruction of the property, the vendor shall not (save pursuant to an obligation to a third party) be bound to keep such insurance on foot or to give notice to the purchaser of any premium being or becoming due

(2) The purchaser shall be entitled to inspect the policy at any time

(3) The vendor shall, if required, by and at the expense of the purchaser obtain or consent to an endorsement of notice of the purchaser's interest on the policy, and in such case the vendor (keeping the policy on foot) may require the purchaser to pay on completion a proportionate part of the premium from the date of the contract.

22. Special notice to complete

(1) At any time on or after the completion date, either party, being ready and willing to fulfil his own outstanding obligations under the contract, may (without prejudice to any other right or remedy available to him) give to the other party or his solicitor notice in writing requiring completion of the contract in conformity with this condition

(2) Upon service of such notice as aforesaid it shall become and be a term of the contract, in respect of which time shall be of the essence thereof, that the party to whom the notice is given shall complete the contract within 16 working days after service of the notice (exclusive of the day of service): but this condition shall operate without prejudice to any right of either party to rescind the contract in the meantime

(3) In case the purchaser refuses or fails to complete in conformity with this condition, then (without prejudice to any other right or remedy available to the vendor) the purchaser's deposit may be forfeited (unless the court otherwise directs) and, if the vendor resells the property within twelve months of the expiration of the said period of 16 working days, he shall be entitled (upon crediting the deposit) to recover from the purchaser hereunder the amount of any loss occasioned to the vendor by expenses of or incidental to such resale, or by diminution in the price.

Appendix D

Con 28B, Oyez, Requisition on Title

Short description of the property

re ....

Parties

....

to ....

oyez

REQUISITIONS

ON TITLE

(For use where Enquiries before Contract have already been answered)

Please strike out any requisitions not applicable.

1. PREVIOUS ENQUIRIES

If the enquiries before contract replied to on behalf of the Vendor were repeated herein, would the replies now be the same as those previously given? If not, please give full particulars of any variation.

2. OUTGOINGS AND APPORTIONMENTS

(A) On completion the Vendor must produce receipts for the last payments of outgoings, of which either he claims reimbursement of an advance payment or arrears could be recovered from the Purchaser.

(B)   (i) In the case of a leasehold property or property subject to a legal rentcharge, the receipt for rent due on the last rent day before the day of completion, as well as the receipt for the last fire insurance premium, must be produced on completion.

    (ii) Does the former receipt contain any reference to a breach of any of the covenants and conditions contained in the lease or grant?

(C) Please send a completion statement.

3. TITLE DEEDS

A. *Unregistered land*

    (i) Which abstracted documents of title will be delivered to the Purchaser on completion?

    (ii) Who will give to the Purchaser the statutory acknowledgment and undertaking for the production and safe custody of those not handed over?

    (iii) Why will any documents not handed over be retained?

B. *Registered land*

    (i) When was the land or charge certificate last officially examined with the register?

    (ii) If the Land Registry has approved an estate lay-out plan for use with official searches of part of the land in the title, on what date was it approved?

    (iii) If the Vendor's land certificate is on deposit at the Land Registry, what is the deposit number?

4. MORTGAGES

(A) All subsisting mortgages must be discharged on or before completion.

(B) In respect of each subsisting mortgage or charge:

    (i) Will a vacating receipt, discharge of registered charge or consent to dealing, entitling the Purchaser to take the property freed from it, be handed over on completion?

    (ii) If not, will the Vendor's solicitor give a written undertaking on completion to hand one over later?

    (iii) If an undertaking is proposed, what are the suggested terms of it?

5. POSSESSION

(A)   (i) Vacant possession of the whole of the property must be given on completion.

     (ii) Has every person in occupation of all or any part of the property agreed to vacate on or before completion?

     (iii) What arrangements will be made to deliver the keys to the Purchaser?

Or

(B) The Vendor must on completion hand over written authorities for future rents to be paid to the Purchaser or his agents.

6. NOTICES

Please give the name and address of any solicitor, residential tenant or other person to whom notice of any dealing with the property must be given.

7. COMPLETION ARRANGEMENTS

Please answer any of the following requisitions against which X has been placed in the box.

☐   (A) Where will completion take place?

☐   (B) We should like to remit the completion monies direct to your bank account. If you agree, please give the name and branch of your bank, its sorting code number, and the title and number of the account to be credited.

☐   (C) We should like to remit the completion monies by Speedsend. If you agree, please give the address of the most convenient Trustee Savings Bank branch and state whether you maintain an account there.

☐   (D) In whose favour and for what amounts will banker's drafts be required on completion?

The deed and documents of title remain to be examined and the right is reserved to make further requisitions which may arise on such examination, the replies to the above, the usual searches and enquiries before completion, or otherwise.

Note.—The Requisitions founded on the Abstract of Title or Contract must, of course, be added to the above.

DATED   198 .   DATED   198 .

Purchaser's Solicitor.   *Vendor's Solicitor.*

oyez   The Solicitors' Law Stationery Society plc. Oyez House, 27 Crimscott Street, London SE1 5TS   *(revised 2.84)*   2.86 B'HAM.

5032056

Conveyancing 28B

Appendix E

Law Com. No. 166, Transfer of Land, The Rule in Bain v. Fothergill

Item IX of the First Programme

To the Right Honourable The Lord Havers, Lord High Chancellor of Great Britain

Introduction

1. Under Item IX of our First Programme we undertook to examine conveyancing with a view to its modernisation and simplification. In this report, as part of that examination, we recommended that the rule of law, known as the rule in *Bain* v. *Fothergill*, which restricts the damages recoverable by a purchaser of land for breaches of contract by the vendor occasioned by defects in his title, should be abolished by legislation. A draft Bill to implement our recommendation appears in Appendix A to this report.

Background

2. In August 1986 we published a working paper[1] requesting views on our provisional proposal that a purchaser should be entitled to claim damages for loss of bargain, even if the vendor's inability to complete the contract is occasioned by a defect in title.[2] Our reasons are fully set out in the working paper, which we now produce in full as Appendix C to this report.

3. Our provisional view that the rule in *Bain* v. *Fothergill* should be abolished has been confirmed for two reasons. Firstly, we received overwhelming support from the organisations and individuals[3] who responded to our working paper whether directly or indirectly.[4] Whilst the rule is not without its champions[5] the majority of those from whom we received comments agreed, for the reasons set out in the working paper, that there is no longer any justification for its retention. Secondly, since our working paper was published, the Court of Appeal has given judgment in *Sharneyford Supplies Ltd.* v. *Edge*,[6] a case in which the judge at first instance had applied the rule and thus limited the purchaser's claim to damages. In the course of unanimously reversing the decision of Mervyn Davies J., their

---

[1] Working Paper No. 98. Transfer of Land: The Rule in *Bain* v. *Fothergill*.
[2] Para. 4.2 of the working paper, in Appendix C.
[3] A list of those who responded is contained in Appendix B.
[4] See, for example, "No More Pain and Botherfull?" [1987] Conv. 1–4; "Banning Bain" (1986) 130 S.J. 733; R.S. Evans and P.M. Rank, "The Rule in *Bain* v. *Fothergill*—An Early Demise?" (1987) 85 L.S.Gaz. 26; Howel Lewis, "*Bain* v. *Fothergill* and the Maggots" (1986) 136 New L.J. 1129; M.P. Thompson "What Must a Vendor do to Perfect his Title?" [1986] Conv. 60–64.
[5] See para. 10 below.
[6] [1987] 2 W.L.R. 363. Leave was given to appeal to the House of Lords, but we understand the case has now been settled.

Lordships voiced strong support for abolition of the rule in *Bain v. Forthergill*. Balcombe L.J. expressed the view:

> "But even limited in this way to defects in the vendor's *title*, the rule in *Bain v. Forthergill* is today impossible to justify. Its rationale depends, and has been seen, on the difficulties of making title to land under English law. Now that registered title to land is the general rule, this rationale is no longer valid, if indeed it ever was. [Counsel] for the defendant, submitted to us that the rule still serves a useful purpose in Yorkshire. In my judgment it serves no useful purpose anywhere within England or Wales, and I note that this view is shared by the Law Commission in its Working Paper (No. 98 of 1986). The rule has been almost universally condemned. In *Day v. Singleton* [1899] 2 Ch. 320 it was described by Lindley M.R., at p. 329 as "anomalous;" an expression repeated by Megarry J. in *Wroth v. Tyler* [1974] Ch. 30, 56. In *Malhotra v. Choudhury* [1980] Ch. 52 it was described by Stephenson L.J., at p. 68, as 'exceptional and anomalous.' For a convincing criticism of the rule see McGregor on Damages, 14th ed. (1980) para. 702. Nevertheless the rule is binding on this court, unless and until the House of Lords declines to follow its own previous decision, or the law is altered by Parliament."

Similarly Kerr L.J. stated:

> "I would only add my entire concurrence, as at present advised, with the provisional views expressed by the Law Commission in Working Paper No. 98 (1986) on the desirability of abolishing the rule in *Bain v. Fothergill*, subject to the right of vendors to stipulate expressly, if they wish to do so, for a limitation of their liability in damages to compensate the purchasers for the loss of their bargain in the event of some defect in the vendor's title. The history of the cases cited in the Working Paper and in the judgment of Balcombe L.J. in itself illustrates the basic injustice of the rule whenever a vendor is, or reasonably should be, aware of the defect in his title which cause the problem. Nowadays this must surely be the position in virtually every case of a defective title. The decision of that court in *Day v. Singleton* [1899] 2 Ch. 320 was no doubt influenced by this consideration, since it is difficult, if not impossible, to square it with the apparently absolute nature of the rule in *Bain v. Fothergill*. But fortunately it is binding on us, together with Malhotra v. *Choudhury* [1980] Ch. 52, and marked the beginning of a lengthy series of cases, now including the present one, in which our courts have again and again sought to escape from the clutches of the rule."[8]

In agreeing with the judgment of both Kerr L.J. and Balcombe L.J., Parker L.J. added,

> "I also entirely agree that the rule in *Bain v. Fothergill* should be abolished at the earliest possible moment. It is not only anomalous and illogical. It is also unjust."[9]

[7] At p. 371G.
[8] At p. 377F.
[9] At p. 378C.

Sharneyford Supplies Ltd. v. Edge

4. In *Sharneyford Supplies Ltd.* v. *Edge*,[10] the defendant contracted to sell a maggot farm to the plaintiff company with vacant possession on completion. The farm was in fact occupied by business tenants protected under the Landlord and Tenant Act 1954 and the defendant vendor was therefore unable to give vacant possession. The plaintiffs claimed damages for breach of contract under two heads: (a) the cost of investigating title and other conveyancing expenses, some £472.05; and (b) loss of profits amounting to £131,544. At first instance Mervyn Davies J. held that the rule in *Bain* v. *Fothergill* applied and the plaintiff could therefore only recover the £472.05 conveyancing costs. In unanimously reversing his decision the Court of Appeal accepted that Mervyn Davies J. had addressed the correct question in applying the rule in *Bain* v. *Fothergill*: had the vendor shown that he had done all that he reasonably could to remove the defect in his title? However whilst the judge at first instance concluded that the vendor had done so, the Court of Appeal held that his failure to give the tenants notice to determine their tenancy, either at common law or under section 25 of the Landlord and Tenant Act 1954, meant that he had not done all he reasonably could to acquire vacant possession of the farm.

5. Despite the submission on the vendor's behalf that a notice of not less than six months is required under section 25 of the 1954 Act, and therefore any such notice would have expired long after the completion date, Balcombe L.J. was prepared to say that the tenants, if served with formal notice to determine their tenancy, might have given up possession. Relying on *Day* v. *Singleton*[11] and *Malhotra* v. *Choudhury*,[12] Balcombe L.J. concluded,

" . . . it matters not that the attempt to clear the title might have failed: it must at least have been tried."[13]

6. On the question of whether the vendor's obligation extended to paying the £12,000 sought by the tenants to surrender their tenancy,[14] Parker L.J. considered that the rule in *Bain* v. *Fothergill* ought not to apply whenever the vendor could fulfil his obligation to give vacant possession by payment of money. He compared the position to the case of a vendor who fails to redeem a mortgage owing to lack of resources.[15] On the contrary, Balcombe L.J., whilst appreciating the logic of the argument, considered that the rule should not be abrogated in that way. There are, he suggested, few defects in title which could not be removed on payment of a sufficiently large sum. Kerr L.J. having decided that the vendor's essential first step was to serve a notice to quit, expressed no view on this issue.

---

[10] [1987] 2 W.L.R. 363 C.A. reversing Mervyn Davies J. at first instance, [1986] Ch. 128.
[11] [1899] 2 Ch. 320.
[12] [1980] Ch. 52.
[13] [1987] 2 W.L.R. 363 at p. 375A.
[14] See para. 2.27 of the working paper, in Appendix C.
[15] *Re Daniel* [1917] 2 Ch. 405.
[16] For a full discussion of this point see paras. 2.29–2.35 of the Working Paper in Appendix C.

Misrepresentation Act 1967

7. There is some uncertainty surrounding the effect of section 2(1) of the Misrepresentation Act 1967 on the rule in *Bain* v. *Fothergill*. This uncertainty relates to whether damages are recoverable for any misrepresentation of good title occurring merely by virtue of entering into the contract for sale itself and whether those damages would extend to loss of bargain. If so, this would be a way of by-passing the operation of the rule in *Bain* v. *Fothergill*.[16] In *Watts* v. *Spence*[17] a husband contracted to sell the house of which he and his wife were co-owners, but without his wife's consent. The purchaser sued for damages for breach of contract. Graham J. held that the purchaser could recover damages for loss of bargain under section 2(1) of the Misrepresentation Act 1967, which were not limited by the rule in *Bain* v. *Fothergill*. At first instance in *Sharneyford Supplies Ltd.* v. *Edge*, Mervyn Davies J. declined to follow *Watts* v. *Spence* and so did not award damages for loss of bargain under section 2(1). On appeal, Counsel did not argue the point, but Balcolmbe L.J. commented *obiter*,

> "[Counsel] for the plaintiff, very wisely did not attempt to argue this ground before us. In the circumstances I need only say that, like the judge, I find the criticism of *Watts* v. *Spence* in McGregor on Damages, 14th ed., paras. 1486–9 entirely convincing."[18]

The uncertainty in relation to the effect of the Misrepresentation Act 1976 on the rule in *Bain* v. *Fothergill* therefore remains. However, in view of our recommendation that the rule in *Bain* v. *Fothergill* should be abolished, no more need be said at present about this problem.

Should a vendor be able to limit his liability to pay damages?

8. We sought views on this question in our working paper.[19] Of those who supported the abolition of the rule in *Bain* v. *Fothergill*, the majority who answered this question agreed that the vendor should be able to include an express term in the contract limiting his liability for defects in title. It has however been suggested to us that, if the use of such clauses becomes widespread, it might be necessary to consider whether the Unfair Contract Terms Act 1977 should be extended to embrace contracts for the sale of land. In order to convey the majority of conveyancing contracts, section 3 would need to be extended to contracts where neither party is acting in the course of a business.

9. However, from the responses we received, there was no general view that the Unfair Contract Terms Act 1977 should be extended to contracts for the sale of land. We therefore remain unconvinced at present that any provision should be made to prevent the parties, by express agreement, limiting the damages payable by the vendor should his title prove defective.

---

[17] [1976] Ch. 165.
[18] [1987] 2 W.L.R. 363 at p. 376C.
[19] See paras. 3.19–3.29 in Appendix C.

Support for the rule in Bain v. Fothergill

10. A number, albeit small, of those who responded to the working paper were opposed to abolition of the rule in *Bain v. Fothergill*.[20] It was considered that the rule has served a useful purpose for over 200 years[21] and continues to be a valuable weapon for a vendor. Little would be gained, it was said, by its abolition, particularly if express terms reintroducing its effect became standard conveyancing practice. It was also suggested that the cost of conveyancing would increase if the rule was abolished because of the extra work of solicitors (and counsel) investigating title before contract to ensure that appropriate special conditions were included in the contract. Since a vendor's solicitor is already supposed to investigate title for the purpose of drafting the contract for sale, we question the basis of this suggestion. In any event, given the uncertain scope of the rule in *Bain v. Fothergill* we query whether, if the rule were retained, a vendor and his conveyancer could safely rely on it.

11. The point was also made that if the rule in *Bain v. Fothergill* were abolished an anomaly would arise in relation to the position before and after completion of the contract. Where a vendor conveys land for valuable consideration and is expressed to convey "as beneficial owner" certain covenants for title are implied into the conveyance by section 76 of the Law of Property Act 1925. Under these covenants for title, damages can only be recovered for defects in title created by the vendor himself or by a predecessor through whom he derives title otherwise than as a purchaser for value. Therefore, it is said, if the rule in *Bain v. Fothergill* were abolished, where there is a defect in title which has been created by a previous vendor, a purchaser would be able to recover substantial damages for that defect if discovered, as it should be through investigation, before completion, but could not sue in respect of that defect on the covenants for title after completion. However, the purchaser's inability to sue after completion in this situation stems from the limited obligation undertaken by the vendor under the implied covenants for title. Under our proposal, the purchaser's causes of action would remain unaltered; what would be different is his ability to claim substantial damages before completion. At the moment, the anomaly is greater as a result of the way in which the rule in *Bain v. Fothergill* has been applied by the courts. The rule does not apply where the purchaser is able to sue after completion on the covenants for title[22] but can apply before completion even though the defect in title was created by the vendor.[23] As a result, a purchaser who could have a cause of action either before or after completion in respect of a defect in title created by the vendor, may only be able to recover substantial damages once the contract

[20] For a public defence of the rule see Stefan Farren, "The Bane of Fothergill?" (1986) 136 N.L.J. 1205. See also M.P. Thompson, "*Bain v. Fothergill*—A Reply to Mr. Farren," (1987) 137 N.L.J. 83.
[21] Perhaps the best example is that recounted by Sir Arthur Underhill of Mr. Charles Swinfen Eady's first case in which he "reminded" his leader Mr. Horace Davey Q.C. of the then recent case of *Baines* (sic) v. *Fothergill. Change and Decay* (1938) pp. 124–125.
[22] *Lock v. Furze* (1866) L.R. 1 C.P. 441.
[23] See recently, for example, *Ray v. Druce* [1985] Ch. 437.

has been completed. Before completion, if the defect had by then been discovered and the contract rescinded, he may be limited to recovering his conveyancing costs. This particular anomaly would disappear if the rule in *Bain* v. *Fothergill* were abolished. The parties to a conveyance can agree on wider covenants for title, but we are currently examining the covenants implied by statute in both registered and unregistered conveyancing. Consideration will inevitably be given to whether covenants for title should become absolute, when they would, in effect, correspond with those implied into the contract for sale.

Conclusion

12. We remain convinced that the continued existence of the rule in *Bain* v. *Fothergill* is undesirable and unjustified. We therefore *recommend* that the rule be reversed by legislation. A draft Bill giving effect to our recommendation appears in Appendix A.

Draft of a Bill

An act to abolish the rule of law known as the rule in *Bain* v. *Fothergill*

Be it enacted by the Queen's most Excellent Majesty, by and with the advice and consent of the Lords Spiritual and Temporal, and Commons, in this present Parliament assembled, and by the authority of the same, as follows:—

Abolition of rule in *Bain* v. *Fothergill*

1.—(1) There is hereby abolished the rule of law (known as the rule in *Bain* v. *Fothergill*) restricting the damages recoverable for breaches of contract occasioned by defects in title to land.

(2) Subsection (1) above applies only in relation to contracts made after the commencement of this Act.

Short title, commencement etc.

2.—(1) This Act may be cited as the Sale of Land Act 1987.

(2) This Act shall come into force at the end of the period of two months beginning with the day on which it is passed.

(3) This Act extends to England and Wales only.

INDEX